CHORAL CONDUCTING

CHORAL CONDUCTING
A Symposium

Edited by

HAROLD A. DECKER
University of Illinois

and

JULIUS HERFORD
Indiana University

Prentice-Hall, Inc., Englewood Cliffs, New Jersey

Printed in the United States of America

ISBN: 0-13-133355-0

Library of Congress Catalog Card Number: 72-94347

10 9 8 7 6 5 4 3 2 1

PRENTICE-HALL INTERNATIONAL, INC., *London*
PRENTICE-HALL OF AUSTRALIA, PTY. LTD., *Sydney*
PRENTICE-HALL OF CANADA, LTD., *Toronto*
PRENTICE-HALL OF INDIA PRIVATE LIMITED, *New Delhi*
PRENTICE-HALL OF JAPAN, INC., *Tokyo*

CONTENTS

PREFACE

The authors of the following chapters are each presently involved in the training of the professional choral conductor at an American college or university. The chapter which each has written is an important facet of the choral musician's study: (1) *choral tone and diction* (Howard Swan); (2) *rehearsal techniques* (Lloyd Pfautsch); (3) *historical research with emphasis on editorial techniques* (Walter S. Collins); (4) *twentieth-century choral repertoire* (Daniel Moe); and (5) *analytical and historical score study* (Julius Herford).

This symposium does not intend to exhaust all study areas necessary for the choral conductor's development but, rather, limits itself to five significant aspects which appear here. The authors and editors of this volume uniformly agree that specific techniques must be combined with historical and structural studies as they relate to the knowledge and performance of choral literature. The choral conductor of today cannot afford to limit himself solely to the study and practice of choral techniques: he must be a musician and scholar of depth and scope. His goal is not only technical skill but also an awareness and sensitivity to musical style. Musicology has provided the performer with tools which must become an integral part of his craft.

Walter S. Collins is professor of music at the University of Colorado in Boulder. His musicological research has centered on the music of Thomas Weelkes. He is chairman of the national Choral Editing Standards Committee of the American Choral Director's Association.

Harold A. Decker is a professor of music and director of choral activities at the University of Illinois and was formerly head of the voice and choral departments at Wichita State University in Kansas. He is a past president of the American Choral Director's Association.

Julius Herford is professor emeritus of music and has been director of graduate studies in Choral Music at Indiana University. Previously he was in charge of Historical and Analytical Studies at Westminster Choir College and coached conductors and musical performers privately at his New York City studio.

Daniel Moe, formerly director of choral activites at the University of Iowa, is professor of choral conducting at Oberlin College. He is also a composer of choral music and a member of the Inter-Lutheran Commission on Worship.

Lloyd Pfautsch is director of choral activities at Southern Methodist University. He is also a composer of choral music.

Howard Swan was formerly professor of voice and director of choral activities at Occidental College. He is presently Visiting Professor at California State University in Fullerton. In recent years he has also been a member of the choral staffs at the Meadowbrook and Blossom Summer Festivals.

The contributors are indebted to Dr. James G. Smith of the University of Illinois Choral Department faculty, who compiled the Selected Reading List, and we extend our appreciation to the many students, colleagues, and members of the choral profession who have offered suggestions and encouragement in the preparation of this book, which had its inception during the spring of 1966. Without the complete understanding and cooperation of all the authors this book would not have been possible.

We recognize the fact that in this rapidly changing world music is no exception. There have been many new developments since this book was conceived which obviously cannot be included. We trust that the examples of music found here and the references which are included will be significant in illustrating choral principles even if they are somewhat outmoded by the alterations of time.

The Editors

CHORAL CONDUCTING

INTRODUCTION

Harold A. Decker

The history of choral music in America is to a large extent reflected in the history of religious expression. Fostered in the colonial psalm-singing congregations, in the singing schools, and in the singing societies of the nineteenth century, choral music has, for the most part, been adopted in our day by institutions of higher learning. In the 1920s a surge of interest in choral singing was inspired by such college and university leaders as Peter C. Lutkin, Archibald Davison, F. Melius Christiansen, and John Finley Williamson. Not only did the dynamic effect of their strong personalities leave an imprint on many of their students, but the choirs conducted by their successors came to be identified with the tone quality and style of the various choral schools.

A decisive change occurred in more recent years, as the emphasis of the choral musician shifted from sound or sonority per se to the totality of music, from mere subjective interpretations to a closer perception of the composer's work. The performer then becomes the servant of the music itself. An equally significant new influence has been the widening scope of choral repertoire through musicological research and through the rapid accumulation of new music since the Second World War. The two poles of historical or stylistic awareness and present-mindedness complement each other, and one often serves to illuminate the other.

The widened knowledge of choral literature, the scope of which is enormous, has made clear that the *chorus* has not been a homogeneous instrument throughout history. The large urban community chorus of amateur singers is a relatively young musical ensemble, its origin not earlier than the time of Joseph Haydn's oratorios. The choruses of Handel's oratorios were still performed by small, highly skilled, professional ensembles of boys and men. The Renaissance choruses of the Sistine Chapel and St. Mark's, as well as those in the courts of England and Western Europe, were also comprised of highly trained professional singers and instrumentalists who devoted their lives and talents to musical performances.

The search for authentic performance practices is only in its infancy. The choice of authentic editions, stylistically sensitive interpretations and the appropriate selection of vocal and instrumental forces still present puzzling uncertainties. Similar problems are found in the area of choral tone as it relates to the various historical periods. Today's conductor must recognize the authenticity and vitality of the music he chooses to perform. Music of the "past" must become "present" to him, to his performing musicians, and to his listeners.

The church, with its boy-choir training schools and professional male adult singers, was once the bulwark of choral singing. Church leaders today, reeling from the impact of changing philosophies and changing times, often seek to appeal to the younger generation through experimentation with music and the forms of worship. New folk and jazz musical settings of time-honored, traditional services are increasingly prevalent, particularly in urban communities. Although a new vitality and the involvement of youth may be achieved through these changes, there is little opportunity for church music from the past to be included in such programs. Often church musicians find themselves neither prepared for nor interested in the "new expression." As a result, many church musicians have accepted positions in secular institutions of higher learning. To further complicate the situation, as the churches have accepted roles of more active social leadership and additional community responsibility, financial support for church music programs as we have known them has decreased. A certain objectivity is required to evaluate this rapidly evolving new music. Certainly a revitalization is in order; yet, music must continue to meet high professional and aesthetic standards of composition and performance.

Serious choral music today generally falls into three basic catagories: (1) the more or less conventional nineteenth-century style of composition favored by many churches and secular choirs, (2) the so-called *avant garde* classification, which virtually eliminates any vestige of conventional music, and (3) music which is rooted in the past yet speaks a contemporary language that incorporates unresolved dissonance and atonality, aleatory and improvisatory techniques, elements of chance, and often a dramatic emphasis on the text.

John Cage has shaken our complacency by challenging composer, performer, and listener alike in his writings about music. His statements have resulted in some facetious, even ludicrous performances, but they have also revealed new concepts and attitudes to the present-day composer by stressing the involvement as well as the entertainment of the listener. From Cage and his compatriots come music for prepared instruments and compositions which rely on such diverse techniques as "structured silence" and multimedia. Although many of these new techniques may grow dull when used repeatedly throughout a composition, there are contemporary composers who have skillfully absorbed them into their own musical expression; therefore, it behooves the practicing choral conductor to remain open to new and exciting musical expression in the choral idiom.

We live in an age of materialism which inevitably affects our general attitude toward the arts. Mass communication brings "commercial" music into every home, but all too rarely does it provide genuine aesthetic experiences. This is a never-ending problem for the practical choral musician, who must educate as well as entertain. The fact is that present-day choral concerts must do both: they must involve the audience as well as the performers. Multimedia presentations which appeal to several of the senses, not only the auditory, have proven to be a very practical solution to this problem.

It is interesting to note that the governments of Canada and England subsidize their most talented artists and composers, and through mass communication the finest musical programs possible are made available to all economic and social groups. Such support has produced a vital musical life in both countries. Similar governmental support and similar results can also be found in many Western European nations. We can only look forward to the day when the arts in our own country will have similar governmental support. As our society becomes more and more automated, it is essential that self-expression through the fine arts be made available to men in all walks of life. Herein lies an imaginative new role for the choral conductor.

The writings contained in this book are not intended to represent a uniformity of thought; yet, the reader will recognize a common direction which is neither fanciful nor achieved by casual agreement but is conditioned by inevitable trends in our time. May our endeavors be of practical and concrete use, based on experience and on a never-ceasing search, and may they serve to clarify the purpose and meaning of the choral conductor's work.

ONE

THE DEVELOPMENT OF A
CHORAL INSTRUMENT

Howard Swan

Artistic choral singing is a comparatively new cultural form in America. Although a few great choirs sang in Boston, New York, and Bethlehem, Pennsylvania, during the first two decades of this century, it was not until the late twenties that the "*a cappella* choir" movement was born. As choral performances became more popular and important during the past thirty years, those responsible for the direction of choirs were from the very first curious about and interested in the techniques which are the foundation of choral expression.

Perhaps there is no subject more important to satisfactory performance and at the same time more difficult to discuss than that of choral tone. Should tone be practiced apart from the score? To what extent can its principles of development be taught in a group situation? Why are there so many differing, yet excellent examples of choral sound? These and many other similar questions have been asked repeatedly of choral specialists. And, there are no simple answers.

The great American choruses are directed by men and women who possess the intelligence, industry, and skill to select and apply techniques with satisfying results for each conductor. These choices must be made by every person who leads a choir. Consequently, the pages which follow contain no description of a particular method or set of procedures characterized as "best." Rather, the thoughtful director is offered his option of many techniques which have proven to be valuable and effective. There will be some discussion of special vocal problems and a summary of the relationships which exist between tone and matters of style and interpretation. But the selection and employment of the several ideas and skills is left to each conductor; this choice is both his privilege and his responsibility.

No two choruses in America sing with an identical sound. The kind or quality of tone produced by a choral ensemble is influenced primarily by the thinking and actions of its conductor with respect to

1. The basic processes of singing: phonation, tonal support, resonation, and extension of range.
2. The degree of emphasis upon one or more of the fundamental choral techniques of blend, rhythmic exactness, phrasing, balance, dynamics, and pronunciation.
3. The interpretive and stylistic requirements of the musical score.
4. The personal and technical resources of the conductor which he uses to communicate with his chorus in rehearsal and performance.

Some statements to the contrary notwithstanding, there are no standards of vocal beauty or quality which are accepted by all musicians. Teachers of singing and choral conductors will agree that a beautiful tone is not breathy, is sung to the center of a pitch, possesses some degree of intensity, accompanies a sound which is normal in pronunciation and is comfortably sustained. Yet, in spite of the work of Bartholomew, Seashore, and others, authorities do not agree upon a proper vibrato rate for a singer, nor do they think alike concerning the importance of vocal registers, the modification of vowel sounds, and the estab-lishment of a dynamic level to be used by a chorus for most of its singing.

Since it is impossible to reach a unanimous opinion concerning the elements which constitute good tone quality, it follows that specialists are hopelessly divided in their choice of methods to be used in securing from their singers a high level of achievement. For many years the teaching of voice has varied from studio to studio as emphasis was placed upon this or that pedagog-ical principle. Each teacher likes his own method, for with its use he secures from his students a performance which is satisfying to his own ears.

Choral conductors, even more so than teachers of singing, are divided in their opinions concerning vocal technique. Some refuse to employ any means to build voices. Either they consider such procedures to be unimportant, or they are afraid to use an exercise which is related to the singing process. Sometimes the choral director cloaks his own ignorance of the singing mechanism by dealing directly with the interpretive elements in a score and thus avoids any approach to the vocal problems of the individuals in his chorus. There are also those conductors who insist upon using only the techniques learned from a favorite teacher. These are applied regardless of the nature of a problem or its desired solution. Finally, there are some who without an orderly plan of procedure utilize a great number of vocalises, devices, and methods secured from many sources with the desperate hope that the tone of their chorus somehow will show a marked improvement.

Why does a choral conductor attempt to solve vocal problems by avoiding them? Perhaps he thinks that the requirements of a particular musical score will call forth from his chorus an appropriate response and the ability to master any technical difficulty. If a composition is sung correctly—if notes are right in pitch and duration—does this procedure guarantee automatically a beautiful sound? Strangely enough, this curious kind of thinking will reject the use of similar procedures by an instrumental ensemble, for all agree that some skill is necessary to play any instrument. Does not a singer also need a considerable measure of technical understanding to use his voice properly? Unfortunately, it is too easy to sing, but it is a difficult task to sing well. It seems sensible to believe that a special quality of teaching and learning are essential for the development of a choral tone which is adequate for the demands of any musical composition.

In contrast to the man who believes that a score somehow possesses the power within itself to solve all vocal and interpretive problems is the conductor who unduly emphasizes factors related to sound. He teaches his audience, his choir, and himself to respond only to aesthetic elements in the music. He draws from his choirs a sound which is his trademark with colleagues and listeners. This never changes—whether the chorus is singing Palestrina, Bach, Brahms, or Stravinsky. Everything in the score is subordinated to sound—to a tone which continuously is the same in spite of obvious musical variations found in one score or among several.

It needs to be emphasized at this point that every element in a rehearsal or performance, whether technical, emotional or interpretive, will affect a singer and will influence his tone. These factors may or may not be designed to call forth a predetermined result. However, the words which a conductor speaks to his chorus and the manner in which he says them, his gestures, his concept of phrasing, the length and vitality of his beat, and the roundness, squareness, or angularity of his pattern—all these and a hundred other elements exercise their influence upon the color, volume, and production of tone sung by the chorus.

The conductor who is conversant with the historical development of music understands that interpretive factors shift radically with every period of composition and for every composer and his writings. Ideally speaking, the tone of the chorus also should change with the interpretive ideas if a performance is faithful to the requirements of the music. Unfortunately for proper interpretations and historical accuracy, it is not possible for the average singer to effect a marked change in the character of his vocal production to meet the needs of every new composition. Nor can the conductor adjust completely his beat, his thinking, and his instructions to the chorus to care in a different manner for the proper rendition of each piece.

If tone can be changed at will, why is it that a chorus which has been conducted by the same person produces what in essence is an identical sound regardless of the selection which is sung? In the hands of an artist some interpretive changes are immediately apparent; it is not necessary for Brahms to sound exactly the same as Palestrina. With amateur singers, however, it is impossible to secure a wide range in tonal variation as the chorus moves from piece to piece.

A conductor may expect to hear the tone he desires from his ensemble only if he understands how voices will respond to various suggestions, exercises, techniques, etc. which he uses in rehearsal. His first responsibility is to select the tone which he wishes his choir to produce. This will be made with the knowledge that he prefers certain tonal attributes and must reject others. For example, it is not possible for a chorus to sing with a perfect blend and at the same time use a dynamic level which extends from *mf* through *ff*. Again, if an excellent choral blend is achieved at the expense of the elimination of vibrato from the voice of a singer, something important in color is lost. An emphasis upon rhythmic precision detracts from the ability of a chorus to sing a beautiful *legato* line. Too much stress upon factors relating to pronunciation and articulation will affect both the balance and the blend of the chorus.

Although this premise is difficult to accept, these are the facts: the conductor of any nonprofessional chorus must choose that kind of tone which he desires to hear from his ensemble. Stylistically speaking, he knows that this preferred tone will be right for certain compositions and will not be as useful for others. His preference for a particular type of tone carries with it the necessity for compromise. A choir which utilizes a beautiful blend will sing superbly a sixteenth-century composition but will not perform as acceptably a piece from the Romantic period of music. A chorus which has been taught to sing with a restricted dynamic level will perform the older music in good taste but at the same time cannot do an effective rendition of a selection which demands rhythmic sharpness or vast tonal sonorities. Intensity in tone is an exciting ingredient and one which aids in establishing communication with a listener. Such is often accomplished, however, at the expense of intonation problems caused by excitement and tension in the singers.

If a conductor's choice of tone is all-important for aesthetic and interpretive reasons, how can he be sure of his judgment? First, he will learn by experience. He finds that a given series of vocalises produces a result with which he is either pleased or disappointed. He uses recordings, both as a means for developing a tone quality which he admires, and for the more important objective of improving his own ability to hear. He studies his own conducting style so that each motion and verbal instruction is relevant to the building of the tone which he wants to hear from his chorus. His knowledge of the vocal potential of his singers is essential. This calls both for an understanding of voice as it may develop normally in a singer who has no unusually poor habits and also the ability to care for the vocalist who presents special problems.

If one judges by the numerous articles, books, and lectures which concern themselves with vocal technique, there is more than one "right way" to sing.* This diversity of opinion is reflected not only by teachers of singing but by those master conductors who have gained proper recognition for the excellent singing of their choirs. These directors exercise in America a profound influence upon a vast company of others who listen to their recordings, their concert performances, television, and radio broadcasts, and by so doing hope to gain the same results with their own choruses. Some of these artist-conductors teach their ideas and methods throughout the country by means of a succession of clinics, demonstrations, and master classes, and each man has his own devoted band of disciples.

How does the novice decide upon the degree to which he follows one teacher and excludes another? Some methods will be contradictory both in practice and execution. Does the conductor with limited experience know this? Can he evaluate the ideas of each teacher as he makes his own contribution both to tonal integrity and to matters of stylistic accuracy and authentic performance practice?

SCHOOLS OF CHORAL SINGING IN AMERICA

There are six schools of thought which in theory and practice now influence choral singing in America. While an imaginative and resourceful conductor will add to the knowledge which he has gleaned from a greater teacher and so compose his own "variations upon a theme," with few exceptions every director in the country has received his initial help from and to some degree includes in his work the principles of one of these six systems of choral development. Each contains both a philosophy and an analysis of choral sound voiced by a master teacher and put into practice by his followers. Always there are one or more choirs of exceptional musical stature who can demonstrate effectively in song the principles by which they have been trained and to which their conductors subscribe.

The basic philosophy of each of these great schools of choral development may be summed up by these brief statements:

School A. A choral tone which is alive, vital, and responsive is secured by emphasizing and encouraging the physical and emotional development of each singer in the choir. To a considerable degree the director is concerned with the growth of the individual—personally, intellectually, and musically—and gives

*For a detailed discussion of the many approaches to the teaching of singing, see V. A. Fields, *Training the Singing Voice* (New York: King's Crown Press, 1947).

somewhat less attention to the needs of the group. The success of a chorus has an immediate relationship to the achievement of each individual in it.*

School B. A singer's tone is like the color of each orchestral instrument and should be developed accordingly.†

School C. Every singer in the chorus has a primary responsibility to subordinate his own ideas concerning tone production, rhythmic stress, and pronunciation to the blended and unified sound made by the total ensemble.‡

School D. By following the natural laws of good speech which are related to proper pronunciation and articulation a singer and an ensemble can develop a beautiful quality of tone.§

School E. Good tone quality is induced by the physical motivation of an individual or a chorus. It is the consequence of a perfectly executed coordination of the entire vocal mechanism.¶

School F. Good tone has three concomitants: a rhythmic drive subordinated to the demands of a score, a knowledge on the part of conductor and singer of the shape of a musical phrase, and an understanding of the laws of vocal energy as they may be applied to a musical composition.**

Mode of Procedure: School A

The advocates of this school of thought believe that the potential vocal ability of each prospective singer must be discovered as soon as possible, then carefully tested and classified before a chorus can be formed. Consequently, the first audition or conference is most important since the information desired by the director will be more comprehensive than that ordinarily found on the card form used for such purpose. In addition to the customary evaluation of musical potential the conductor observes these physical characteristics of the candidate: his weight, walk, and posture; the shape and size of the throat; the sharpness or

*School A is an exposition of the principles of John Finley Williamson, the founder and first conductor of the Westminster Choir. Material relating to the procedures used by School A was secured by the author as a member of John F. Williamson's annual summer classes in the years 1936-1943.

†School B is concerned with the techniques for the development of choral tone taught by Father William J. Finn.

‡School C is a review of the principles formulated by F. Melius Christiansen and several of his followers. He was the first conductor of the St. Olaf Choir.

§School D utilizes the principles and procedures of Fred Waring and his associates.

¶School E includes the following group of teachers: Joseph J. Klein, Douglas Stanley, and John C. Wilcox.

**School F is a compilation of the principles and rehearsal procedures of Robert Shaw.

intensity of his vision and the rate, pitch, and resonance of his speech. The applicant gives some evidence of his imaginative qualifications as he is engaged in conversation by the conductor. Perhaps the primary musical objective in the audition is the determination of the "lift"* of the prospective choir member, which with his quality and range is used to classify him as a singer.

Some authorities claim that the lift is an imaginary occurrence. Others assert that it is quite real and caused by changes in vocal resonance, pronunciation, or is an indication of the overtone series in the human instrument. But the adherents of *School A* are less interested in its cause than its effect and so proceed to chart the lifts by which they classify all voices. They say that a voice changes both in tone color and pronunciation at the pitches shown in Figure 1-1.

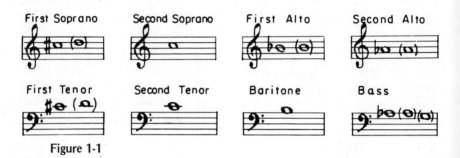

Figure 1-1

These provide the clue to the vocal registers and indicate also the points at which vocalises will be used to induce a satisfactory degree of vowel modification.

Unlike many conductors who experiment with the placement of vocal sections in their choirs, those who favor the principles of *School A* insist upon a regular and unchangeable seating of their singers (Figure 1-2). Because ensemble

2 Tenor	1 Tenor	2 Bass	1 Bass
1 Alto	2 Alto	1 Soprano	2 Soprano

Figure 1-2

tuning is accomplished primarily with the use of an A-major chord the four outer voices (first soprano, second alto, first tenor, second bass) are placed together in the chorus so that they may hear each other easily as they sing the root of the chord (second tenor and second soprano sing the fifth; baritone and first alto the third).

*"Lift" is a coined word which John F. Williamson used in his teaching.

As soon as the classification process has been completed, the director turns his attention to correcting the posture of his chorus. This involves more than the usual admonition to his singers "to sit or to stand tall." The chest is held high with the abdominal wall drawn inward. The head is placed well back on the trunk of the body and the neck shortened. Somewhat unusual is the request for a quiet jaw and an active tongue. Practically speaking, the singer's jaw is not allowed to sag nor is the mouth opened to any considerable extent.

Most of these postural elements would be acceptable to any teacher; there is nothing particularly startling about them. On the other hand, the physical movements used to develop a correct posture for each chorister are somewhat unorthodox. One such exercise is accomplished in this fashion: the hands are clasped firmly behind the head with the elbows brought forward in front of the face so that they almost touch. The singer is urged not only to keep his rib cage high but to use his arms to pull up and away from the waist, without, however, lifting his shoulders.

The emphasis upon physical activity does not stop at this point. If the unfortunate singer is overweight, he will be instructed to vocalize with his hands held high above his head while he is walking or standing on his toes. The singing of higher pitches depends upon spreading wide the back ribs and is accomplished by stretching the arms forward and pulling hard as the tone is sung.

According to *School A* it is most important to know whether a primary objective is to quiet a conscientious person or to stimulate a lazy one. Most young singers will try too hard. In some cases it is necessary to loosen a tight abdomen by asking an individual to bend over, to crawl, or in an extreme situation to lie on his back while practicing his singing. It is claimed that these unusual and relaxing body positions are particularly helpful in the elimination of a *tremolo* from the voice.

As the chorus begins vocalization procedures, whether in the first moments of a rehearsal or the first weeks preliminary to a year's activity, the basic exercises are sung in *staccato* fashion. The emphasis is upon an attack which is vital, precise, and produced with a maximum amount of intensity. The vowel *uh* as sounded in the word *sung* is used by the women; *ooh* as pronounced in *soot* is sung by the men. These vowels are claimed to be the "purest"—also, they are formed easily with a small mouth opening and the use of a half-smile by the singers.

Until some concept of support and control is established, the range of the vocalizations is limited at the top by the pitch of the second lift (an interval of a fourth above the first lift). However, sopranos and altos are asked to vocalize in unison, as do the tenors and basses. In general, the women sing softly (but intensively), while the men are encouraged to produce a big tone. Because of their tessitura and dynamics the sopranos and altos will use the lighter (in weight) part of their voices—whether this is defined in terms of "mixed register," "middle register," "head voice," "lighter mechanism," or any other similar phrase. On the other hand, the men are employing the "low register," "low mechanism," or "weighty tone." Regardless of the terminology the vocalizations produce eventually a choral balance which has been predetermined. Instead of a chord sounding equally among the four, six, or eight parts of the chorus, the lower pitches (sung by the men) will carry the greater volume. This "pyramid" or "steeple" effect is desired by the adherents of *School A*. In defense of this somewhat unusual concept of choral balance they point to the sound of any musical chord which is heard with the bass or root dominating all other pitches.

Extension of range is taught by (1) proper application of physical vitality, and (2) modification of vowel pronunciation above the second lift. As the singer proceeds high in the scale he learns that *oo* modifies to *oh, ay* to *ee, ah* to *uh*, and so on. *School A* says it in this way: "In ascending scales closed vowels open and open vowels close. As low voices approach the pitch D (fourth line) and the high voice to F-sharp (fifth line), all vowels are pronounced with a tinge of the *uh* sound. At the extreme upper limits of a singer's range all vowels will have the sound of *uh*."*

The increase of physical vitality needed for the phonation and support of the upper tones is supplied by asking the women and the men to produce in a spoken sound and then to simulate with a sung vowel the sensation of a scream or a shout. The women begin with the *uh* prefaced by the consonant *v* (which produces a sound remarkably like the wail of a siren), the men with the use of the vowel *ay*. In the initial stages the vocalise takes the form of a descending *arpeggio*. Eventually, this is succeeded by ascending *arpeggios*, ascending scales, and finally by sustained pitches using all vowel sounds.

While some conductors may scoff at this method for establishing a singer's ability to produce high tones, it can be affirmed that the combination of (1) intensity, (2) vowel modification, and (3) the employment of a different quality or registration brings very quick results even for vocalists of limited experience. However, not all teachers would be satisfied with the quality of the higher pitches. The men sing with a tone which is big and dark and the women with a sound which at times could be characterized as shrill by some listeners. Although the sopranos and altos have comparatively little difficulty in producing tone at the softer dynamic levels while maintaining support and intensity, it is difficult for the men to show this same evidence of control. In all but the most exceptional cases their normal dynamic panel for the tones above the staff will lie between *mp* and *ff*.

Since the primary objective of *School A* is to plan for the improvement of each member in the chorus, special exercises are provided for this purpose. These are based upon the pedagogical principle of direct and physical control of the vocal mechanism by each singer. Included are these vocalises:

1. The use of an intensified hum with the tongue held between the teeth by men who are inclined to stifle resonance.

*This statement and the material relating to problems of diction which begins on p. 14 are taken from an unpublished leaflet used by John F. Williamson in his classes.

2. The admonition to all choristers to take and use more breath for the lower tones and less for the higher ones.
3. Instructions to the women to substitute *vuh* for a hum on higher passages while the men replace the hum with *ooh* as in *soot.*
4. The practice with many pitch consonants and nonsense syllables and phrases both in speech and song to establish resonance in male voices.
5. Experimentation with tongue positions to eliminate nasality in tone.
6. The use of such words as *set* and *black* to destroy hootiness in an overly dark tone used by altos.

The diagnosis of and help with vocal difficulties is made constantly after repeated analyses of the individual and his personal and musical requirements. Suggestions for the progress of each singer grow out of his familiarity with simple everyday experiences and with the sounds which he hears and feels in his speech. Accordingly, a conductor who chooses this method (*School A*) for the development of choral tone must be able to diagnose quickly and almost instinctively every physical and mental action of his singers.

In the evolution of choral tone there are four steps or stages which may be followed by the conductor who accepts the precepts taught by *School A*:

1. The classification of voices accomplished basically with the help of the lift.
2. The creation of a correct posture for each individual including his coordination of the parts of the vocal mechanism related to the processes of support and phonation.
3. The development of a skill to pronounce properly any vowel on any pitch.
4. The singer's understanding and practical application of procedures related to techniques for good diction, that is, the ability to sing words in an acceptable manner.

School A teaches diction by means of a series of rules governing the use of vowels, diphthongs, and consonants. A somewhat unusual device is a list of suggested words rather than syllables to carry sample vowel sounds. The claim is made that singers will remember how to use words, while they tend to forget syllables in choral situations where there is the objective to pronounce in a uniform fashion.

Vowels

Fundamental	Subordinate	Diphthongs
soon	soot	*vow* (ah + oo)
so	sod	*vie* (ah + ee)
saw	sung	*voice* (aw + ee)
psalm	sat	*view* (ee + oo)
say	set	*say* (ay + ee)
see	sit	*so* (o + OO)

Consonants

I. Vocal Consonants (have pitch)	II. Voiced Explosive Consonants (carry sound but not pitch)	III. Pure Explosive Consonants (initiated with air)
m	b	p
n	d	t
ng	g	k
l	j	ch
r		
v		
z	IV. Sibilants / Aspirate	
zh	f / h	
th	s	
w: vowel "oo"	sh	
y: vowel "ee"	ch	
b: at beginning of a word	th	

If voiced explosives are not produced with an audible sound, they become pure explosives; that is, *b* is sounded as *p*, *d* as *t*, *g* as *k*, and *j* as *ch*.

Some unusual, helpful, and occasionally controversial statements are the following:

1. When the vowel *ah* in a monosyllable precedes *s, f, th,* and sometimes *n*, it always carries the medial *ah* sound (as in *task*, and *and*).
2. All unaccented syllables carry the sound of *uh* as in *sung*, together with the vowel already present in the syllable (as in *angel, lovely,* and *mortal*).
3. In ascending scales closed vowels open and open vowels close toward the common sound of *uh* as in *sung*. This occurs as the low voice approaches D (fourth line) and as the high voice approaches F-sharp (fifth line).
4. Because the tone is partially or completely stopped in order to make a consonant it is impossible to create an absolute *legato* in singing.
5. All consonants are made with the breath in the mouth. (Do not exaggerate the sounds of consonants to the extent of employing too much breath or energy for their phonation.)
6. All explosive consonants should be separated from the vowels which follow, for example: "p—eace"; "t—ear"; and "g—od."
7. Voiced explosive consonants have the sound of *uh* at the end of a word. At the beginning of a word they are treated as pure explosives.
8. When a nasal consonant (*m, n, ng, l*) at the end of a word is above D in the low voice and F-sharp in the high voice, it is treated as a voiced consonant. (Add the sound of *uh* to save the singer's throat.)
9. The consonant *r* preceding a vowel in a word which is a verb is rolled. When it precedes a vowel in a word other than a verb, it is burred or touched

very lightly. When a word ends in *er*, the *r* has the sound of *uh* as the vowel in the word *sung*.

10. All perfect diction is a result of phrasing according to mood or emotion.

In sum, every precept and technique taught and practiced by *School A* is directed towards the physical, musical, and emotional maturation of the individual singer. Because of this basic principle a choir trained by these methods sings with a tone which is big, dark, intensive, and colorful. This last term carries the implication that a singer is less restricted in the nature of his tonal contribution to the sound of the total ensemble than perhaps is true of those trained by other methods and who strive for different objectives. An *A* choir sings with an unusual balance, that is, not equally distributed among the sections of the chorus. The singers will not produce an impressive blend, their precision in attack and release possibly may be accomplished in a superior fashion, the softer dynamics will not be forthcoming, and clarity of articulation is commendable but often is gained at the expense of a *legato* flow in the line. Together with all choral attributes, phrasing is conceived as the result of mood or emotion. The interpretive process takes place when the conductor learns for himself the mood expressed in a composition and then by intensity from within gives to his group that same mood. They in turn project this to the listeners. The conductor never forces his chorus to do his will; he allows his singers to create for themselves. The audience will listen because emotion is universal. In the last analysis every facet of choral endeavor is dictated by mood.

Mode of Procedure: School B

Perhaps no group of conductors places as much importance upon the value of vocalizations for the purpose of building a choral tone with its necessary components of blend, balance, dynamic control, color, and even interpretive factors as do those who subscribe to the principles of *School B*. For them, vocalization is an art. It calls for a definite plan of exercises which is comprehensive enough to correct abuses and then to develop positive qualities. These exercises are used, however, according to a diagnosis of choral needs and an acceptance by the conductor of the kind of repertoire which he wishes his chorus to sing. The practice of vocalization is concerned with both physiological and musical objectives.

Because each step in the vocalization process is considered significant, every sound sung by a chorus is tabulated carefully and rejected if harmful to vocal production, or it is accepted with a concise explanation relative to its contribution to good singing. So it is that no vowels are used for purposes of vocalization unless they are preceded by consonants. The claim is made that consonants help physiologically by giving the tone a focal point in the mouth and relieving a "squeeze" in the larynx; they aid psychologically because after practicing frequently with consonants the singer will seek the same freedom when singing pure vowel sounds in words.

F, p, and *m* are consonants which serve best to compress the air in the mouth rather than below the cords. *P* is considered too explosive for beginners but is used in later periods of vocalization, while *m* is used to stimulate resonance. But most unusual is the claim that rehearsal with different vowels will produce results related to the color of orchestral instruments. According to *School B* the use of *ee* will make a string tone, *oo* leads to a sound like that of a flute, *ah* simulates reed tone, and *aw* is used if the sound of a horn is the effect which is desired.

Several "combinations of timbres" are presented of which this is one example:

Soprano I	one half, *foo* (flute)
	one half, *mee* (string)
Soprano II	two thirds, *fee* (string)
	one third, *fah* (reed)
Alto I	one half, *mah* (reed)
	one half, *maw* (horn)
Alto II	one half, *mah* (reed)
	one half, *maw* (horn)
Tenor I	entire group, *mee* (string)
Tenor II	entire group, *mah* (reed)
Baritone	entire group, *mee* (string)
Bass	one half, *mah* (reed)
	one half, *mee* (string)

Other possible combinations of tonal color involve the practice of all voice sections with *mee* or *fee* to build a string sound and the use of *mah* or *fah* to cultivate a reed timbre. Another arrangement would eliminate string tone from the choir by vocalizing in this fashion:

Sopranos I and II	*foo*
Altos I and II	*maw*
Tenors I	*maw*
Tenors II	*mah*
Baritones	*mah*
Basses	*mah*

It is asserted that these voices will approximate the color scheme of flutes, horns, and trombones.*

*From *The Art of the Choral Conductor* by William J. Finn. Copyright © 1960 by Summy-Birchard Company, Evanston, Ill. All rights reserved. Used by permission. Pages 245-246.

Because of the higher tessitura for soprano voices they are heard most readily by an audience of listeners. Therefore, the conductor begins with this section as he seeks to build the color scheme of his choir. One hears flute, string, and very light reed tones in lyric and coloratura voices. There is also, in the middle registers of some lyric voices, a resemblance to the sound of the clarinet. But the dramatic sopranos sing with a tone of brighter color which is quite analogous to the heavier strings, the French horn, and on rare occasions the softer sounds of a trumpet. The conductor develops the tone of his sopranos (and other choir sections as well) according to the nature of the repertoire which will be sung. Regardless of the arrangement of timbres these principles are inviolate:

1. The older music cannot be sung with a "robust" soprano tone.
2. Most vocalization should be done at a dynamic level of *pp*. Never should the level go beyond *mp*.
3. For a considerable period of time all vocalizations should be sung downward.
4. While vibrato enhances the quality of solo voices, it is disastrous to choral unisons relative to pitch and pronunciation.
5. The ratio for a beautiful soprano blend is that of two lyric voices to one of dramatic timbre.*

School B claims that a majority of singers usually classified as altos are in reality mezzo-sopranos. String, reed, and brass qualities are found in their voices. For some music a compound of these three voices is desirable; at other times one of the three is accentuated. With the exception of polyphony the alto part is often written awkwardly: "It serves only to take up the loose threads in a composition." This also is true in orchestration—witness the lack of vigor of the viola and the almost inaudible sound of the English horn when an instrumentation is moderately full. In reality, "the ideal alto tone quality is a distinctive, vital coloring, sufficiently self-assertive to arrest attention to itself and possessed of elements not common to other voices."†

How is this "ideal" quality to be secured? These are the principal points with which a conductor is concerned:

Objective: To develop elasticity in the mezzo voice.
Exercise: Use *staccato* vocalizations in rapid passages followed by *legato* singing in sustained phrases. Do not allow the mezzos to drag up the scale the weight of the low tones. Sing softly at first; use a *mf* dynamic during later periods of rehearsal.
Objective: To temper an excessive reed or string vibrancy which is natural in this kind of voice.

*Unpublished lecture of William J. Finn, July, 1934.
†From *The Art of the Choral Conductor* by William J. Finn. Copyright © 1960 by Summy-Birchard Company, Evanston, Ill. All rights reserved. Used by permission. Page 145.

Exercise: Sing *pp*. Vocalize with the syllable *tat*, which will resemble the bleat of a sheep. Continue until excessive vibrancy has been eliminated.

Objective: The avoidance of a guttural quality in low tones.

Exercise: Vocalize alternately upper and lower octaves. Use the syllable *pee* as a corrective for throatiness. Guard against the singers exceeding the natural volume of their voices.

Objective: Train the mezzos to relate their voices to the tenors rather than to the soprano section.

Exercise: Vocalize the two sections together. The nature of the vocalization depends upon the tessitura of the line in the composition. For example, if both tenors and mezzos are called upon to sing in the lower range of their voices, use *mee* (string) for the mezzos and *mah* (reed) for the tenors.

According to the proponents of *School B* there are three types of tenor tone: (1) thin and reedy, (2) string—with adequate resonance in the upper range but a meager quality in middle and lower registers, and (3) a sturdy middle register type whose upper notes probably are inelastic. A well-balanced tenor line requires a blend of these three qualities. Because type (1) is inclined to produce tones of excessive vibrancy, *voh, vaw,* and the "bleat" are recommended to reduce the pungent sound in these voices. On the other hand, type (2) needs to project a reed and string quality and thus should practice with *mah* and *mee*. Rapid *staccato* passages using widely spaced intervals are recommended to improve the dry, stiff, and undistinguished tones sung by type (3). In working with tenors one should seek to copy the tonal texture of a clarinet playing between these pitches:

School B divides baritones into two classes: the string voice which is effective for low polyphonic parts and all homophonic music, and the round voice which is more suitable for singing medium and high contrapuntal passages. These two vocal timbres parallel the sounds of the viola da gamba and the instrumental baritone found in contemporary wind ensembles. Basses are classified in this fashion: the basso-cantante who sings fluently and with resonance in any part of his range but loses elasticity on the upper pitches; the somewhat uncommon basso-profundo who does well in performing vertical compositions and is of doubtful help in singing polyphony; and the string-staccato bass who produces an incisive, pungent tone and usually possesses a more accurate sense of pitch than do the two other kinds of bass voices. Baritones are considered to be the most valuable voices in the chorus for constructing a satisfying ensemble blend.

After vocal defects have been eliminated and tonal timbres developed insofar as possible, the next task of the conductor is to make the chorus into a unified ensemble. The order of procedure is first to blend each part within itself and then to work with the outer voices, that is, the sopranos and basses. The third step is to establish the altos and tenors as the choral axis and finally to make the baritones the means by which blend may be modified in the choir. This blending process in the development of the choral instrument is succeeded by the rehearsal of vocal problems related to the recognition and control of dynamic levels.

Because the advocates of *School B* are interested primarily in the performance of polyphony, they do not consider problems of diction to be as important as do those conductors who hold to other philosophies of choral tone. *School B* speaks of acoustical difficulties related to the singing of high and low pitches and of short notes and noisy accompaniments which must be overcome with diligent practice. They suggest a whispered scale and a dictionary guide to pronunciation as aids to vowel formation. Drill and exaggeration are recommended for the articulation of consonants. These are not to be sustained; rather, they must be articulated deftly and disposed of quickly. In certain circumstances one of the two elements (words or music) must grant precedence to the other. Which shall it be? The answer is emphatic. For concert performances, if there is a conflict, music must be granted first consideration.

In sum, the following statement reflects the philosophy of *School B* relative to the tonal development of a chorus:

> Vocalization is the disciplinary basis of singing . . . . [It] is indeed more than a disciplinary force; it has personality; it is the real factor of choral destiny; it is the animating energy of growth . . . . The comments of musicians . . . upon being asked to make the color-scheme the basis for their training can readily be imagined: "The chorus is not a symphony orchestra," "sopranos are not reasonably to be paralleled with flutes, oboes, strings, and horns," "is a choirmaster to have several groups of sopranos, each group singing only when its particular effect is desired?" Etc., etc. Yet, the majority will inevitably adopt the color-scheme as a fundamental dogma of choral musicianship, and address themselves to the technical processes by which it is developed . . . . The structure of a standard chorus is analogous to that of a symphony orchestra. But it is many-colored and sensitive beyond the mechanical limits of an orchestra . . . . Considering the fact that singers learn by imitation it is recommended that vocal exercises be accompanied whenever possible by the instrument whose timbre is being sought . . . . Just as the richness of symphonic effect depends upon the set-off of strings against woods, woods against brasses, etc., each orchestral choir fulfilling or complementing the suggestions of the others, so the consummate art of chorophony depends upon the correlation of polychrome voices, lyric flute-sopranos trading with lyric reed-sopranos, giving lucidity to dark contraltos, borrowing harmonic authority from solid basses or a quasi-vibrato from high cello-tenors.*

Conductors who follow the teaching of *School B* believe in the validity of every vocalization. Each prescribed exercise leads to a result which is always the same. For a considerable period these vocalizations are prefaced with humming,

*From *The Art of the Choral Conductor* by William J. Finn. Copyright © 1960 by Summy-Birchard Company, Evanston, Ill. All rights reserved. Used by permission. Pages 70, 117, 134, 166, 233, 235, and 258.

and are sung down the scale at a *pp* level, with the use of *staccato*. Lyric voices are preferred for all choral sections. Dramatic voices can be "lyricized," but the opposite process should not be attempted. Larger voices must be surrounded with smaller ones. The chorus which performs artistically will have a limited complement of singers. While it sings all forms of choral music, it will excel in the rendition of polyphony. Finally, the timbre, color, and interpretive qualities of many instruments can be reproduced by singers if they receive the proper guidance presented in an orderly and progressive fashion.

Mode of Procedure: School C

In the building of a satisfactory choral tone *School A* is interested primarily in the physical, vocal, and emotional development of the individual. *School B* employs a series of prescribed exercises to produce colorful timbres analogous to those of instruments. In contrast to these two philosophies *School C* emphasizes the cardinal principle of blend as the key to beautiful ensemble sound.

Blend is born when each singer succeeds in subordinating his own unique vocal quality to the emerging sound of the group. The degree of blend desired is variable and is dependent upon the wishes of the conductor. It is both unique and significant as a technique, since many vocal qualities considered ideal in the solo singer must be subordinated and often eliminated from the voices of chorus singers if a successful blend is to result.

Any discussion of choral techniques is certain to underline sharply opposing points of view relative to blend. The mastery of this particular skill presents an interesting paradox. On the one hand every conductor desires and expects to secure a blended tone from his ensemble, for he recognizes that this is a vital and necessary element in the production of beautiful choral quality. Yet with every step he takes to create accuracy and unanimity in choral sound he is forced to alter and sometimes to destroy other skills which are vitally important to successful choral singing. To the degree that he moves toward a perfection of choral blend the conductor must demand from his singers a change in their thinking concerning vocal techniques. They must rebuild their concepts of pronunciation, dynamics, tone color, phrasing, *vibrato* rate, and rhythmic vitality—all of which may be completely valid when they sing as individuals apart from a chorus.

Because blend as an aesthetic quality cannot be measured in absolute terms conductors who hold generally to the precepts of *School C* disagree among themselves with respect to the degree of blend which is desirable. Thus, some assert that a choir may learn to sing with an acceptable amount of uniformity if their practice is restricted to the improvement of pitch discrimination and a common pronunciation. Others believe in drill on these particular techniques to achieve uniform dynamic levels, uniform rhythmic vitality, and uniform phrasing. While a majority of directors insist that the presence of a wide *vibrato* in any choral section will be harmful to blend, others would be concerned only if such a *vibrato* is found among the sopranos and altos, or in yet a different situation, among the sopranos and tenors. Some will have nothing to do with dramatic voices, while other directors will admit a few of these singers to the alto and bass sections of their choirs.*

Although the speed and wave of an individual *vibrato* may be measured and classified, this kind of evaluation is rejected by those who are interested primarily in choral blend. The realists are willing to accept the premise that in a hypothetically perfect unison no vibrato of any kind is present. At the same time it is difficult to find a director who admits to the use of straight-tone singing (without vibrato) by his choir. In speaking of a solo *vibrato*, a wide *vibrato*, or simply an "inordinate" amount of *vibrato* in a voice, a typical conductor will characterize the sound as a "*tremolo*," a "flutter," a "noise," or a "variation from pitch." Such definitions are valid only for each conductor who makes them; they exist because of his own stipulations concerning the tone which his choir must sing.

When a conductor strongly emphasizes uniformity and blend, there are times when he is required to voice his thinking relative to the solo voice. He may state boldly that a soloist who is both intelligent and responsive to direction can be effective both as a choir member and as an individual singer. Sometimes there is the assertion that a soloist should be able to sing with two kinds of vocal production—one for his own purposes and the other to be used as a member of the ensemble. This dichotomy will be possible if his voice is not too full or his vibrato too prominent.

A chorus learns to sing with a beautifully blended tone quality only to the extent that each individual in the chorus consents to give up, to take out, or to submerge a measure of his own sound. So it is that imitating or "matching" voice to voice and section to section becomes a most important and necessary procedure. However, it is at this point that the advocates of *School C* are criticized most strongly by some conductors and particularly by those who teach voice. A statement by the American Academy of Teachers of Singing reflects this attitude:

> The practice of having all voices within a section imitate any one voice is . . . not conducive to good choral tone. In the singing of "forte" passages this becomes particularly noticeable. Natural, free emission of tone by each individual need never be sacrificed in order to achieve the desired result in choral singing. A student of singing should be encouraged to participate in choral groups, but only if by so doing he can, as an individual, enhance his vocal development, free from strain or tension. In such groups where "imita-

---

*Much of the material which appears in this section comes from conversations held by the author with Olaf C. Christiansen, Paul Christiansen, and Weston Noble and from statements published in the volume by Leland Sateren, *Those Straight Tone Choirs*, Augsburg Publishing House, Minneapolis, Minn., 1963. The reader also may wish to refer to several articles written by O. C. Christiansen in *Choral News* (Vol. I, No. 2; Vol. II, No. 1; Vol. IV, No. 3), published by Neil Kjos Music Co., Chicago.

tion," the so-called "straight tone," or other dubious methods are practiced he has nothing to gain and much to lose.*

The continuous rehearsal of listening, imitation, and matching techniques, which is obligatory when blend is the all-important choral element, leads to other results which are both questioned and criticized. Some strong advocates of *School C* procedures concede that theirs is an *"a cappella* tone" and as such is best suited for the rendition of music without accompaniment. This music is sacred and possibly liturgical in origin, and to a considerable degree is lacking in subjectivity. Critics may point out this restriction in choice and amount of repertoire, but such is happily accepted by the adherents of *School C*. They are complaisant with the knowledge that many compositions including fifteenth- and sixteenth-century polyphonic works receive their finest and most authentic renditions from choirs taught to subordinate individual emotion in favor of an impersonal interpretation projected by the entire group.

The comment is often made that these choirs sing with a basic low-keyed dynamic extending from *pp* to *mf*. It is alleged that this produces a monotonous interpretation which is not helped by a kind of unvaried phrasing. If a defense is needed, the reply follows that color in singing may be found not only in dynamic variation or in stressing the literal meaning of words but rather is developed in the treatment of the innumerable variations in pronunciation of every vowel sound. To state the argument simply: the production of a unique and satisfying tone quality is the principal goal for any chorus; all other aspects of interpretation, including matters of style and performance practice, at times must be subservient to tonal perfection.

While the usual differences among all conductors exist also in *School C*, there is general agreement concerning basic procedures for the development of choral tone preferred by these directors:

1. The selection of singers for the chorus is especially significant. In addition to the usual musical prerequisites the prospective chorus member must not sing with an "excessive *vibrato*." In many cases singers, particularly women, who use a very fast *vibrato* are preferred. The applicant's auditory perception is important; one authority suggests as an audition test the measurement of an ability to repeat and to imitate musical phrases.

2. The importance of numerical balance. While the number of singers assigned to each section may vary slightly according to the size of the choir, a good balance is possible if the first soprano and second bass sections are equal in numbers and the second alto part is almost of the same size. Second sopranos and first altos are equal while the tenor section is approximately two thirds as large numerically as the alto or bass parts. A suggested balance for a choir of 46 members: 8 *first sopranos*, 6 *second sopranos*, 5 *first altos*, 7 *second altos*, 4 *first tenors*, 4 *second tenors*, 4 *baritones*, and 8 *basses*.

Choral Singing and the Responsibility of the Choral Director, American Academy of Teachers of Singing, 1964. Reprinted by permission.

3. The placement of sections within the choir will depend upon the preference of the conductor. However, if he is consistent in his desire to draw from his chorus their best blend, he will not change formations during the progress of a performance nor employ the "quartet" or "scrambled" arrangement currently popular.

4. Vocalization techniques and rehearsal. The objectives sought by the director may be defined in terms of good choral unisons in pitch, color, and dynamics together with a unified rhythmic concept. While the conductor is the final arbiter, he is often helped by a "model" voice in each section whose quality is imitated by the other singers. Long periods of drill are essential for the development of sensitive listening skills. Vowels used at first are *oo* and *ee*; in subsequent rehearsals all fundamental and subordinate vowel sounds are practiced. In some situations pronunciation is taught by means of a chart which carefully details the differences in the color of vowel sounds. Most vocalization is accomplished with the use of the softer levels of dynamics. The matching or imitative process takes place both within and between the voice sections, and the primary materials are the scores being prepared for performance. Unisons are sought first in the opening chords, then in cadences, and finally in other sections of the compositions. Emphasis may be made upon the use of lips and tongue to shape vowel sounds. The practice to achieve a unified rhythm consists of some use of body movement and the sensing by the group of the precision with which vowel sounds are pronounced and the exactness with which they must fall on the beat.

In sum, choral conductors are sharply divided in their opinions concerning the principles and procedures advocated by *School C*. The controversy centers about the musical relationship of an individual to the chorus in which he sings. *School C* asserts without apology that uniform pitch, pronunciation, and dynamics are necessary factors for fine choral singing. Therefore, the elements which are unique to individual expression cannot be tolerated.

Choirs of great reputation have been and are now developed according to the ideas delineated in the preceding pages. They sing with precision and with restraint and usually are content to perform materials representative of one or two areas of musical composition. A listener is made aware of accuracy, of blend, of a unanimity in the total ensemble effort—and an individual *vibrato* is never heard.

Musicians who are dissatisfied with the singing of these choirs voice these objections: the absence of dynamic color and variation, a "sameness" in tonal quality, and, most important—the submergence of individual creativity and expression, which may result in the added complaint that "straight-tone" singing is employed by the chorus.

In the midst of argument there is this certainty. Every choral conductor is required to make a decision concerning the degree of uniformity which he desires from his choir. He cannot ask for the ultimate—the very best in musical endeavor from singers thinking and performing as *individuals* and at the same time expect absolute perfection in those elements which are related uniquely and directly to *ensemble performance*.

Mode of Procedure: School D

Any chorus which purports to sing with an acceptable tone uses habitually a diction which is accurate, understandable, and beautiful in quality. While terminology in this area continues to be confused, a satisfying diction includes three processes: the formation or molding procedure involving the mechanism of the vocal organs (articulation); a dynamic or energizing procedure (enunciation); and the integrating or combining procedure whereby vocal sounds are united into rhythmic groupings of syllables, words, and phrases (pronunciation).* Because a choral conductor is concerned with the speech habits of more than one person, to these three processes must be added a fourth essential—that of uniformity.

Every treatise dealing with the choral art devotes much space to a consideration of the problems of diction. No thoughtful conductor will ignore the obligation to spend a considerable amount of his precious rehearsal time in working with these techniques which are so much a part of good singing. Because of this requirement a conductor must make four decisions:

1. The degree of blend—of uniformity which he sets as a standard of achievement for his choir.
2. His acceptance of the responsibility for learning the basic principles of voice production.
3. The plan or system by which he proposes to teach diction to a chorus (by its very nature diction is involved and integrated with other components of a vocal training program; one cannot teach diction without also teaching singing).
4. His expectation and desire to hear his choir change in their performance of other choral techniques.

These alterations are the consequence of, first, an intensified study and rehearsal of practices related to the improvement of diction, and, second, the conductor's choice of method by which he teaches the topic.

Perhaps it is safe to say that most conductors have thought of diction only as the means by which their choruses were taught to pronounce alike and to make what they sang intelligible to audiences. In some places there is the additional understanding that the manner of pronunciation is closely allied to the shaping of a phrase. But, while there can be no deviation from some principles (as for example, the use of a good dictionary to indicate the correct pronunciation of a word), one questions whether every director of choral music

*From *Training the Singing Voice* by V. A. Fields, King's Crown Press, 1947, p. 191. By permission of Columbia University Press, New York.

is aware of the many results which follow intensive rehearsals devoted to techniques of diction. He may believe that as a chorus is learning these skills he has only the responsibility for judging whether the sounds made by his singers are right or wrong, good or bad. Yet, there is the opportunity at this point for an extraordinary number of decisions leading to consequences reflecting every phase of choral endeavor—the pedagogical, the qualitative, the rhythmic, and some aspects of the technical. The questions which follow may clarify such implications.

1. Is diction best taught by the employment of phonetic symbols, diacritical markings, illustrative symbols, with the use of key or sample words, by imitation, or by a combination of these methods? Does the chorus learn best by using one system or by varying the approach?

2. Many authorities claim that singing is sustained or exaggerated speech. If a considerable amount of speaking is practiced by a chorus to improve diction, will this affect the singers' concepts of rhythm, pitch, intensity, stress, and tempo? Do these factors change as one moves from speech to song?

3. Some hold that "interpretive diction" consists of three distinct styles—*legato, staccato,* and *marcato*—and that each must be mastered to meet the particular needs of a score. If a singer is asked to change his rhythmic and dynamic concepts, will this affect his subjective evaluation of his tone production and quality?

4. How much should lip, tongue, and jaw help with vowel placement? Where are vowels formed? Where do they resonate and is this the same for all vowels?

5. If one agrees that different vowel sounds are sung with greater ease on one pitch or in one tessitura rather than another, which vowel should be selected for initial use? Is this "favorite" vowel the same for all voices?

6. If one bears in mind its acoustical composition, can one vowel be used by all voices singing simultaneously on more than one pitch? Is unison vocalization desirable?

7. Is there validity in the declaration that a vowel sound must be changed or modified in pronunciation as a singer ascends a scale?

8. If it is true that consonants partially or completely block the voice passage, do they help or hinder the production of a satisfying tone quality? If their exaggeration is needed for purposes of intelligibility, there may be a dichotomy at this point. If so, how is it resolved?

9. Is the formation of consonants to be taught by (a) a consciousness of their placement, (b) the kinesthetic or "muscular" approach, (c) the use of sample words or syllables, (d) a classification according to their origin (labial, dental, etc.), (e) a procedure involving the sensory or "feeling," or (f) a combination of these processes?

10. Is rhythmic intensity which implies a sensing of the movement in music hindered or helped by an exaggeration of vowel and consonant sounds?

11. As one sings a word should he think in terms of its component sounds or its literal meaning? Does one approach affect the other?

12. How are the principles of good diction related to changes in vocal register?

13. Will the projection of pitch consonants and the extent of their duration help to shape a musical phrase and thereby influence the style of a composition?

14. Is it valid to say that the manner in which the principles of diction are applied will affect timbre, intensity, pitch, the duration of note values, balance, and stylistic factors?

15. The American Academy of Teachers of Singing says that "vowel exercises should always have a prominent part in the period of vocalizing prior to the actual rehearsal of choral literature."* Does a choral director conduct his practices in this fashion or should he decide for purposes of diction to use only program materials?

To these questions could be added many others which continue to emphasize the influence of diction upon almost every facet of choral technique and expression.

There should be no quarrel with the widely held opinion that a mastery of diction is vitally important for every choir. It is fortunate that this subject has received such an extended and thoughtful treatment in the classroom, in textbooks devoted to choral art, and as a topic for many demonstration clinics. Yet, most conductors continue to think of diction in terms of two objectives—the establishment of a choral blend and the development of a satisfactory method of communication. Because of apathy, ignorance, or thoughtlessness they fail to recognize that diction is related to other choral techniques; it cannot be practiced as a thing apart. Since this is true, the thoughtful conductor is required to make his decisions concerning: (1) the selection, order, and degree of emphasis upon procedural detail, (2) standards for blend and uniformity, (3) the possibility for necessary compromise between interpretive styles and quality of diction, and, most importantly, (4) his intelligent choice of a method by which he builds the individual voices in his choir.

Since beautiful diction is recognized as essential to fine choral singing, the influence of teachers who emphasize this skill in the building of choral tone is considerable. One proposal which has been both popular and helpful to conductors is based upon a system of "tone syllables."†

Tone syllables are the simplest units of sound to be found in all words. In first rehearsals they are spoken slowly and pronounced with an "exaggerated distinctness." According to the proponents of this method, "after discipline is

---

*From *Choral Singing and the Responsibility of the Choral Director*. American Academy of Teachers of Singing, 1964. Reprinted by permission.

†Fred Waring, *Tone Syllables*. © Copyright MCMXLV, MCMXLVIII, MCMLI, Shawnee Press, Inc., Delaware Water Gap, Pa. International Copyright secured. All rights reserved. Used by permission.

achieved, this exaggeration will be almost automatically tempered and refined by good taste, and the mechanics of the method will not be apparent in the actual performance."

There are four primary rules to be followed when a conductor chooses to have his chorus work with tone syllables.

Rule 1: Be conscious of all the vowel sounds and sing them with what will seem like exaggerated distinctness.
  (a) English vowel sounds: *a, e, i, o, u*
      w, y—when they are used as vowels
  (b) Diphthongs:
      ay, oh, ou, oy, wah, I, you
  (c) Triphthongs:
      your, wear, way, wide, yore

The claim is made that since vowels and a few consonants are the only sounds on which tone can be sustained, *legato* singing is a natural result of singing all the possible sounds in each syllable.

Rule 2: Be conscious of all consonants which have pitch, and sing them with exaggerated intensity and duration.
  Pitch consonants: *m, n, ng, l, r*

These sounds are given "extended treatment." It is stated that "the hummed consonants are merely a closing of the lips or a movement of the tongue and therefore the proper use of these consonants will in no way affect or interfere with freedom of tone production." Not all authorities would accept this premise; they would ask about the use of these consonants at higher pitches and with louder dynamics.

Rule 3: Establish a calculated continuity of tone from word to word and from syllable to syllable.
  (a) *Pitch consonant followed by a vowel:*
      When a word or syllable ends with a pitch consonant and the word following begins with a vowel, the consonant is sung as if it belonged to both words on both pitches.
  (b) *Pitch consonant preceded by a vowel:*
      When *m, n, ng*, and sometimes *l* begin a word or a syllable and are preceded by a vowel, they are sung as if they belonged to both words or syllables on both pitches.
  (c) *Final consonant followed by a vowel:*
      When a final consonant is followed by a vowel, it should be pronounced as if it were the first sound of the following word or syllable.
      It is claimed that this technique aids in maintaining a *legato* phrase, assures a continuity in mood, and helps to assure the simultaneous pronunciation of all final consonants.

(d) *Consonant followed by a consonant:*
When a consonant which has little pitch tone precedes a consonant which carries more sound, "bring out" the first consonant. When two pitch consonants are doubled, move smoothly from one consonant to the next and preserve their liquid quality unless the text calls for a dramatic effect. Some explosive consonants, *t* for example, need a momentary delay between the two sounds.

School D cautions that "consonants are not tied across to the next syllable at the ends of phrases. Phrases should be ended where they make sense musically and textually."

Rule 4: Give subsidiary vowel and hummed consonant sounds a proportionate, rhythmic amount of the full time value.

Illustration:

If the word "home" (*ho-oom*) has a whole-note value in a moderate 4/4 tempo, the four beats would probably be divided thus: *ho-o-o-oom*. The *oom* would be allotted the last beat, the last fourth of the total duration of the word . . . . The final consideration in determining the amount of time which should be given to subsidiary vowels and consonants is the style of the music being sung. The appropriate fraction of time to be given to subsidiary tone-syllables (especially hummed consonants) varies with the period, tradition, mood and intent of the music.

These rules advocated by *School D* are imaginative and helpful. Since tone syllables are printed with the notation of many pieces of octavo music, their practice is made easy by the use of such visual aids. With the faithful application of these principles a chorus should greatly improve their blend, their uniform quality of pronunciation, the clarity of their enunciation, and the ability to sense and to maintain a beautiful *legato* phrasing. The two rules which provide for the "carry-over" of consonant sound and a consideration of proportionate time and rhythmic value for each vowel and pitch consonant can be exciting and full of possibilities for the imaginative and resourceful conductor.

As with every other proposal for working with problems of diction, however, tone syllables can prove to be detrimental to the conductor who is determined to use them as his sole instrument for tonal and interpretive results. They are most effective at moderate tempos; therefore, a director may slow the speed of a selection for the sake of clarity. Although the originator of this plan has urged caution at this very point, the older styles of music sometimes are heard with a curious pseudocontemporary sound because a thoughtless director has not realized that in these compositions a musical phrase is more important than textural clearness. The carry-over of the consonant sound often results in a distasteful scooping from pitch to pitch. Sometimes the ardent disciples of this school will modify dynamics as they did their tempos, and while this practice produces an effect which is excellent for recording and broadcasting purposes, it cannot support the variety in interpretive techniques that one wants and expects of distinguished choral singing. Finally, as with all other plans centered upon diction, if there is a great involvement with tone syllables, the production of choral tone is affected—sometimes to the detriment of the individual singer. It is not that this approach, or any other plan for the cultivation of good diction, has in its procedures that which is fundamentally opposed to principles of good singing. A proper answer, as always, is in the manner a conductor uses these processes: he selects his techniques with a full understanding of their objectives, and more importantly, their probable consequences.

Mode of Procedure: School E

Six basic systems related to the development of choral tone are discussed in these pages. The precepts, procedures, and practical techniques for five of these were formulated by choral conductors. The sixth owes its instigation and influence to several teachers of singing whose ideas have been considered revolutionary and perhaps even dangerous by a large group of voice specialists and directors of choruses. Others use this novel approach and are almost rabid in their enthusiasm for results which they claim it achieves for their singers.*

School E calls its method of teaching "scientific." Whenever possible, use is made both of principles and instruments which possess validity for two areas of learning closely related to the process of singing—physiology and acoustics. *School E* offers no apology for what is obviously a mechanistic approach to singing. The final objective is to realize completely the potential inherent in each singer in the chorus and whenever possible to teach him how to become an excellent soloist rather than simply a member of the ensemble.

A few examples may serve to illustrate the unusual and even startling nature of these teaching techniques. While some differences in method and detail have existed in the past among vocal instructors, their pupils usually have been told to think, to feel, or to focus their tones. This is nonsense, declares *School E*. Since each vocalist requires a maximum effort from the muscles used in his singing, his first responsibility is to strengthen these together with the other body organs which are necessary for the production of sustained sound. At a certain stage in their growth these will begin to function properly. Good tone quality primarily depends not upon "focus" but upon the correct coordination of all of the physical processes which are involved in singing.

There are other departures from techniques which had been thought of as constituting a normal pedagogy for the teaching of voice. It is the usual practice to ask a student to think or to send his tone forward and upward. No, says *School E*, the proper sensation is backward and downward. Traditional teaching decrees that throatiness is a negative factor in fine singing. Yet, the approach

---

*The reader is directed to the following publications for detailed presentations of the vocal methodology espoused by School E: Joseph J. Klein, *Singing Technique*, Princeton, N. J.: D. Van Nostrand, 1967; Arnold Rose, *The Singer And the Voice*, London: Faber and Faber Ltd., 1962; Douglas Stanley, *Your Voice*, Pitman Publishing Co., 1945; and John C. Wilcox, *The Living Voice*, Carl Fischer, 1935.

advocated by *School E* claims that since vowels are both shaped and resonated in the pharynx good singing in truth is throaty singing. For a correctly phonated tone the traditionalists teach that the tongue should lie flat in the mouth with its tip touching the lower teeth. But, *School E* replies that as physical coordination is achieved for purposes of singing the tongue naturally will assume a high position in the mouth in order that the throat can remain open. The traditionalists propose that range be extended by beginning vocalizations in the middle of the voice where one sings most comfortably. *School E*'s answer is that in all but unusual cases work should first take place in the lower part of a singer's voice with a later emphasis on practice with the higher pitches. The advocates of *School E* explain that the middle range is the last part of an individual's voice to be properly coordinated. Again, the traditionalists caution that after taking his breath a singer should wait an instant before beginning his tone—this to induce poise and control without tension before phonation. On the other hand, the adherents of *School E* call for a vigorous attack to be made following inhalation at the very second that the body is energized and ready to apply an intensity to the tone. This intensity is created by a properly coordinated process of inspiration.

Those who support the principles of *School E* declare that vocal progress is measured by the ability of a singer to (1) extend his range, (2) increase his volume, (3) improve the quality of his tone (this applies primarily to factors of resonance), and (4) develop a clear and natural vibrato. In the first stages of learning how to sing, muscular techniques are consciously controlled only for the purpose of building a suitable vocal instrument. There can be no concern for the artistic elements in singing until the time that the voice has been properly prepared by much repetitive practice.

According to *School E* the correct phonation and support of a tone demands an unusual coordination of the various parts of the breathing mechanism. Two sets of muscles, one responsible for inhalation and the other primarily concerned with the process of exhalation, work against each other to produce an equilibrium, a continuous state of tension during the singing of a tone.* One authority describes this as "the diaphragm 'holding back' against the inward and upward pressure of the abdominal wall until a perfect equilibrium is reached."† This process takes place automatically for an instant when a singer is asked to bark like a dog or when he sings properly *staccato* exercises.

During the process of singing, the swallowing muscles must never be allowed to function or a tight throat and a constricted tone will be a result. The larynx must not rest against the hyoid bone—sometimes it is necessary to keep these two organs apart by employing manipulative exercises. The looseness of the jaw is an essential factor for effortless singing; this may be accomplished by

---

*From *Singing Technique* by Joseph J. Klein, p. 17. Copyright © 1967 by Litton Educational Publishing, Inc. By permission of D. Van Nostrand Company.

†W. T. Bartholomew, "A Survey of Recent Voice Research," *Proceedings of the Music Teachers Nation Association*, XXXII (1937), 115.

the instructor placing his hand gently over the jaw and stretching it to help the student experience the sensation of producing a tone without an accompanying body tension.

School E believes in two vocal registers, each produced by different sets of muscles which operate to stretch the vocal cords. In both male and female voices the lower register is sung primarily with the use of the crico-thyroid group of muscles; the falsetto, or upper register, is produced with the action of the arytenoid muscles. Most women will use falsetto register muscular adjustment to sing their entire range. Because these particular muscles do not adjust well at lower pitches, a woman whose voice has not been trained according to the principles of School E cannot sing with correct intensity and volume in the lower part of her voice. On the other hand, the untrained male singer will employ his lower register adjustment to the exclusion of his arytenoid muscles and push his "heavy" quality as high as it can go. By so doing he deprives himself of the opportunity to sing with softer tones throughout his range and to produce higher pitches with ease.

The normally "weak" register in both men's and women's voices can be strengthened by practice. At first, vocalizations are restricted to the lower register. According to School E, both men and women move from the lower into their upper registers at about E-flat on the top space of the staff. After this register has been "isolated" for a period of time, that is, by practice confined to the lower part of the scale, vocalization is moved to the upper register. Both sets of muscles eventually become strong enough to coordinate with each other, and thus the blending process for the entire voice takes place. A three-octave range is claimed for every vocalist who has been trained in this manner, and he should be able to sing both with control and dynamic variation on every pitch in his scale.

In sum, the conductor who chooses to employ the principles of School E in the tonal development of his chorus must be aware of consequences which reach into every phase of choral activity. Perhaps more than is true of any other school of thought, these particular precepts exert a marked influence upon his teaching and upon the way that he will use his knowledge of psychology and physiology. Nor does this influence end with the utilization of new techniques which lead inevitably to results which are different. Of the gravest importance to the director and his students is the truth that E means the acceptance of standards for a choral program which are bound to be unlike any other list of objectives.

Regardless of their differences in opinion concerning procedures to be employed in building tone, all conductors agree that a fundamental goal for any chorus is to sing together beautifully as an ensemble. This is achieved only by some subordination of individual sound to that sung by the group. At this very point there is conflict with the aims of School E which are designed primarily for the development of solo singers. Conductors who use all the methods advocated by this school cannot be vitally interested in matters of blend and balance since these two choral skills demand of each singer some restriction of individual effort, a compromise in concept of volume and pronunciation in order that the sound of the group be more beautiful.

Nor can the proponents of *School E* emphasize principles of good diction until that time when each individual has learned to sing an extended range with proper physical control. Their dictum is firm—the vocal instrument must be built before it can be played upon. For many of these conductors the formation of consonants constitutes a serious problem. The utilization of tongue and lips to make the required sounds has a tendency to disturb the physical coordination which they believe is so necessary for a correct singing technique. "Consonants are noises . . . . most singers need to be restrained from placing too much vocal quality into certain of their consonants," says *School E*.*

This school works for a choral tone which is big, full, and dark. The favorite vowel for practice purposes is a dark *ay* (ā). Intensity and vitality of tone is highly important. However, it should be noted that intensity can change quickly into a state of tension if either the singers or their director are easily excited or if the conductor does not have sufficient skill and knowledge to teach vocal technique.

Before he chooses the principles of *School E*, the thoughtful conductor also will be concerned with some implications relative to interpretive principles. If singers are instructed and admonished over a period of time about the mechanics of singing, is there danger that they will forget how to express themselves through the phrases of their songs? As they make music will they concentrate upon physical procedures rather than interpretive values?

It should also be pointed out that this kind of tone, like others discussed in preceding pages, will be both more effective and authentic when it is used for some types of compositions rather than with others. It sounds best in those selections which call for fullness and volume of tone and which need an urgent and intensified vitality for purposes of communication.

If this system for building tone is so very different, why are many directors enthusiastic about its possibilities and attracted to its use? First, because of its mechanistic approach there is the opportunity to communicate quickly and thoroughly with every individual in a group rehearsal. Second, some conductors like the mature sound which this method develops in their singers. Third, there is considerable evidence to indicate that, when a chorus member understands how to employ these principles, he is comfortable with his voice production and encouraged to continue with his vocal study and practice. But perhaps the greatest value which a conductor and his singers find in these principles is the opportunity to extend the range of each voice in a comparatively short period of time. Unlike any other school of thought, *E* also deals directly and positively with the problem of weakness in a singer's scale. No conductor can avoid facing up to this ever-present difficulty. His tenors and altos in particular must know how to sing through the "hard spots" in their range.

*From *Singing Technique* by Joseph J. Klein, pp. 40-41. Copyright © 1967 by Litton Educational Publishing, Inc.. By permission of D. Van Nostrand Company.

Everyone in his choir will relate his ability to control and phrase, to sing flexibly, and to supply tonal color to the degree of success which he has in singing evenly and comfortably a complete scale.

Mode of Procedure: School F

More than is true of any other school concerned with the development of choral tone the ideas of *F* exist because of the creative genius of a single choral conductor. In attempting to analyze his influence on the choral art in America one is immediately aware of paradoxical truths which make a review of his contributions exceedingly difficult. He is not the usual teacher, if by this one thinks in terms of lectures, demonstrations, the listing of rules, and the writing of textbooks. Yet, as he makes music, conductors from every part of the world come to him to learn. They watch him probe, explore, develop, and communicate the force inherent in a great musical composition as it comes to life in sound, walks for a time with awkward steps, and achieves maturity. This man is a great teacher when one thinks of his study, his knowledge, and the ability to fuse the elements of music into communicative reality. Yet the paradox continues, for those who study with him only partially understand his reading of a score. They are unable to reproduce his unique results.

This man—this "school"—would decry the teaching of tonal principles divorced from other elements of music including form, style, and technique. But the essential qualities which he succeeds in extracting from each composition create a sound which is unusual, distinctive, and familiar to all who hear it.*

How to secure this tone from their own choruses is the ardent desire of a host of choral leaders. In at least two respects they attempt to do this improperly. There are some who try by a process of imitation to gain for themselves this man's results: they copy his phraseology, rehearsal management, and conducting techniques. They are never successful. A larger number analyze his tone only in terms of its final sound. Because it is vital, or it dances, or it has intensity, drive, and urgency, they try to infuse their choruses with a kind of artificial excitement which is generated from the personality of the conductor rather than from any source in the score. This is a most unfortunate experience for the conductor and his choir and obviously leads to a distorted performance of the music.

School F asserts that the nature of every musical element including that of sound depends on the demands of an individual score—even to its component sections, clauses, and phrases. Since all compositions differ in their structure and so present a bewildering array of technical and interpretive requirements, the search for a common denominator by which *School F* builds tone even by indirect means would appear to be a hopeless task.

*The philosophical and technical ideas relative to the development of choral tone given the appellation "School F" are those originated and practiced by Robert Shaw.

It is not possible to dissect the personality of an individual and lay bare for all to see his thought and response to any given musical motivation. Yet from letters, a few pertinent lecture notes, and some highly significant statements one may draw conclusions concerning the musical philosophy of the founder of *School F* and apply these to particular concepts of choral sound. That which follows consists almost entirely of his own words originally written or spoken and a description of some of his rehearsal techniques. Any additional editorial comment appears in brackets.

1. Music is order in sound. It has pitch, color or timbre, amplitude or dynamics.
2. Music is order in time. It has meter, rhythm.
3. Music's order in sound and time is communicable. Song, as one musical form, needs the disciplines of enunciation for its communication.

[The factors of musical speech must never be allowed to disturb the fundamental orderliness of the music.]

The five choral techniques are *pitch, tone, dynamics, speech, rhythm.* These interrelate and influence one another but to some degree can be studied individually.

Pitch

Given are four facts: first, pitches are frequencies of vibration which are related to each other in point of mathematical proportion and acoustical behaviour; second, the voice is an instrument of limited range, but of practically limitless accommodation within that range; third, while Western music has developed according to a quasi-arbitrary system which utilizes only twelve pitches [or their octaves], for almost all of us these twelve pitches are recognizable and reproducible not of themselves, but only in reference to another pitch or other pitches which we accept in reality "on faith" — for the moment; and fourth, by habitual daily reference to a pitch or pitch timbre constant [a tuning fork or a musical instrument] one can indeed develop a pitch memory which shares some of the recognition abilities of what we call "absolute pitch."

It occurs to me that even music which is not formed according to the traditional and physical acoustic relationships [but which utilizes the twelve-note heritage of Western practice] in performance must still relate these pitches according to their acoustical behaviour. In spite of new systems of total tonal organization, minor thirds, octaves, small sevenths, and perfect fifths, for example, continue to exist—in multiple voices simultaneously, or in a single voice successively. We are still privileged—and obliged—in rehearsal to utilize nature's instincts and phenomena in order to "tune up" our pitch relationships.

Absoluteness of pitch is a factor of memory; and though we may now begin forty days and nights or years too late, let's begin. Your insignia of membership in this chorus is a tuning fork. Flog it ten to thirty times a day; each time attempt to sing before you bong; and each day prescribe for yourself after it is sounded a specific interval to reproduce—differing intervals day after day. They say good habits are as easy to form as bad ones.

[As a first requirement for good tone, pitch perception must be practiced.] Two exercises used by *School F* are (1) suddenly asking the chorus to sing a chord in a particular key without making use of the piano, and (2) the assignment of a two-part chord to sing with the choice of interval as unfamiliar and dissonant as the director may wish.

[Fast pitch perception is essential.] Here is a teaching device: direct each section of the chorus to sing very rapidly and for several times a single syllable of a word—then the first and second syllables of a word—then the first, second, and third syllables, etc. For example (in the "Fugue" of Verdi's *Requiem*):

(1)   *Lee—Lee—Lee* (until correct)
(2)   *Lee-beh, Lee-beh, Lee-beh* (until correct)
(3)   *Lee-beh-rah, Lee-beh-rah* (until correct)
(4)   *Lee-beh-rah-meh, Lee-beh-rah-meh* (until correct)

[By forcing the chorus to sing rapidly but requiring it to stop after each syllable, a high degree of concentration allows the group to sing in tune, in time. Of this and all other problems related to pitch *School F* could say:] "Mental laziness and sloppy intonation are a pretty smooth couple."

Tone and Dynamics

[While *School F* does term these two elements "choral techniques," they are not usually rehearsed apart from other technical and interpretive factors to which they are related. In other words, the sound which is heard from a chorus at any given moment is shaped and influenced by many musical forces—principally those of pitch, speech, and rhythm. And the greatest of these is rhythm! Nevertheless, there are a few statements and rehearsal techniques which give some clues to the thinking of this school relative to choral tone and its dynamic expression.]

1. The dimension of music is time—not space. Time is Music's canvas. If Time is Music's canvas, then every instant ought to be used up. There ought to be no fragmentary time without dramatic drive. If momentary silence has a real and pertinent meaning, O.K.; if not, then it has no business interrupting the music. This consciousness should result in a terrific *legato* in choral singing. Furthermore, if Time is Music's canvas, then every song is a new song. Each performance is a first performance; New Time and New Artist. This consciousness is almost bound to force freshness and vitality.

2. There is no such thing as absolute "beauty" of choral tone; there is only dramatic integrity of choral tone. What is right for one bar is wrong for the next. Harshness and angularity are as important to music as polish and roundness. When you come right down to it, beauty has to have its bones and its beast.

3. Tone should range from strenuousness and stringency to sheen and hush; and tenderness with respect to sacred ideas and persons is not to register with the same patent-leather efficiency as "Darling, I love you." But each has its place.

4. Make the tone carry the emotion; not the words.
5. Use vibrato for beauty and not as a sign of fault. We don't want to hear your vocal problems—keep them at home.
6. *"Sostenuto"* doesn't mean simply to sit on something: it has to *crescendo* or to give more intensity to provide its own meaning.
7. Never change the quality of tone in a *crescendo* or *diminuendo*. Neither dynamic device must ever alter the integral beauty of a tone; it should always enhance it.

[Following are three rehearsal techniques:]

1. For purposes of balancing color and weight ask the chorus to sing phrases from their music while vocalizing only with the vowel sounds.
2. To teach *crescendo* and *diminuendo* divide each beat into smaller units:

is practiced as

da - da - da - da - da - da - da - da

This allows the chorus to see and hear the apex of the *crescendo*. Vary the choice of the syllable and also the use of *staccato* and *legato* before proceeding with words. Insist that the singers maintain tempo.
3. In the first stages of rehearsal, which includes the learning of notes, the phrasing, concepts of balance and pitch, etc., the dynamic level of the singing should never be allowed to go beyond *mf* and usually stays at *mp*.
   [It is most important to realize that this singing is of a vital, intensified nature and definitely is not the usual lifeless, emasculated tone that ordinarily is associated with quiet singing. This tonal intensity is gained by rhythmic means which are discussed at a later point in these pages.]

Speech in Song

1. Song is drama. It has an "argument." It has situation and story. I don't think that it is limited to that. That is, song has all the "unboundaries" of music, but its essential defining element is drama. You are obliged, thereby, to do a lot more than make pretty sounds. You are obliged to make sense as well as sensation. Good speech means good sense.
2. Don't pronounce words, pronounce all the sounds of the words.
3. Love the sound of words, but this must not destroy the pulse of the music or the speed and shape of the phrase. For no matter what sounds of speech are prescribed, the principal sound of any syllable must coincide exactly with the rhythmic pulse in the music.

[While *School F* would agree basically with the rules of diction embodied in "tone syllables," this last statement points up a new and exciting direction for the cultivation of speech in song. Not only must a singer make every sound in a musical phrase; he must make them in tempo and with rhythm. What are some of the details involved in this "larger" concept of enunciation?]

School F explains: there are two necessary rules for a singing diction, they are

1. Sing every sound of every syllable.
2. Give to each sound its particular time allotment—"its slot"—as one thinks rhythmically.

Use the dictionary to establish the sound that is properly found in each syllable. Employ a method that has proved itself to learn how to form the sounds.

Because the vowel sound carries the sonority, it must also carry the rhythm. The principal vowel sound. must be sung on the beat or its assigned fraction. Be especially watchful of diphthongs and triphthongs.

Consonants can be divided into three groups: those which have sustained pitch—*m, n, ng*, etc.; those which carry a fractional amount of initial pitch—*b, d, g*, etc.; those which have no pitch—*p, t, k*, etc. Those which have sustained pitch must be given extra duration and emphasis—related, however, to pulse and tempo. Consonants which carry pitch at the end of a word must be given some of the preceding vowel sound.

For example:

is sung:

Do not give the entire fourth count to the *m;* its duration depends upon tempo and pulse of the music. Initial consonants which carry no pitch can be sung on the beat if they are not combined with other consonants. When there are combinations such as *tr, pr*, etc., they must be moved ahead of the pulse, very much like a grace note.

Final consonants which do not carry pitch sound less affected if placed slightly ahead or immediately after a pulse. Normally, they are just ahead of a pulse in the middle of a phrase; just after a pulse when they conclude a phrase.

All final consonants will have a fraction of a vowel sound in front of them. The important thing: what is this beat in the metrical scheme? If it is a strong beat, "borrow elsewhere" to make it so.

[Finally, these general statements relative to words and music.]

1. Text exists on three levels:
   a. it must make sense;
   b. it exists in terms of its own sound;
   c. it exists in terms of the urgency of communication from performer to listener.
2. The great composer does not merely highlight or underline text; he creates a musical fabric in tone or time which matches or transcends or illumines the text, but also is a law unto itself and its own reason for being.
3. Music should comment upon a text. If there must be a choice between text and music, musical language is supreme.
4. [In speaking of musical setting related to text], "A wedding is not a marriage."

Rhythm

[The unique and exciting quality in the sound of a *School F* choir is generated primarily by factors of rhythm. There is nothing artificial in this approach to musical performance. One finds the rhythmic elements in a score and in every way possible makes the chorus sensitive to their form, energy, and pulsation. Finally, this vital force is communicated to the listener as it was originally created with the music, unfettered and unspoiled by other technical and interpretive devices.]

It is not surprising that an art form based in Time should have Pulse as its dominant characteristic . . . . By its nature Pulse implies an inevitability. Without this there can be no proportion.

Rhythmical problems are not primarily problems of reading. The primary problem is that of feeling. The "sense" of rhythm is a complex thing . . . . And the problem as a group is not that of visual identification—two quarter notes equal one half note—but that of getting people to experience two quarter notes simultaneously, physically, psychologically, viscerally, etc. . . . Concerted [ensemble] music has to be concerted around something, and that something is *pulse*.

Music is a game in which there are no "time outs." From the beginning to the end of any single piece or movement there is no "rest time."

There are four major elements in rhythm:

Pulse: its divisions or groupings
Duration: its meaning and measure
Accentuation:
    (a)   That which is artificially contrived by dynamics
    (b)   That which seems to be inherent by metric groupings
Tempo: its significance—change—and control

[*School F* uses these ideas and procedures to help in defining rhythmic elements]:

1. Rhythmic discipline is built first and surest upon the feeling of the smallest common rhythmic denominator. A chorus cannot hold a moderate 4/4 rhythm without a supreme awareness of the four sixteenth notes inherent in every quarter note.
2. Pulse has inner divisions. These divisions are natively felt only in very small groups of twos and threes. [For example, four is a multiple of two.]
3. The pulse must always be delivered with the principal vowel sound.
4. The clue to phrasing is the treatment of the weak beat. Think, *crescendo–pull–stretch–breadth–deepness–thrust*–all these things on the so-called weak beat. A musical phrase derives much of its energy from the weak beat in all rhythms. Sometimes this is done through a short note separated from the note which precedes it.
5. Rests are real and rhythmic. They are as much a part of music as the singing. They are to be felt intensively and observed meticulously.
6. Releases are no less rhythmic than attacks. You let go to pick up again. They match attacks, style for style, spirit for spirit, accent for accent . . . . Borrow time from the phrase you are leaving, give the releases the spirit and accent of the phrase which is coming up, and never be late on the new phrase.
7. Almost 50 percent of poor intonation is due to poor rhythm.
8. One of the basic rules of rhythm is that the greater part of what we call "expression in music" must be done within tempo. While tempo variation can be expressive if sparingly used, it is without meaning if there is not a firm and persistent base from which it can depart. Every time you change rhythm there must be a reason for it.

[Tempo *rubato* can never be license but freedom, and a good reason must exist for such freedom.]
[Some rehearsal techniques follow:]

1. Break the music down into its smallest possible units: ♩ to ♩ ♩ to ♪ ♪ to ♪ ♪ , etc. Sing with numbers or syllables for practice. Instruct the chorus to sing up to a point in the phrase and stop. Continue with this procedure.
2. Separate each dotted note from its following note. Practice with the chorus coming to a complete stop before singing the next pitch.
3. Beat at times ahead of the chorus. This should be done with several phrases or a section of the score and the conductor must keep his tempo steady.
4. Beat the basic rhythm in place of the metrical rhythm.
5. Practice the singing of vowels, consonants, and diphthongs rhythmically. What proportion of the sound does each carry in a syllable? In a word?
6. To repeat: remember that the principal vowel sound must be sung on the pulse. Singers must and can feel the importance of this procedure. [If a

choral conductor considers that rhythm is all-important, is sensitive to its power, and can find and communicate its forms to his choir, the sound which his chorus makes will begin to resemble that produced by *School F.*]

PRACTICAL APPLICATION OF THE VARIOUS TECHNIQUES

The philosophies and procedures endorsed by six schools of thought have been reviewed with the hope that this information will be helpful for the conductor who wishes to plan each step in the development of the voices in his chorus. How can he use this material most effectively?

1. He should not attempt a point-by-point imitation of any system for building tone. Imitation stifles imaginative thinking and the use of individual initiative. His choral situation is different from any other with respect to the maturity and ability of his singers, the choice of repertoire, and the kinds of performances he is asked to present. Because of many personal differences, a selection of communicative techniques and the response to aesthetic elements in music will vary from conductor to conductor. To try to copy another in every particular is to admit failure.

2. He should avoid making a random or indiscriminate choice of a single technique—selected with the forlorn hope that it may provide an instant solution for a troublesome problem. One must recognize that each of the schools sponsors a plan which implies continuity of endeavor. This utilization of one idea or procedure leads naturally to the employment of another, and this in turn to a third, and so on.

3. There are principles and methods which can be borrowed from several of the schools and used successfully if each functions in a logical fashion to implement or to supplement the others. Their selection must not create confusion in the thinking or the singing of the chorus. Because each school holds to different objectives, some of their procedures are opposite in purpose. A thoughtful conductor is aware of these differences as he plans his own program for tonal development.

4. A first step for any conductor is to make his decision concerning the relative importance of particular choral skills. Is he most interested in ensemble blend? In the principles of good diction? In the development of the vocal ability of an individual singer? Which of these or other techniques is of primary importance for his purposes? His choice will point the way to the use of procedures advocated by the several schools.

5. Too often a choral director is defeated in purpose by his refusing to believe that the process of singing by an individual or a group is taught most efficiently by separating it into component parts. This conductor perhaps is fearful of his own ability to teach vocal techniques or he is overwhelmed by what he imagines are the complexities of choral sound. His pedagogical difficul-

ties are caused by his trying to hear "everything all at once." However, like every other art form, singing is a proper mixture of vocal, technical, and psychological principles which can be formulated in such a way that the "whole" is greater than the sum of its parts. A conductor who is serious about the business of building his own choral instrument will develop the sound which he wishes to hear first by listening, then by analysis and by teaching particular vocal and choral skills. This becomes the ideal method by which any conductor formulates his concept of good tone quality. He must identify the various elements which by their implementation and coordination "make tone." He listens for their reproduction in sound—in recordings, in his own rehearsals, and in live performances. After a time he will be able to teach toward the refinement of these skills in a practical and logical manner and according to his own tastes and concepts of proper choral sound. Thus, he will knowingly borrow some techniques, stress others, and discard those procedures which he considers unimportant. Finally, he will have his chorus singing the tone which he wants to hear, and he knows what he has to do to secure it.

Regardless of their differing opinions about tone all conductors would agree on the elements or "characteristics" which are related to choral singing. The methods by which these are taught lead to the creation of distinctive tone qualities. What are these factors—these "choral characteristics"—which every conductor must hear, analyze, and teach?

Elements of Choral Tone (Choral Characteristics)

Tonal Elements in One Voice
phonation (attack) and release
support and breath control
resonance
pronunciation of vowels and articulation of consonants
extension of range
color, timbre, texture
amplitude
vibrato: rate and prominence

The tonal elements in each single voice relate directly to these group characteristics:

Tonal Elements in the Chorus

blend:	related to factors of pronunciation, amplitude, color, vibrato rate
balance:	related to factors of amplitude, extension of range
intonation:	related to factors of pitch perception, support, extension of range (and other elements not pertinent to this discussion)
diction:	related to factors of pronunciation and articulation
rhythmic vitality:	related to factors of attack and release, support, pronunciation of vowels and consonants, precision, and accuracy

These tonal elements also will influence the nature of expressive or interpretive devices—for example, dynamic controls, flexibility, and phrasing— and are also important to the conductor in making his choice of tempo and determining some matters of musical style and performance practice.

Before he uses in rehearsal various kinds of devices, vocalizations, and so on, which have been inspired by his own thinking or obtained from other sources, a conductor should develop within himself a concept of the tone which he hopes that his chorus eventually will sing. At this point he must not try to identify this concept in terms which are timeworn or vague in their powers of definition. For example, to use such words as "pure," "clear," "forward," "free," or "comfortable" in describing tone quality before an auditory image exists in the director's mind is to court disaster. Rather, he should begin to mold his ideas of tone by listening to choral performances, both live and recorded, and while doing so should recognize and isolate the choral characteristics which are distinctive for each particular quality of tone. If he likes the sound, why? Is it because of the beauty of the blend? Is it the degree of resonance employed by the singer? Is the resonance produced with equal skill by all the sections of the chorus? Now, does this factor of resonance affect for good or ill the fullness of the voices (amplitude), their balance, or their rhythmic vitality? Most important, can the listener-conductor suggest or guess at the means by which this quality of resonance was developed?

This kind of analysis as one listens should proceed with all choral charac- teristics. Which are predominant in the tone? Does their stress or accentuation or submergence affect other tonal factors? To repeat: as a conductor I like or I disapprove of a particular choral sound. I must be able to answer in detail my own question: why do I react as I do to a particular quality?

More often than not a listener is aware only of the interpretive elements in performance. If he does notice tone, very seldom will he attempt to separate those elements which are responsible for almost everything which he hears. A successful teacher of singing knows that as he instructs a beginner he can be concerned with only one or two techniques at a time. He does not teach "voice"; he talks or works so that his student concentrates on one problem, then another, and then another. The conductor must follow an identical pedagogical scheme as he teaches himself. If he will practice for the refinement of his listening skills and include in this practice a desire to develop his capacity to recognize each choral characteristic, his tonal concepts will expand at a rapid rate. The "what" (identification of characteristic) is succeeded by the "why" (influence of characteristic upon other factors of tone). It then becomes only a short time before he is able to cope successfully with the "how" (teaching techniques by which characteristics are developed and refined).

Before a conductor plans in detail his rehearsals for tonal development, he should turn his attention to the offerings of the six schools. Now he sees them in a new light. Because he has trained himself to hear clearly the factors or characteristics which engender tone quality, he is able to evaluate the ideas proposed by the schools in terms of their usefulness for his own purposes. He accepts or rejects these procedures as they may help or hinder the development of a tone quality which he will create. Instead of resigning himself to a process of imitation or blundering along in an aimless fashion by trying first one device and then another, he is able to predetermine the tonal consequences of the techniques which he chooses to stress in rehearsal. To put it simply, he now knows what he is doing to build his instrument.

An evaluation of the principles and procedures of the six schools in terms of choral characteristics might proceed in this manner:

School A

Fundamental Premises
(1)   Individual differences among singers are recognized and a vocal method is formulated to allow for these differences.
(2)   Every musical composition is classified according to the mood or emotion which it expresses. Performers are able to communicate this emotion to their audience.

Tonal Elements in One Voice	*Rehearsal Techniques:* *Principles and Practice*
phonation and release	Sharp attacks with use of *staccato* and *marcato* vocalizations; releases conditioned by word endings.
support and breath control	Emphasis on a variety of postural aids; basic vowel is *uh* produced with half-smile.
resonance	A shout for the men, a scream for the women; utilization of pitch consonants and thin vowels in syllables, i.e., *ming, lee, name*, etc.
pronunciation and articulation	Of great importance (see diction rules pp. 13-14); practiced by memorizing and applying the rules listed in the chart.
extension of range	Modification of vowel sounds at lift; use of scream and shout to extend full voice upward; no consideration of registers; sensation of body support and amount of energy shifts with changing pitches.
color, timbre, texture	Determined by individual concepts of the mood or emotion expressed in the text; basic tone color is dark.
amplitude	Men—big voices; women—full, dark, but lighter (in weight) than the sound of the male voice;
vibrato	the opportunity to develop a natural vibrato is encouraged.

Tonal Elements in the Chorus	
blend	Theoretically developed by following principles for good diction appearing on pages 13-14; however, the voices are too large to sing with a significant blend.
balance	Bass is predominant because choir voices have been developed so that the male sound is larger than that sung by the women; a "steeple" balance.
intonation	Choirs may flat because of the weight and thickness of the male tone; they may sharp because of the driving, energized attacks and the emphasis upon emotional factors.
diction	Encouraged—but sometimes to the point where *legato* phrasing seems impossible to achieve.
rhythmic vitality	Excellent in areas of precision, accuracy, and exciting use

	of energy; rhythm is not necessarily related to techniques of phrasing.
We hear:	Full, dark, weighty, and vibrant tone sung in all parts of the range; emphasis on meaning of text; dynamic contrast; unusual balance.
We do not hear:	Emphasis on blend; emphasis of rhythmic phrasing; lightness or a thin tonal texture; effective *legato* singing.

School B

Fundamental Premises

(1)   All singing tone is like instrumental tone in color and timbre.

(2)   All vocalizations will have their effect upon tone quality.

Tonal Elements in One Voice	*Rehearsal Techniques:* *Principles and Practice*
phonation and release	All attacks are made precisely but with a minimum amount of physical effort.
support and breath control	Linked mentally to the contours of a musical phrase.
resonance	All dramatic and robust voices must be "lyricized," that is, taught to sing with less volume and energy.
pronunciation and articulation	Not stressed.*
extension of range	Employ light "string" and "flute" qualities with higher pitches; extensive use of descending scale passages for vocalization.
color, timbre, texture	All colors and timbres are developed according to kinds of vocalization; texture is clear, thin, flexible, and floating.
amplitude	The best voices are the small ones; most vocalizing is done at *pp*.
vibrato	No individual vibrato should be heard in the sound of any choral ensemble.
Tonal Elements in the Chorus	
blend	Very important and quite possible to achieve because of the small tone and clarity of texture.
balance	Inner voices are the most important.
intonation	Choirs may sing under the pitch because of the lack of energy applied in support of the tone.
diction	Never to be stressed to the point where a *legato* passage is disturbed or the arch in the phrase disappears.
rhythmic vitality	Not stressed.
We hear:	A small, bright, thin, floating tone; an excellent blend; an extremely soft dynamic used much of the time; literally, a "polyphonic" tone.
We do not hear:	Big voices; vibrato; rhythmic vitality; excellent diction; dark tone; effective singing of any selection which demands some degree of personalized mood or emotion in its interpretation.

*When the phrase "not stressed" appears, this does not mean that the school in question is unaware of or does nothing with this particular choral technique. It believes that other skills are more important. Such information is of great value to a conductor who is attempting to develop his own ideas of tone quality.

School C

Fundamental Premises

(1)   While ideas and tastes may vary, the most important objective for a choir is to sing a tone which, because of its character and beauty, an audience continuously wishes to hear. The sound of a choir is its greatest asset.

(2)   By its very nature good ensemble quality exists only as individual concepts disappear.

	Rehearsal Techniques:
Tonal Elements in One Voice	*Principles and Practice*
phonation and release	"Matching" vowel sounds continuously through the phrase; balance and tuning maintained to the end of the phrase.
support and breath control	Not stressed.
resonance	Not stressed.
pronunciation and articulation	Unified by "matching procedures."
extension of range	Not stressed.
color, timbre, texture	Very important; lyric voices favored; color is gained from unified drill with a variety of vowel sounds.
amplitude	Softer singing stressed so that a wider range in dynamics is possible; dynamic change within vocal sections for purposes of expression.
vibrato	The use of a "solo vibrato" is discouraged.

Tonal Elements in the Chorus	
blend	Important; achieved by matching vowel sounds and by the careful placement of singers in each vocal section.
balance	Important; achieved primarily by planning the number of singers and their placement in each vocal section; the formation of the choir for performance does not change.
intonation	Important; tune all chords constantly; begin with unisons.
diction	Practice precision.
rhythmic vitality	Some choirs advocate an "urgency"—a pull from note to note to increase intensity; others "float" through a phrase; vowels must be sung on the beat; when used tastefully, *rubato* is important.
We hear:	Almost the ultimate in possibilities for choral blend and balance; precision of attack and release; excellent intonation; an "impersonal" tone; maximum use of softer dynamics.
We do not hear:	Rhythmic elements expressed in sound; big tone; vibrato; qualities of extreme resonance or brilliance; great dynamic contrasts.

School D

Fundamental Premise

There is no factor in choral singing as important as diction. A unified pronunciation is the only way to combine all elements of singing so that music sounds and moves properly, beautifully, and gracefully.

	Rehearsal Techniques:
Tonal Elements in One Voice	*Principles and Practice*
phonation and release	Every singer must reproduce every vowel and consonant sound and give to each a proportionate time value in the musical phrase.

support and breath control	Not stressed.
resonance	Exaggeration of pitch consonants.
pronunciation and articulation	(See phonation and release.)
extension of range	Not stressed.
color, timbre, texture	Exaggeration of vowel and consonant sounds.
amplitude	Provides basically for a kind of *legato* singing which tends to set limits on volume.
vibrato	Not stressed.

Tonal Elements in the Chorus

blend	Important; each singer must learn to make every syllable at precisely the same instant as his fellow singers.
balance	Not stressed.
intonation	Achieved effectively by insisting that all pitch consonants be sung on the pitch of the vowel which follows.
diction	This is the most important choral characteristic (see fundamental premise).
rhythmic vitality	Implied in the use of proportional time values for syllabic sounds; if this technique is used without the addition of certain tonal and interpretive devices, musical styles may be distorted.
We hear:	A tone which is sung comfortably but usually without evidence of intensity; a tone which possesses limited rhythmic qualities; splendid diction; excellent *legato* phrasing; literally "speech in song."
We do not hear:	Great dynamic variation; brilliance; changes in color or texture adequate to stylistic requirements; a tone which lends itself to all rhythmic demands; evidence in sound that each singer has been taught to use his vocal instrument.

School E

Fundamental Premises

(1) A satisfactory choral tone will be obtained only when each singer in the group understands how to realize completely his own vocal potential.

(2) A singer who possesses an instrument adequate for solo or ensemble performance (a) provides excellent physical support for his tone, (b) has the ability to sing a range of three octaves, (c) coordinates effectively the two registers in his voice, (d) sings with greatly increased powers of resonance, and (e) sings with a tone that is full, big, dark, and "operatic" in its sound.

Tonal Elements in One Voice	*Rehearsal Techniques:* *Principles and Practice*
phonation and release	Attacks are made vigorously and with great intensity which is maintained to the end of a phrase.
support and breath control	Important; mechanistic pedagogy used almost exclusively; constant practice to develop antagonistic action of "holding" muscles; use of conscious controls to loosen jaw, free tongue, inhibit swallowing muscles, etc.
resonance	Important; resonance is formulated primarily in a pharynx which is free of obstruction or tension; practice to free the tongue and other vocal organs which normally impede the proper development of resonance.
pronunciation and articulation	Not stressed; considered somewhat of an obstacle to proper tone production.

extension of range	Important; implies the acceptance of the principle of "weak and strong" registers in each voice and the necessity to strengthen and coordinate these with repetitive practice.
color, timbre, texture	Important; finished tonal product calls for more low than high format; basic vowels for practice: dark *aw, ay* (o, a); texture is thick.
amplitude	Important; all dynamic panels are conceived in terms of relative fullness or "big" sound; employment of vocalization with full voice particularly in beginning stages of development.
vibrato	Every singer is encouraged to sing with his natural vibrato.

Tonal Elements in the Chorus

blend	Acquired only by a limited attempt to tune vibrato rates; must not be secured at the risk of imposing restrictions on individual voice production; the large ensemble sound precludes the development of "blend" as one usually thinks of the meaning of the term.
balance	Not stressed.
intonation	Some tendency for choruses to sing under the pitch because of the prominence of vibrato and the fullness of the tone; thus, at times, singers cannot hear exact pitch.
diction	Important only for purposes of communication.
rhythmic vitality	The tone possesses qualities of vitality and precision but is not a flexible instrument.
We hear:	A chorus of solo voices; this does not mean that all elements of ensemble are lacking: the huge and vital sound is thrilling for those compositions which demand this particular quality of tone; the sound is produced easily and comfortably by singers uninhibited by problems of range and who perform with confidence and pleasure in their own vocal powers.
We do not hear:	A tone exemplifying the usual choral standards for blend, balance, diction, and flexibility; the last term is defined to mean clarity and dynamics of ensemble sound.

School F

Fundamental Premises

(1) Every instant of musical time must be used up in singing: there is no fragmentary time without dramatic drive.

(2) There is no such thing as abstract beauty of choral tone; there is only dramatic integrity of choral tone.

(3) If a conductor and his chorus are sensitive to the rhythmic elements in a score and are able to recreate these by sensing or feeling or experiencing them, all expressive devices including tone will meet the requirements of the composer and his music.

Rehearsal Techniques:

Tonal Elements in One Voice	*Principles and Practice*
phonation and release	Important; conditioned by rhythmic factors in each phrase which must be related to the ending of the preceding phrase and the beginning of the following one.
support and breath control	Important; proper support comes from sensing the vitality inherent in the smallest unit of musical time expressed in sound.

resonance	Not stressed.
pronunciation and articulation	Important; all vowels are sung on the beat and consonants are sounded to meet the requirements of pulse and tempo; every sung sound has its time allotment.
color, timbre, texture	Important; tone, and not words, carries emotion; to some extent tonal color and texture are variable.
amplitude	Rehearse at softer dynamic levels; amplitude comes from an increasing measure of vitality in the tone.
vibrato	Allowed but not stressed.

Tonal Elements in the Chorus

blend	Important: the tone is the aural representation of all rhythmic elements in the score; it has movement, direction, pronunciation and regulated by rhythmic requirements.
balance	Not stressed.
intonation	Constant rehearsal leading to pitch memory; poor intonation is due in part to a poor rhythmic sense.
diction	Pronounce all the sounds in words and not the words themselves.
rhythmic vitality	Important; the tone is the aural representation of all rhythmic elements in the score; it has movement, direction, precision, vitality, urgency—a sense of "going somewhere"; practice with the treatment of the weak beats, the feeling of the smallest time unit, the separation of dotted notes and the relationship of musical and physical movement.
We hear:	Vigorous tone; *elasticity* in tone; rhythmic elements sounding as though they are sensed or felt by the singers; diction used primarily to shape a musical phrase; evidence of sound always in motion; variable and exciting uses of color; tone quality correlating and implementing other interpretive elements rather than being heard for itself alone.
We do not hear:	Tone exploited as an aesthetic experience; emphasis upon expressive qualities of *rubato* and tempo changes; the accentuation of words to exploit their meanings; elements of musical sound and interpretation divorced from the score.

It is obvious that the six schools offer an enterprising conductor a varied and exciting list of principles and practices which will help him build his own choral instrument. If he is timid or unsure of procedures, the outline which follows may be of assistance. These are the precepts and techniques "borrowed" by the author which have been found useful in the development of his choir's tone.

From School A

1. A desire to understand and teach with the potential vocal ability of each singer as an important objective. This begins with the first audition, which is designed to explore individual idiosyncrasies, capacities, and so on, and is not limited to the one purpose of determining choir membership.
2. The use of range, voice quality, and lifts for deciding upon voice classification.

3. The employment of postural aids, (with the exception of the jaw position; I favor a dropped and loose jaw).
4. The utilization of a great many *marcato* and *staccato* types of vocalization.
5. A limited use of the "scream" or "siren" device to extend range and establish the feeling for head tone, particularly with the mezzo and contralto voices.
6. Some application of the rules found in the diction chart (pp. 13-14).

From School B

1. The employment of descending scales sung at *pp* to teach the singers a feeling for buoyancy and lightness (of weight) in the tone. This is necessary for the performance of much of the older music.

From School C

1. The utilization of the matching principle for purposes of blend. However, the choir does not rehearse this technique over long periods of time, nor is it used with every new piece of literature.
2. When the choir sings sacred polyphony of the fifteenth and sixteenth centuries (and only for this particular style of music), the women are asked to use a vibratoless tone and the men a "head tone" quality. This is established with the use of *oo* (ōō, women) and *oh* (ō, men) sung with descending scales. In order to protect the voices the dynamic panel is not allowed to exceed *mp* or *mf*, and attacks, releases, and the choice of tempos are conditioned to take care of this "temporary" tone production. This quality of tone enhances personal interpretive and stylistic ideas relative to the performance of sacred music of this historical period.

From School D

1. We learn to exaggerate consonant sounds, to think syllables rather than words for purposes of drill for unified pronunciation (but not for interpretive reasons), and to begin new words with the final consonants of preceding ones—especially in unison passages or where *legato* phrasing is needed.
2. We use the important principles concerning the treatment of diphthongs and triphthongs.

From School E

1. In first rehearsals singers are taught to control by physical means (a) breathing for the attack, (b) support for the tone, and (c) tongue and jaw action. This mechanistic pedagogy is succeeded at a later period by an approach which emphasizes sensory and psychological principles of instruction.
2. We utilize in many ways the principle of isolating and then coordinating the registers. The high range of the men is developed with the use of an "energized" falsetto which eventually becomes a part of their normal tone

production. All women vocalize at comfortable pitches in the lower register and then simulate their sensations of support and pronunciation used for the lower voice as they move to higher points in the scale. If there is no tension, the coordination of physical factors needed for the production of a pleasing tone is quite successful. Increased power and sonority comes with vocalizing in the lower register, and for both men and women this full or "mature" sound carries on up the scale and is possible to produce on any pitch. On the other hand, soft and controlled tones and what might be termed the "sweetness" in the women's voices (in addition to the ability to sing the higher pitches) comes with the practice in the high register. The development of both registers allows the singers to "mix" tonal colors magnificently from the technical standpoint; any choice of color is related, of course, to the interpretive requirements of the score. It is also useful for singers to know whether they are using a "heavy" or a "light" production when they are singing lines which in pitch hover about the weaker spots in the range. Very often intonation at these points is affected by the registration used by the singers. Thus, if proper register development takes place, this can affect the control of dynamics, the nature of pronunciation, the extension of range, and the establishment of an acceptable intonation.

From School F

1. To develop rhythmic precision, the choir
    a. Breaks down many notes into smaller durational units; these are both spoken and sung with numbers or with syllables which are appropriate to the mood and style of the musical selection.
    b. Uses the technique of singing to a given point in a phrase (perhaps it is to the midpoint in a word) and stopping suddenly; two or three syllables may be added and the process is repeated.
    c. Sings only the last few syllables in a phrase; then, several preceding syllables are added and sung, and this procedure is rehearsed many times.
    d. Sings only vowel sounds in each word to be certain that these are felt and sung exactly with the pulse.
2. The practice for the development of pitch memory.
3. The very important concepts of the relationship of sound and time must come from the explanations of the director which are reinforced by his conducting techniques in rehearsal and performance. These are concerned with
    a. The movement of sound.
    b. The accumulation and dissemination of energy in music.
    c. The nature and shape of a musical phrase.
    d. The vital truth that music must always be doing something (even in rests).

It should be evident that every choral conductor, including the author, will be happy and successful with the sound of his instrument only if he goes beyond the principles and techniques advocated by the six schools. To their methods selected by him for use with his choir he adds his own precepts. These must be chosen according to several criteria. The first of these is the conductor's understanding of himself. How does he communicate best with his choir? What styles of music does he enjoy—does he feel "most comfortable" with in directing? In what manner does musical sound appeal to him? Then, he should consider the level and experience of the musicians in his chorus together with the time available for rehearsal. Furthermore, he must accept the premise that no choir can sing all music equally well. For, if he is convinced that the blend of his choir is a primary objective, he should know that rhythmic vitality and tonal amplitude will suffer. The reverse of this precept also is true. Choral blend and individual vibrato do not go hand in hand. If he has decided upon the extensive use of any particular vowel for purposes of vocalization, his choice will affect such important attributes of sound as texture, color, amplitude, vitality, and phonation. If the conductor is drawn to the expressive power of a text, he will ask his chorus to "bend phrases" by the use of a tempo *rubato*—and by so doing the rhythmic elements in the phrase may be distorted. These and many other choices made by the conductor not only affect choral tone but also will determine the selection of repertoire and the degree of historical accuracy with which the music is performed.

THE AUTHOR'S METHODOLOGY

It may be helpful to the reader to know how the author has used these suggested criteria in developing his own methodology. This augments his "borrowing" from the several schools which were described on pages 48-51.

As a teacher of singing, I am concerned with the vocal growth of each individual in the chorus. This includes the development of his ability to phonate properly, and to support, control, and resonate the tone. He is encouraged to use vibrato and must learn to extend his range.

As a conductor, my principal desire is that my chorus learn to communicate to an audience all the musical, aesthetic, and textual elements which are in each score they sing. Every rehearsal principle and technique is dedicated to this purpose. Therefore, I consider that the tone of the choir is important as it may contribute to communication. Furthermore, of all the choral characteristics, I believe that the color of tone is most helpful as an agency of communication. It accomplishes for song that which stress, pause, pitch change, and accentuation do for speech. Also, color in tone, unlike other tonal ingredients, is capable of a limited change from song to song.

Many conductors will utilize the principles of diction as the means for developing tone color. While acknowledging the importance of this approach, I prefer to believe that the primary sources for color are found in two places: (1)

the dynamic, harmonic, and rhythmic characteristics of each musical phrase, and (2) the expressive quality of the text which will vary greatly with the historical period of the composition. To these two sources for tone color I give much time and attention.

With these objectives as a background for my thinking and planning I review my consideration of choral characteristics. I remind myself that from the several schools I have taken principles, techniques, and so on, which will be useful in the development of these characteristics:

1. For the tonal elements in *one voice* I have "borrowed" ideas relative to my instructional approach, the nature of phonation and release, resonance, pronunciation and articulation, extension of range, and amplitude.
2. For the tonal elements in *the chorus* I have "borrowed" ideas relative to blend, intonation, diction, rhythmic vitality, and color.

What remains for me to add? I want to utilize techniques which hopefully will help to solve problems relating to (1) phonation, (2) support, (3) vibrato (4) color, and (5) choral balance. (In the areas of phonation and color I wish to use techniques to supplement those which I have "borrowed.") As I consider these areas which need attention, I recognize that the schools have furnished materials for the tonal development of the ensemble but that I will wish to develop other techniques as I work with individual singers.

Vocalizations are used in the solution of these problems and each exercise is selected with these conditions in mind:

1. The amount of rehearsal time to be devoted to a specific vocalise.
2. Selection of material from choral literature or other sources.
3. Choice of vowel or syllable.
4. Presentation of the vocalise to selected singers, a section of the chorus, or the entire ensemble.

Exercises to Help with the Process of Phonation (Attack)

1. For extremely breathy voices I use with care the whispered glottal stroke followed by soft speech employing the same technique. The student then is asked to "think" the glottal stroke as he uses staccato with sung sounds.
2. For a singer who habitually uses a glottal attack I prefer that he vocalize with *kl* combined with a vowel sound to rid himself of this problem. I believe that the aspirate *h* advocated by many teachers to help with this particular difficulty leads inevitably to other vocal problems.
3. My choir sighs, pants, blows out scores of candles, and counts both with speech and sung vowels. We stretch and sing with our backs against a good solid wall for the first few weeks of rehearsals. We slowly speak and sing nonsense phrases filled with sustained pitch consonants to develop the sensation which should accompany intensified tone. These exercises help both with processes of attack and support for the tone.

4. Normally, the choir will be asked to take breath through the mouth *and* nostrils. Inhalation in this manner is accomplished quickly. At times we experiment with breathing only with the nose for the sake of calmness, or only with the mouth to secure depth of breath.

5. My choice of "basic" vowel sounds are, for men, *o* and *aw*, and for women, *uh* and *ah*.

6. I do not employ humming as a device for initiating a tone: for listening purposes, possibly for building resonance, for teaching comprehension of dynamic levels of sound, yes; for attack, no.

7. I believe that the most important principle related to attack or phonation is the degree of intensity with which the sound is begun. This is variable and depends almost entirely upon the nature of the phrase which follows. The chorus must know the speed and the degree with which energy is to be accumulated and dispersed. Therefore, the singers must be taught to initiate many kinds of attacks, and they are helped in this endeavor (1) by the way in which I prepare and indicate the attack with my fingers, hands, wrist, arms, breath, mouth, eyes, and chest, and (2) the kind of picturesque speech which I can employ in rehearsal: an "attack" may be driven, clipped, caressed, stroked, cut, hit, sobbed, sighed, and so on. It may question, command, or plead. It may be thoughtful, joyful, solemn, triumphant, mysterious, doubtful, worried, or enthusiastic. And, with the exception of the first phrase in the selection, it continues something which already has begun.

Exercises to Help with Processes of Support and Breath Control

1. To basic exercises which are sung *marcato* by the men and *staccato* by the women (this because of the difference in the "weight" of their tone), we add a vocalise which calls for an extremely rapid *crescendo* and *diminuendo* of a single tone followed by another step higher sung in the same fashion and continuing in this manner throughout a scale. Obviously, a singer cannot perform the exercise successfully without using a significant amount of diaphragmatic control. The choir does not breathe or break the pattern of sound between pitches.

2. I believe that it is helpful for the singer to develop a higher level of support for higher pitches and that less breath (in quantity) under greater pressure is needed to sing properly these tones. The opposite is true when lower pitches are sung. Perhaps it is unnecessary to say that the basic process for support remains undisturbed regardless of pitch, tempo, or dynamic change.

3. Support is helped immeasurably if the singer learns (1) to "balance" the intensity of all vowel sounds, and (2) to modify the pronunciation of vowels with respect to range and dynamic.

4. With the exception of a few musical phrases which because of their "special"

nature are performed with great care and concentration, other passages ordinarily are not given their proper due and consideration by a choir. At some point *before* a passage is concluded, the thoughts of conductor and choir are already upon the next phrase while they continue to sing the preceding one. This happens, I believe, because this is the way that we have been taught to read. Also, we conductors condition our choirs and ourselves to think in terms of *beginning* and not *ending* a phrase. Regardless of tonal methods, "schools of thought," or what have you, this neglect of rehearsal for the release of sound at the end of a phrase is the most glaring fault in contemporary choral singing. Too many of us are content if our choirs release their tone at the same time and with some consistency in dynamic. We do not insist that what was begun with the singing of the phrase must be completed.

Exercises to Develop a Natural Vibrato

1. As the voice matures so will the vibrato of the singer.
2. The vibrato is made more pleasing, more useful, and will blend to a remarkable degree if members of the chorus learn to
    a. Sing *legato* scales at almost every imaginable tempo with emphasis upon those which move quite rapidly.
    b. Sing vocalises which employ many different kinds of rhythmic variation.
    c. Concentrate upon listening for the vibrato rate in their own voices and in other voices in their section of the choir.

It is possible to blend and to tune vibrato rates if there is sufficient desire and an accompanying measure of concentration on the part of every singer.

Methods to Help Improve Tonal Color and Choral Balance

Color and balance are achieved only if the members of the choir (1) understand and thereby communicate the meaning both in the text and the musical form of a phrase, (2) are able to hear at all times the sounds sung by the entire choir, and (3) are seated in their voice sections and the sections are placed within the choir so that the result is an optimum for tonal values. To implement these procedures we use these techniques:

1. Depending upon the period of its composition we speak of the expressive quality of the text and the music which accompanies it. Like all conductors I use various forms of picturesque speech, metaphor, and analogy to attempt to paint a vivid word picture. However, I believe that there is danger in indicating that the chorus see or think or imagine exactly in the same way that I do. I prefer to stimulate *their* imaginative and communicative powers rather than insisting that they follow my own.

2. When the auditory can be accompanied by the visual and the sensory, it

is easier to comprehend. Therefore, we diagram phrases on a blackboard and endeavor to trace in them the speed, direction, and degree of their energy accumulation and dissemination. We try to find the musical logic for a proper use of rubato, inflection, and accentuation. We learn the fundamental qualities in short and long notes, in high and low pitches, in contrast or in repetition, whether such be in length of phrase, in tempo, in dynamic, or in rhythm. I "measure" volume of sound by using an imaginary distance between my hands, and the chorus memorizes concepts of dynamics both by hearing sound and by feeling the energy which they produce to make it. We find that there are two score ways to pronounce or to color every vowel sound depending upon its musical context.

3. Since I believe that the contribution of each singer is vitally important, his placement and that of his section becomes most significant. He is seated in a particular place only after days and weeks of singing with prospective partners, and the process of finding the permanent spot where he can sing most comfortably and effectively goes on for some months. The same procedure applies to the placement of the several voice sections; it is seldom that one finds in two successive years the vocal sections in my choir appearing in the same place. Although I understand all the reasons for a standard seating plan, I believe that since persons and voices change from year to year we may gain by our willingness to experiment with placement.

The process of building a choral instrument is an exciting and challenging experience for every conductor. The sound of his choir will reflect both his success and his failure to utilize properly the technical and interpretive aspects of music. But once a conductor knows the basic processes of singing, once he is familiar with the demands of the score, and once he can evaluate his own personal and musical resources, then, and only then, can he develop his tonal concepts with a judicious employment of procedures which have been tested over a long period. To these he adds his own techniques—and at this point, he is well on his way to becoming in time that very rare person—an artist.

TWO

THE CHORAL CONDUCTOR
AND THE REHEARSAL

Lloyd Pfautsch

PURPOSE OF THE REHEARSAL

The primary and most commonly recognized goal of choral rehearsals is the concert appearance. The public performance not only provides motivation for purposeful and disciplined rehearsals but constitutes a pause in choral development at which time the chorus and its conductor may present a summation of their progress in choral refinement. The choral concert thus reveals much about the chorus and its conductor. In addition to demonstrating how carefully rehearsal time has been spent, the concert reflects the conductor's musicianship, musical tastes, knowledge of repertoire and style, understanding of the human voice, understanding of people (in the choir and the audience), and especially his abilities as a rehearsal technician.

Generally, however, we tend to forget that there are other, perhaps even more beneficial results from intelligent choral rehearsing than a praiseworthy public performance. A chorus is a community of singers led by a conductor in service to the choral art. Together they are willing to learn and work in a curious interdependence (as we shall see later) to enlarge their understanding and appreciation of choral music and to develop their voices and choral techniques. In particular, they can, and should, aspire to the following:

1. An expanding encounter with the vast repertory of choral literature, along with a growing sensitivity to stylistic integrity.
2. A gradual mastery of the scores being studied and prepared for performance as the "blueprint" of the composer's notation is realized in sound. The printed score should arouse the imagination so that the inner life of the music can then be reborn in sound (a stimulated imagination will add new and varied dimensions to performance).
3. The development of technical disciplines so that the voice, the ear, the lips, the tongue, the breathing mechanism, and so on—all become more proficient and responsive in carrying out the demands of the music, thus eliminating technical barriers which inhibit choral development. The gradual absorption of choral disciplines creates good rehearsal habits.
4. The cultivation of flexibility and versatility comparable to that expected of soloists. An atmosphere of artistic endeavor encourages individual responsibility and personal musicianship, particularly sight singing.
5. A more expressive and effective communication between conductor and chorus, encouraging responsiveness.
6. The development of an awareness of how important and essential it is for each singer to listen to himself and to others, and to hear and comprehend the interreliance of all parts.
7. A constant and unsparing effort to approximate choral ideals, thus creating a corporate sense of satisfaction, stimulation, exhilaration, entertainment, and educational advancement.

In recent years a much greater versatility has been expected of choruses than was the case twenty-five years ago. Contemporary composers are writing choral music with a variety of unfamiliar sounds which challenge both the chorus and its conductor to develop new vocal and rehearsal techniques. Choruses are expected to perform a greater variety of choral literature and to do so in the appropriate style. It is in the rehearsal that the choral community fortifies itself for meeting these responsibilities.

The choral conductor is responsible for making effective use of rehearsal time. Many conductors are skillful and adept in rehearsing, while others are clumsy and inept. A few have a charisma which helps them as they rehearse, even though the techniques they employ are the same as those of other conductors. And some conductors rely on personality, dictatorial demeanor, or blind loyalty. But regardless of how conductors rehearse, all are required to prepare for this responsible leadership. How they prepare foretells the measure of success they will achieve.

PREPARATION FOR REHEARSAL

Preparation begins with experience: singing in a choral group, listening to choral groups, observing other choral conductors, and learning from what one does in his own rehearsals. It is most important that the background of every choral conductor include the regimen of singing in a choral ensemble. In no other way can he appreciate the significance of individual contribution to the ensemble sound, individual responsibility in following the conductor's directions, and individual reaction to different rehearsal procedures. Without this experience, a choral conductor will lack empathetic understanding of the individual and the group. Experience in choral singing will also lead to the choice of a model singer and a model conductor—be they actual individuals or the idealistic composite of those qualities considered worthy of emulation.

No choral conductor outgrows the need for listening to other choral ensembles and learning from such experience. Opportunities for listening include formal concerts, recordings, and rehearsals. A concert performance by any choral group will reveal how they have rehearsed under their conductor's guidance. Although recordings always present an incomplete choral sound, they disclose many good and bad rehearsal procedures while also demonstrating how much a conductor knows about the choral problems which are peculiar to recording—for example, arranging the voices for a balanced pickup by the microphones. Both concerts and recordings provide opportunities for enlarging one's exposure to repertoire and performance practices. No choral conductor can ever acquaint himself with the entire repertoire performed in his professional environment or available on hundreds of recordings. Yet his preparation involves the need for continual attentiveness to choral sounds *other than those produced under his direction*, with emphasis on variety, style, technical proficiency, and musicality. Again, the role of models is significant, especially in the early stages of a choral-conducting career. However, a choral conductor will always need to engage in an objective criticism of the preferred model or models lest he become and remain a slave to that source of stimulation and never develop any independence as a choral conductor. (It goes without saying, of course, that, while this independence is to be a goal for all choral conductors, it is ultimately more procedural or philosophical than environmental since no choral conductor can avoid the influence of the choral community on his own choral work.)

FRAMES OF REFERENCE

No choral conductor ever outgrows the stimulation one can experience when reading books and periodicals available in the choral field. The choral art is not an exact science: there is no *one authority* or *one school* which has discovered all the knowledge pertinent to the choral art. Any writing is thus, at best, a partial presentation, disseminating what the author has discovered within his own experience and study. Furthermore, the more one reads, the more obvious it becomes that most of the ideas presented have been encountered before. Some choral conductors may consider this fact reason enough not to bother reading more than a few basic books. However, if these ideas are repeated in writings on the choral art, then they must have significance; even though the ideas may be basic, the writer's discussion and application will have an individual touch that can enlarge the reader's understanding. This book, for example, does not pretend to be an all-inclusive presentation of what is to be known about the choral art, and most certainly this particular chapter will not cover all that could be included in a discussion of the choral rehearsal. Naturally, the writer hopes that his presentation will be both informative and provocative, but he will follow his own admonition to continue reading and to welcome the exposure to different approaches and ideas as a professional responsibility.

More generally, the interest in enlarging one's knowledge and understanding should not be limited to the choral art, for every choral conductor should be eager to know more about other areas of human knowledge. While there will always be limitations of time, energy, and personal propensity, it is important to broaden oneself in the other arts, in the social and natural sciences, in history, in philosophy, in theology, and the like. There are choral conductors who need to be reminded that there is other music besides choral music. Exposure to the creative efforts of a dramatist, novelist, poet, painter, sculptor, or choreographer can enhance artistic sensitivity. Opening one's mind to the thinking of philosophers, theologians, politicians, scientists, economists, and so on, can contribute a breadth of knowledge which not only suggests a more complete human being but also helps the choral conductor relate more effectively to the other human beings with whom and for whom he works. This openmindedness also encourages learning from the other disciplines as well as willingness to change, to experiment, to adopt, and to appropriate.

LEARNING FROM MODELS

It was mentioned earlier that certain conductors are endowed with charisma. Many conductors are able to produce good choral music in spite of technical and musical inadequacies, while other less charismatic ones produce results which contradict their recognized musical training and ability. Not every good musician is a good rehearsal technician, just as a good rehearsal technician might not necessarily be a good musician. A fine singer does not necessarily become a good choral conductor. Why is it that a chorus will work for one conductor and not for another? Why will singers produce good vocal tone for one conductor and not for another? How does a chorus sense that one conductor has empathy with vocal technique while another does not? Why does a chorus overlook the musical integrity of one conductor while overlooking the lack of it in another? How do some conductors manage to establish an esprit without even talking about it, while other conductors alienate the singers as they employ the generally accepted methods of rehearsing? The answers to these questions will reflect the kind of preparation each conductor has considered important as well as the extent of his preparation. When thoroughness of preparation combines with charisma, the rehearsals are distinctive.

A most important warning should be given to young choral conductors.

Stated simply, the warning is BE YOURSELF. In watching other conductors work, listening to other choral groups, and reading what others have to say about the choral art, appropriate what will work for *you*. What you borrow must be meaningful for you. Do not employ another conductor's rehearsal techniques *just because they work for him*. Seek to understand the purpose behind the procedure and adapt the procedure to your own way of working. There is great danger in the matching of attire, humor, jargon, stance, and conducting gestures and mannerisms. The results usually are not the same, and when they are not, either great consternation overwhelms the imitator, or he deceives himself into thinking that he hears the same results achieved by his model just because he has imitated it. Thus, the choral conductor's *self-image* will determine the type and quality of preparation for rehearsing, the specific procedures employed in rehearsing, and the boundaries of effectiveness while rehearsing. It often seems easier to mimic the successful conductors than to pursue the reason behind their success. However, such pursuit can lead to a more profound understanding of why they do what they do; then this knowledge should be applied with *your own personal touch* in a manner that is *your* way of sharing this knowledge. Never forget to BE YOURSELF!

SCORE STUDY

The study and analysis of scores is an aspect of rehearsal preparation which choral conductors must accept as routine. This responsibility requires personal discipline, patience, and an inquisitive mind. As the details of a score are mastered through study, mnemonic development can be a by-product which every choral conductor will find beneficial if not essential. The particulars of score study and analysis are presented elsewhere in this book. They merely need to be reaffirmed at this point so as to emphasize continuous dedication to this phase of rehearsal preparation.

SCHEDULING OF REHEARSALS

Scheduling rehearsals is another prerehearsal consideration. Many rehearsal times are determined by tradition, by space limitations, by schedule exigencies, or by an authority higher than the choral conductor. In such situations the conductor will need to adjust. It is often easier for one person to make the necessary adjustments than to ask many to adjust. When the conductor has a voice in scheduling rehearsals, he should entertain the following considerations:

School (High School, College, and University) Choirs

Is the purpose of the group an educational opportunity for many to gain experience singing in a chorus, or, in addition to being educational, is it also a select group with a public relations factor in concertizing, or is it strictly promotional and committed to entertainment?

The purpose of the group will dictate the amount of time required for rehearsing. The location of the rehearsals in the schedule will hopefully be related to the purpose and the time required. To service large numbers of students or to assure an abundance of good singers for a select group, a minimum of schedule conflicts is necessary. The locations of the rehearsal in the schedule will hopefully avoid hours when physical, mental, and vocal fatigue can be problematic. The location of the rehearsal in the schedule will enable the conductor to have adequate time for checking the setup, last-minute preparations, unforeseen complications, and a few moments by himself.

Church Choirs

Again, the purpose, which should be obvious, is often overlooked. While the commitment to serving the worship experience of a congregation should be predominant, the conductor must never neglect educational responsibilities or forget that the church choir is a community of singers which needs or expects social interaction in a manner and at a degree of importance quite different from school or civic groups. The scheduling of rehearsals will need to consider other church activities, the complexities of business, professional, and family obligations, and the proximity to Sunday. The amount of time involved must allow for adequate preparation, organizational matters, and socializing.

Civic Choruses

Again, the purpose of the group is important. Is it a musical adjunct to the local symphony orchestra, a service choral organization which represents the city at various gatherings, or a group that contributes to the cultural life of the city by affording the best singers in the city an opportunity to perform choral masterworks?

The scheduling of rehearsals will require consideration of business, professional, and family obligations, the rehearsals of other choral groups such as church choirs, and the availability of rehearsal facilities. The length of rehearsals must allow for adequate preparation, organizational business, and breaks for rest, socializing, and so forth. The frequency and length of rehearsals are not as important as how the rehearsal time is used. Some conductors can accomplish more in one hour of rehearsal than others can in three.

REHEARSAL ENVIRONMENT

The rehearsal environment is very important. Although some excellent choral performances have been prepared under adverse conditions, it helps to have a room with good acoustics, lighting, seating, and temperature control. A well-lighted room with activating colors will help attract, arouse, and maintain a spirit of involvement. It is important that the chairs provide a degree of comfortable support while also encouraging correct body posture for singing. Each conductor will have to decide if he prefers a permanent or flexible seating arrangement on a flat surface or on tiered risers. This decision will not necessarily be the norm, for many choral conductors have to work within an environment which is determined by someone else, unless they have a room specifically set aside for choral rehearsals which they may have helped design. Temperature control cannot be overemphasized, especially since the advent of year-long temperature-control systems, which are usually fallible. Lack of constant and dependable thermostatic control frequently ruins rehearsals. A hot, stuffy rehearsal room is enervating, and, while a cold rehearsal room may seem initially activating, it quickly becomes depressive. Visual aids such as bulletin and chalk boards are necessary for announcements, reminders, publicity, listing the rehearsal sequence, and explanations. Systems for music storage should be adequate, accessible, and practical. In recent years, the importance of tape and phonographic equipment has become universally accepted although often regretfully limited. How a conductor uses this environment ultimately determines whether it controls him or he controls it. (For example, much valuable time can be lost through excessive taping during rehearsals.)

SEATING

Organization and preparation for seating arrangements must be planned with care. Every choral conductor will have a predilection for certain arrangements. A few varieties are shown in Figure 2-1. The exact seating arrangement will be

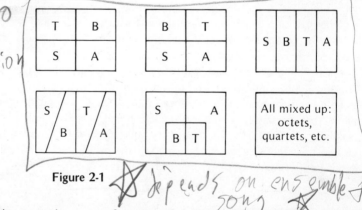

Figure 2-1

dependent on the type of seating. Rehearsal rooms which have permanent seating will limit the possible arrangements to varying degrees. Other rooms will allow for mobility and variation since the chairs will be movable. The following suggestions might prove helpful when planning seating arrangements:

1. The seating should vary with each choral group, with change in personnel, with the repertoire, and with reference to the arrangement which will be used for concert appearances.
2. The conductor must decide if he wants the arrangements to be consistent or if he prefers to change them frequently. Regular arrangements encourage the individual singer to develop a sense of security within the choral ensemble, while shifting arrangements encourage his sense of personal responsibility to the total choral ensemble sound.
3. Place weaker voices near the stronger, the inexperienced singer near the experienced, the singer with modest musicianship near one whose musicianship is advanced, and the person who is blessed with a good voice but who has difficulty in sight-singing near one who reads quickly although his voice has limitations.
4. Whatever the arrangement, it should assist the individual in relating to his own section as well as to the total ensemble sound.
5. The eventual arrangement should help the group develop a sense of ensemble and balance, interdependence and independence, and personal as well as corporate responsibility.
6. Singing position should be related to the style of the repertoire. For instance, when rehearsing polychoral works, the identity, development, and control of the several choirs can be assisted by various seating arrangements which also enhance the aural effect. The arrangement shown in Figure 2-2 might be used for Andrea Gabrieli's polychoral *Magnificat* for three choirs.

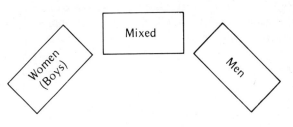

Figure 2-2

7. Do not choose a singing position for your choir based solely on another conductor's preference. What may be right for *him* and *his* chorus may not be right for *you* and *your* chorus. More important, the choice must be based on the structure of the music and the aural effect required by it.
8. Allow enough room for spacing so that the group can stand comfortably with enough room for necessary body movement.
9. As the performance date approaches, employ the concert arrangement consistently in rehearsal so that the group will feel secure and be able to adjust easily to the acoustical environment of the concert hall.

ORGANIZATION OF REHEARSAL

The organization of a rehearsal is the most important responsibility of a choral conductor. Many conductors rehearse in an improvisatory manner, and others are methodical to the point of tedium. A lack of organization is so hazardous that every conductor should develop early in his career a sense of obligation toward rehearsal organization. How one organizes a rehearsal depends on the particular chorus, the time of day, the amount of rehearsal time allowed, the variety of repertoire employed, the tempo, dynamics, and mood of the repertoire, the performance commitments, and the long range plans for the group. The use of rehearsal time can be rigid or elastic. Rigidity does not allow for unexpected accomplishments or complications, although it does limit the danger of aimless procedure. Elasticity allows for change within a planned procedure and allows for what develops in a rehearsal whether it be a problem or an achievement. Any choral group will recognize and appreciate an organized rehearsal prepared by a conductor who is capable of facile adaptations during a rehearsal.

The conductor must not waste rehearsal time, nor should he permit any of the personnel to waste it. Starting a rehearsal on time indicates meaningful purpose; ending a rehearsal on time indicates a respect for the individual's right to determine his own use of time outside the rehearsal. Both policies encourage punctuality. The organized use of rehearsal time indicates to the group that the conductor has made preparation and that he has an appreciation for the time and energy which the singers contribute during a rehearsal. A planned rehearsal which is paced well contributes much to a good rapport between the conductor and the chorus.

WARM-UPS

Young conductors are often eager to rehearse the music at hand but are frequently concerned about the preliminaries. They have read or been told that a rehearsal should begin by calling the roll, singing warming-up exercises and/or singing a familiar work. They may have encountered the idea that warm-ups are not necessary because the singers have employed their vocal mechanisms prior to the rehearsal. In opposition to this idea, there are devotees who favor warm-ups and spend almost one fourth of a rehearsal on them. Are warm-ups necessary? One could answer "yes" or "no," but they are generally agreed to be helpful for the following reasons:

1. Warm-ups have a pedagogical potential, although the conductor does not have to make this obvious to the chorus.
2. They are an excellent way to focus the attention of the chorus on the singing process.
3. Since singing makes greater demands on the human vocal mechanism than

speaking, warm-ups are an effective means of preparing the body and that mechanism for meeting these demands.

4. Since there is more extensive use of the breath in singing than in speaking, the muscles involved in breath support need to be activated and exercised before strenuous singing begins.

5. Warm-ups can help the singers relate breath support to tone production. The use of consonants can assist this process; for example, one can use the exercises shown in Figure 2-3.

Hip, hip, hoh, hoh, hoh Zip, zip, zoh, zoh, zoh *etc.*

Mah, may, mee, moh, moo Fah, fay, fee, foh, foo *etc.*

Figure 2-3

6. Warm-ups can assist in the development of vowel sounds and good tone production, the results being a collective precision in enunciating and sustaining uniform vowel sounds, and a collective sensitivity toward pitch accuracy. When this process is supervised with care and persistence, much of the common sound experienced in the warm-ups can be carried over into rehearsal and performance of the music.

7. The warm-up procedure should vary for rehearsals although the purpose should remain the same. When the same procedure is employed, it suggests mere routine and thereby encourages apathetic participation and a lack of attention. A variety of procedures will prove stimulating, engaging, and interesting to the singers and call on the conductor's imagination and ingenuity.

8. The warm-ups should be consistent with those employed in sound vocal pedagogy. Singing in a chorus may be the only vocal training many of the members will receive, so the conductor can use the warm-ups to share some vocal techniques and disciplines with the singers. Since there will also be a number of singers who have studied voice privately, the warm-ups used should be consistent with what the singers have experienced in private vocal study.

9. The amount of time given to warm-ups should be varied. Determining factors are the time of day, the activities of the personnel prior to the rehearsal, and the necessity for conditioning.

10. Whatever is done in the warm-ups must be purposeful and directed to the music at hand, never routine.

TYPES OF PROCEDURES

The effectiveness of what follows the warm-ups in a rehearsal sequence will depend on how well defined a conductor's musical objectives are, how dedicated he is to pursuing these objectives, and how successful he is in sharing his objectives and dedication with the chorus. The conductor helps to shape the attitude of the chorus toward rehearsal as he creates an atmosphere of artistic endeavor which engenders individual involvement and responsibility. The singers must join with the conductor as they work together for an authentic and meaningful translation of the printed score into aural beauty. The conductor fosters a spirit of collaboration in contrast to one of servility. He should reflect the mood, style, and purpose of the music by word and gesture and direct the singers into an aesthetic experience. The conductor further assists this process by using his voice (and choosing his words) at a pace and dynamic level empathetic with the music being rehearsed. Nothing is more inconsistent than a conductor's shouting directions at a chorus during the rehearsal of a very quiet choral work. Likewise, group interest and attention may be quickly lost if a conductor speaks slowly and softly while rehearsing a loud and fast choral work.

Consider now a few rehearsal pitfalls which choral conductors often fall into:

1. The music is repeated over and over with benevolent allowances for mistakes in the hope that increased familiarity will eventually eliminate the mistakes.
2. Every detail of choral finesse must be mastered as a chorus moves through a choral work phrase by phrase.
3. One specific detail is stressed to the neglect of all others. For example, good diction is emphasized, but balance of parts, dynamic variety, or rhythmic accuracy are not considered.
4. A haphazard approach which features a casual, almost careless attitude by the conductor which is reflected in the chorus and in performances which are perfunctory.
5. Every choral work is rehearsed in exactly the same manner so that the singers anticipate what the conductor will do as he follows a set routine.

No two choral works should be rehearsed in exactly the same manner. There must be a variety both of procedures and in the manner of communication. The entire approach should be consistent with the mood and style of the repertoire being rehearsed. Thus, the following works should be rehearsed with different techniques: a Bach motet; an anthem by Purcell; a mass by Palestrina; an oratorio by Handel or Mendelssohn; a Brahms motet; a folksong arrangement; a contemporary choral work; and so on.

The tempo of rehearsing, like the tempo of the music, should relate to the style, the mood, the text, the composer's directives, the capability, size, and age of the group, and the acoustical environment of the rehearsal hall. Musical form can be pointed out to advantage in the learning process. It is often helpful to ask all parts to sing the melodic lines together in order to point out their similarities as well as their variations. Fugue subjects can be mastered quickly when everyone learns together what is basically the same. Rhythmic problems are also overcome more quickly by corporate involvement in the learning process. In addition to these advantages, the conductor is also keeping the whole chorus involved during the rehearsal. Those sections which lack security, courage, leadership, and sight-singing ability will learn more quickly and develop faster without the embarrassment of struggling by themselves while the rest of the chorus listens.

The choral conductor must cultivate the ability to detect problems quickly and, with a resilience in coping with the unexpected, he must develop an interesting and creative approach. He should discover early in his experience that refinement comes gradually and must not expect to accomplish too much too soon. For example, the pace of rehearsing must not be constantly interrupted at the expense of details or subtle refinements. Mistakes, after all, need not be completely eradicated in one rehearsal, and an inordinate amount of time should not be spent in correcting them. Several rehearsals are often required to consolidate corrections so that the *right way* becomes habitual.

Pauses in a rehearsal should have purpose. When the choral conductor stops a chorus, he should know what was wrong and how to correct the mistake. If an added measure of refinement is necessary, he must make it clear how to effect the refinement. Once again, it cannot be overly stressed that the exact manner of handling a pause will vary with each choral conductor. The danger of imitating and appropriating conducting techniques effectively used by others, but without one's own understanding, is ever present. Thus, the observation of experienced conductors must serve only as a basis for personal adaptation of what was done in relation to why it was done. In order to be ultimately effective, the adaptations must become *your* own way of working and thus the valid methods or techniques will eventually receive *your* personal touch.

The chorus must be trained immediately to watch the conductor and gradually enlarge the amount of eye contact as they become freed from looking at the printed page. This helps develop the important relationships between conductor and chorus: dependence, interdependence, and independence. The manner of communication between conductor and chorus is different in the rehearsal than in performance. The more efficiently a conductor rehearses, the less he will have to do in a performance. The longer a group rehearses, the less a conductor should have to do by way of communication either through words or expressive gesture. As the performance nears, there should be a gradual diminution of helpful gestures, of vocal directives and demonstrations, and of interruptions. Emphasis should be on reminders conveyed through conducting. Thus, the longer a conductor rehearses a chorus, the less a chorus needs him, except for such reasons as providing a focal point, inspiration, and reminders of what has been done in previous rehearsals.

Great patience will be required in rehearsing. The conductor must learn to recognize that the difference of age, capability, and purpose will affect the momentum of rehearsing. These differences will determine whether the process and progress of preparation will be slow or fast. The speed of learning will be related to the age and experience of the singers and to the degree of difficulties inherent in the music. The choral conductor must respond with patient understanding to the varying rates of vocal, technical, and musical development. He must be equally patient with the progress of repertoire appreciation and the singers' sensitivity toward musical style. He should never forget that he has spent much more time with the music and with rehearsal analysis than the singers, so that he is capable of moving at a faster pace than they are. Thus, these conductors should allow their singers the privilege of similar growth experience *during* rehearsals and not expect them to begin rehearsing at the conductor's level of understanding or proficiency.

The day-by-day routine of rehearsing will also demand much patience. The choral conductor must not only know what should be accomplished in a rehearsal, but he must also know how long it will take, with allowances for the unexpected. He will also need to be patient with organizational details which are often more significant to the chorus than they are to the conductor.

PACE OF REHEARSAL

Reference was made earlier to the pace of the rehearsal. How a rehearsal is paced is extremely important, for the results can be fatigue or exhilaration. The whole rehearsal must have changes of pace which depend on a variety of style in the choral literature, an alternation of the familiar with the new, a variation of tempi and dynamics, and a balanced relationship between the vocal demands involving volume, range, and tessitura. These changes will help keep the chorus alert and refreshed and counteract mounting tension and fatigue. Limited disciplinary problems are another by-product. Each choral work rehearsed should have its own pace largely determined by style, tempo indications, rhythm, and the like. Verbal directives and verbal demonstrations should be given within the rhythmic framework and in relation to the dynamic indications. Keep the momentum of a rehearsal going in relation to the tempo of the music, and the singers will be forced to remain alert, ready, and responsive. Sustaining the mood as it relates to the style also assists concentration.

The pace of a rehearsal depends on the frequency of pauses and interruptions, which have the potential danger of lengthy discourses by the conductor or conversations between the singers. Group conversations can be thwarted by the pace and momentum of a rehearsal which never allows time for such exchanges. If the conductor begins speaking immediately after stopping the choral sound, he will inhibit conversation within the chorus. He should speak right to the point with a minimum of words and not lose any valuable time. It is equally important that he talk to the chorus while it is singing: directions and corrections can be given in this manner and be more meaningful because there is an immediate relationship between what was done and what was said. Singing with the group can also save time when the singing is a good model. However, singing with the group should be employed sparingly lest it become a habit and lose its purpose and significance. Some choral conductors spend more time talking than the chorus does singing; other choral conductors sing with the chorus so frequently that they rarely hear the sound of the chorus. This imbalance between singing and talking suppresses the possibility of a well-paced rehearsal.

Periodicity should also be avoided since this implies predetermined pacing that cannot be varied. Vital pacing is the result of the conductor's reaction to mistakes, accomplishments, peaks, climaxes, and so on, each of which appear in rehearsals irregularly and often unexpectedly. Such pacing will also disclose a conductor's attitude toward the learning process and the developing of refinement. Does he know how much to expect from the chorus in rehearsal and how far to go in the process of refinement in one rehearsal? Does he know how to let a chorus and a choral work mature? The answers to these questions affect the pacing of a rehearsal.

HUMOR IN REHEARSAL

Humor is of great consequence in maintaining a well-paced rehearsal. The choral conductors who look on humor with disdain are at the opposite extreme of those who rely on humor to the surfeiting point. Excessive and uncontrolled use of humor or the lack of humor with insistence on sober propriety are equally abhorrent. Conductors frequently say the wrong thing at the wrong time, employ a double entendre or spoonerism, and experience other slips of the tongue; the conductor who is not pompous will quickly learn how to use such episodes to his advantage by permitting himself and the choir to enjoy what has happened. Failure to take advantage of this potential humor can be devitalizing to a rehearsal. There are also those conductors who recognize the importance of humor and collect anecdotes, jokes, and "clever phrases" so that they can use them at the right time or on the right occasion. Some even plan their use at a specific point in the rehearsal. Of more genuine significance is the use of humor that is personal, local, "in-group," unplanned, improvisatory—based on what has happened in the rehearsal. It may only have momentary pertinence which in retrospect is forgotten, but such humor contributes to the pacing of a rehearsal since it is generated by it. This use of humor can reinforce corrective measures, vocal demonstrations, or assist in the understanding of style or mood just as much as it can disturb them. Every choral conductor is responsible for controlling the use of humor: he should know when and how to encourage as well as stifle it. If he is not humorous by endowment, he should solicit help from those in the chorus who have such talent. Every choral group will have at least one singer who can provide this assistance. Never try to mimic a professional comedian or the way another conductor uses humor. Again, BE YOURSELF and work with humor in *your own way*, which is actually what the chorus would prefer anyway. It is amazing how frequently moments of humorous relaxation are followed by a resurgence of interest, energy, and involvement. When properly identified with the pace of a rehearsal, the use of humor is never a waste of time! Humor is one of the forces at work in *group dynamics*.

GROUP DYNAMICS

The importance of group dynamics must not be underestimated. The success of any rehearsal depends much on the role the conductor assumes, his self-image as a person, as a musician, and as a conductor, his attitude toward the group and its purpose, his personal relationship with the individual singers, and his approach to the rehearsal. It also depends on the group's sense of identity as a choral organization, their attitude toward each other and toward the conductor, and the acceptance of their responsibilities during a rehearsal. Although many conductors and choruses do not realize it, the success of their rehearsing together will be related to their attitudes toward other conductors, other choruses, the people who make up their audiences, the composers whose music they rehearse and perform, and the standards of choral excellence they seek to maintain.

INTERACTION

Although the conductor is the prime mover, the interaction of conductor and chorus determines group morale, collective musical and technical discipline, and artistic refinement and growth. It also determines expanding interest in choral repertoire, its study in rehearsal, and its performance. He can be dictatorial or resort to friendly persuasion. He can be patient and persevering or restless and easily discouraged. He can be hypercritical or appreciative of achievement. He can indulge in frequent displays of temper or his demeanor can be well-adjusted and modulated. He can be a stoical disciplinarian, or he can control the chorus with benevolent authority. He can remain aloof from the group or he can be open to their reactions, ideas, feelings, and preferences. In addition to the interaction between the conductor and the chorus, there are also important interactions between the conductor and the sections of the choir, as well as between the conductor and the individual singers, the conductor and the accompanist, the chorus and the accompanist, one section with another, and each section with its individuals. This interaction between individuals of the choir affects the quality of the rehearsal and the deportment of the group. Many choral conductors have difficulty understanding what leadership involves and are insensitive to a balance between reproach and commendation.

DIFFERENCES OF CHORAL GROUPS

The differences of various kinds of choral groups also affect the group dynamics of a rehearsal. Since there are women's choruses, men's choruses, mixed choruses, concert choirs, pop choirs, church choirs, civic choruses, children's choirs, youth choirs, adult choirs, large choruses, and chamber choirs, there will be differences in age, experience, personnel, purpose, and repertoire. Conductors of these various choral groups must approach them with a difference in pacing, humor, and general attitude. A select college choir can rehearse at a much faster and more demanding pace than the average volunteer church choir. The humor employed or even expected in a rehearsal of a men's chorus will be quite a contrast to what is heard in that of a rehearsal of a women's chorus. The manner of correcting mistakes and the discipline differ as the conductor works with choruses of different ages and experience. The terminology and jargon used by the conductor must be related to each group, and in some instances, such as a choir of music majors, he will be understood only by that specific group.

Every rehearsal demands a high degree of concentration on the part of conductor and singer, and the interaction between them is important to maintain this ingredient. All rehearsal procedures should assist the continuity of concentration. Loss of concentration upsets rehearsal momentum. It is always difficult to regain momentum and concentration, and the rehearsal time that is lost can be extensive. In some rehearsals, a singer's span of concentration will be very short, while in others an hour will pass in what seems like ten minutes because of the extended span of concentration elicited. In either instance, the span of concentration will be dependent upon the interaction between conductor and chorus.

It is imperative that the rehearsing of a single choral work be organized as carefully as the total rehearsal. When a chorus turns to a choral work for the first time, the conductor should introduce the work with great care. Some pertinent information or the history, style, composer, poet, or source of the text should be presented in a manner that is appealing, informative, and succinct. Any additional information may be shared subsequently, for the conductor should never deliver a lengthy musicological lecture to his choir. Interesting information, properly spaced, will increase the choir's depth of understanding and appreciation for the work, but often the conductor can let the choral work "speak for itself." Every conductor hopes that the chorus will share his same interest and enthusiasm for the repertoire he selects, but he should be aware of the fact that the response will be both positive and negative. A negative reaction might suggest to the conductor that he reconsider his selection, or, quite the contrary, that he must not lose confidence while the chorus becomes familiar with a work which may not have immediate appeal but will grow on them.

Difficult to Easy

REHEARSING ONE CHORAL WORK

It is wise to sing through a new choral work from beginning to end with reasonable allowances for mistakes. The chorus should hear the musical sound from beginning to end, even if it is far from the sound expected in public performance. A gradual approach to musical details may have the advantage of arousing interest, but it also has pitfalls. For example, too much time can be spent on an early section of the choral work at the expense of a later section which may also be difficult and demanding. Previous study of the score should help the conductor anticipate how the chorus will progress. Before the first reading, he should analyze the form of the work phrase by phrase and then after the first rehearsal note carefully where the trouble spots occurred. In the rehearsals that follow he should begin with the section that is most difficult and work from there to that which presents little difficulty.

To make this clearer, the diagram in Figure 2-4 shows how a choral work can be sectioned from beginning to end.

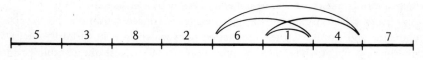

1 = most difficult section
8 = easiest section

Figure 2-4

After acquiring some security in the section designated as most difficult (1), move on to 6 and 4 and bridge them with 1. Then move on to 2, and using the same process, bridge with 8 and 6. Connect 2–6–1 and then 8–2–6–1–7. Move on to 3 and connect with 5 and 8. Then connect 3–8–2–6, 5–3–8–2–6–1, and finally 5–3–8–2–6–1–4–7, as the whole work is put together. The advantages of this procedure are as follows:

1. Most of the rehearsal time will have been spent on the difficult sections.
2. The conductor has avoided the pitfall of "getting stuck" in the difficult sections.
3. The easier sections receive the proper amount of attention and time.
4. The total work and its formal organization is mastered more easily and understood more quickly.
5. The amount of rehearsal time involved in preparing the choral work for performance is shortened.

USE OF PIANO AND INSTRUMENTS

At this point, it seems appropriate to discuss the use of a piano and accompanist. The *a cappella* tradition, which enjoyed many years of prestige, has been supplanted by an interest in a more varied choral performance. In addition to unaccompanied music, accompanied works may require piano, organ, brass, woodwinds, strings, percussion, or even band or orchestra. The piano may substitute in rehearsal for most instruments except percussion and is especially adaptable in substituting for the organ, brass, woodwind, and string sounds. Such keyboard assistance calls for an imaginative and skilled pianist. However, not every gifted pianist proves to be a good choral accompanist, as keyboard responsibilities in a choral rehearsal require ensemble techniques which differ greatly from those demanded for solo and recital performances.

ACCOMPANIST

Some choral conductors argue that the piano should never be used in a choral rehearsal. They emphasize the dangers of constant use, of complete dependency on the piano by singers, and of retarded sight-reading. They also point to the differences between the tempered pitches of the sound produced by the piano and the nontempered pitches produced by the human voice. Most choral conductors recognize these dangers, but they would also add that, when used with discretion, the piano can be of great assistance. Excessive dependence on the piano in a choral rehearsal can be a detriment, yet this does not mean that the singers cannot learn to hear each other and make efforts to produce a homogeneous ensemble sound through individual vocal adjustments as they follow the conductor's directives and demonstrations just because the piano is used. The vocal sound is primarily the result of vowel formations and as such is much more varied than the sound of the piano. Thus, the singers should not listen to the piano as musical sound to be imitated (when it is doubling the voice parts and not contributing an accompaniment) but should merely let this sound be a helpful reminder of pitch and rhythmic accuracy. When the piano does not function as an independent accompaniment, it should be used sparingly and then only as a valuable assist in speeding up the learning process.

The accompanist must be a facile reader. He should be able to play with ease from the open choral score, especially when a piano reduction is not provided. The ability to play from an orchestral score and to provide a continuo part from the open score is also helpful. Working from vocal scores with piano reductions of orchestral parts, the choral conductor and accompanist should study the orchestral score thoroughly and mark the piano-vocal score in accordance with important instrumental parts. The accompanist should carefully prepare his accompaniments ahead of time so that he makes a minimum of mistakes in rehearsal. He should be able to follow the conductor's directions and learn to anticipate the conductor's actions and reactions. He should mark the score at the spots where the conductor has asked for specific assistance or support, where problems occur, or where the accompanist has significant responsibilities. The use of paper clips to section a large work will assist quick and easy reference.

The accompanist must also be empathetic with the singers by breathing and phrasing with them, even thinking with them as they produce the vowels and consonants, which is their musical instrument. He must likewise be as one with the conductor. Every choral conductor rejoices when he has an accompanist who almost thinks as he does during a rehearsal, who does not have to be told what voice parts need assistance, who is constantly alert to mistakes, who reacts intuitively to rehearsal procedures, and who can help momentum, interaction, humor, and so forth. The accompanist must also learn to play the parts a fraction of a second ahead of the beat in order to help the singers enter with rhythmic accuracy and avoid a late response. He should also be able to know when playing the voice parts in octaves will help the singers hear their parts more easily. It is an added bonus if the accompanist is capable of improvisation. Such skill can provide variety during the tedium of part rehearsal. He should also be sensitive enough toward the rehearsal momentum to know when to play and when not to play. It will be of additional help if the accompanist is gregarious, for the conductor can often use him as a foil in helping to relieve tensions that can build up during a rehearsal. For example, when used judiciously, repartee (of a respectful variety) between a conductor and his accompanist can be a most significant source of humorous relaxation. Of course, above all, the accompanist must be a good musician who is capable of contributing his own dimension of artistry to both the rehearsal and performance.

When other instruments are involved in a performance, it is essential to use them for several rehearsals prior to the final rehearsal in the concert hall. The singers need to hear and adjust to the sounds of the instruments, and the instrumentalists need to adjust to the dynamics and balance of the chorus. Each group will need to note the slight changes in conducting techniques employed by the conductor as he coordinates the contributions of both voices and instruments to the total sound. It will be most helpful if the rehearsal hall provides adequate space for combining the two groups with a minimum of confinement or restriction. Working together in this manner is of special educational significance to school choral and instrumental groups. The costs involved when professional instrumentalists are used limit the possibility of attaining the balanced relationship so necessary between choral and instrumental forces.

REHEARSAL SHORTHAND

Like an accompanist, the singers should mark their own music, and should be taught to do so even without being told. When a conductor does give special directions he should do so clearly, quickly, and in proper sequence so that the singers can easily follow him to the specific point or problem. He should take advantage of rehearsal numbers or letters when they are provided in the printed score, but whenever they are missing, he can determine his own system of dividing the choral work into sections under alphabetical designations and also number the measures.

Mistakes in rhythm, consonant articulation, vowel production, phrasing, dynamics, balance of parts, and so on, should be indicated immediately and marked with reminders. The choral conductor, however, must never overwhelm the chorus with a barrage of corrections. He must know which corrections are of primary concern and how others rank in order of importance to the rehearsal sequence. The chorus and conductor should be responsive to what the composer or arranger has added to a score by way of written directions, musical terminology, and musical signs or symbols. Obviously, they should be understood by all, and so the conductor is responsible for explaining less familiar musical terminology. These terms may be underlined, encircled, or highlighted.

Use of a *rehearsal shorthand* has practical significance, it is not difficult to learn, it need not be employed in exactly the same way by all singers. The most important consideration should be that the individual singer employ markings which *he* understands immediately and which remind *him* of what *he* is to do. A list of some marks that may be employed is given in Figure 2-5.

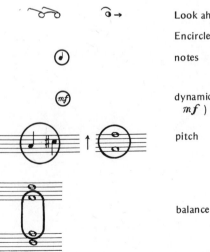

Look ahead, watch out for

Encircle problem spots:

notes

dynamics (or write in large script
mf)

pitch

balance

 pitch for entrance

How_lovely   Consonant connections

How lovely   Voiced consonants

$\overset{s}{\text{place}}$ / $\overset{dz}{\text{gods}}$ Final consonants

$\overset{d}{} \overset{\text{ɔ}}{}$
How great   Dipthongs

Ha-oo Eh-ih

Remember   Medial consonants

unto / us   Two vowels in sequence

God / omnipotent   End consonant and begin vowel without connecting

V   Lift in phrasing

9   End of phrase

9 //   Take a breath

   Cut off (where to add the "D" in *Lord*)

          Full note value

glo̲-ry of the Lo̲rd   Textual nuance

glō-rў ŏf thĕ Lōrd   Syllabic nuance

Figure 2-5

Some of the standard musical signs or symbols which singers should know and be able to add to the score as directed are given in Figure 2-6.

Symbol	Meaning
.	Staccato
＞	Marcato
ʌ	Heavy accent
ɼ	Very staccato
—	Slight accent with breadth (tenuto)
͡ ŕ ŕ	Slurred staccato
⌒	Phrase (musical and textual)
⌒	Fermata (long pause on note)
＜p.＞	Messa di voce (crescendo and diminuendo in relation to note value)
◁	Crescendo
▷	Diminuendo
sfz	Sforzando (sung with immediate stress)
fz	Forzando (sharply emphasized)
sub. p	Suddenly soft
sub. f	Suddenly loud
ten.	Held or sustained longer than note value

Figure 2-6

PEDAGOGICAL RESPONSIBILITIES

The listings in Figure 2-5 and 2-6 suggest that a conductor has pedagogical responsibilities in a rehearsal. There are many conductors who think of themselves primarily as teachers when they rehearse. Indeed, any performance by a chorus will reflect the conductor's effectiveness as a teacher during rehearsals. The sounds of his chorus will be a commentary on his ability to transfer his knowledge, to enlarge and refine his pedagogical techniques, to arouse and maintain dedication to vocal and musical disciplines on the part of the singers, to shape the syllabic and melodic nuances, to expand the knowledge and technical proficiency of the chorus, and to lead the group to artistic performance. When a foreign language is involved, the conductor, if he is not proficient in that language, may need to ask assistance from others. He can invite colleagues in the language departments to check phonetic accuracy, although more advanced choruses will frequently have members who are qualified to provide such assistance.

The conductor must not confuse teaching with lecturing. Although occasionally the information or ideas he wishes to share with the chorus may be presented in the manner of a lecture, the choral conductor should then be brief, and, as indicated before, he must never indulge in lengthy discourses. Whatever a choral conductor presents to the chorus, he should do so with enthusiasm, and he should develop an active imagination so that he can communicate with the chorus in different ways. An imaginative conductor will search for new ways of explaining, demonstrating, and sharing the old routine principles; in other words, a choral conductor must be willing to experiment as he teaches. The reactions and responses of the singers will help the conductor decide which of the new methods should be retained for refinement and which should be discarded as inconsequential. Thus, the teacher can learn from the student, although the singers are rarely aware of the fact that the conductor is experimenting.

LEARNING BY LISTENING

The chorus must be taught to listen. The act of singing requires that the singer listen to his own voice, even though he will never hear it as others do, and to those around him. He must place his emphasis on good tone production, blend, balance, intonation, vowel formations, consonant articulation, dynamics, and phrasing. The choral conductor should encourage the singers to listen to the sound which the score solicits before attempting to reproduce it. Hearing the pitch ahead of time in the "mind's ear" results in better intonation and assists sight-singing proficiency. The singers should also be taught to listen to the music's harmonic, contrapuntal, and rhythmic activity, and to be aware of the contour of verbal and melodic phrases, in their own as well as the other parts. Since vocal scores contain all the parts and usually an accompaniment or a piano reduction of instrumental parts, singers have a great advantage in that they can see as well as hear the contributions of other performers while the instrumentalist only sees his own part.

The conductor must also guide the singers to an awareness of the variable acoustical environments. They should learn to adjust their voices and appreciate their choral environment whether it be in a rehearsal room or a concert hall. Of course, none of this will be possible if the singers have not been taught to listen to the conductor when he speaks or demonstrates and to watch his gestures express the music he conducts. Once he has established this liaison, the responsiveness of the group will depend on his effectiveness as a teacher. There will always be a few conductors whose native endowment includes pedagogical aptitude, while other conductors will need to work diligently on acquiring and cultivating teaching skills.

CORRECTIVE PROCEDURE AND DEMONSTRATION

One of the teaching skills is a knowledge of how to introduce, develop, and complete a rehearsal procedure or routine. For example, when correcting a rhythmic mistake a choral conductor may know what should be done, but, in attempting to correct the mistake, he may alienate the chorus by his manner or by spending an inordinate amount of time, and by not appreciating the necessity of gradual mastery. How a corrective procedure is introduced can determine its success or failure as well as the response of the singers. How a corrective measure is devleoped can make it a tedious or an exhilarating process. How the corrective procedure is closed can establish a recognition of need for additional work on the problem, create the sense of failure and frustration, or produce a feeling of satisfaction and achievement.

Demonstration is another important part of a conductor's pedagogical responsibility. The generous assortment of tape and phonograph recordings of choral works can be used in demonstrating style, performance practices, tone production, and other attributes of choral performance. The emphasis might either be on exemplary models or on a careless choral performance. Taping during rehearsal can also provide the conductor and chorus object lessons in which the chorus demonstrates to itself what the conductor prefers or dislikes.

The choral conductor must be willing to use whatever potential he has in demonstrating for the group what he wants to hear from them. The use of his own voice is especially valuable. He can demonstrate good or poor vocal technique, correct or incorrect vowel and consonant production, proper and improper use of breath, accurate and faulty rhythm, subtle or meaningless nuance and phrasing, and spirited or ineffective projection of style or mood. It will be necessary for the conductor to mimic what he does not desire to hear so that the chorus can easily observe the difference when he provides the contrasting demonstration of what he prefers. The conductor must not be reticent in personal demonstration. While a well-trained voice is an asset, the purpose and the quality of demonstration is more important. The point can be made with modest vocal abilities, but any self-consciousness will limit the effectiveness of a demonstration involving mime. He must "let himself go" in order to accomplish the desired results in a choral rehearsal. He can use movements associated with the dance to assist the shaping of phrases, the contours of melodic lines, and the mood of a text. In his evocations or verbal demonstrations, the imaginative use of metaphor and analogy can increase a depth of understanding.

Use of individual singers for demonstration can be as dangerous as it can be helpful. Great care must be exercised in singling out any singer for this purpose. The choral conductor must know which individuals he can turn to and which ones to avoid. Their demonstration should always be pertinent and preferably have an impersonal quality; that is, there should be no excessive reference to a highly trained voice or to a singer with vocal limitations. The demonstration by an individual singer must never result in embarrassment, and it should always involve the possibilities for a successful and satisfying contribution to the purpose of the demonstration. Such demonstrations by chorus members can have an impact on the group if they proceed skillfully. Conductors themselves demonstrate so regularly and, in some cases so profusely, often in exactly the same manner, that such a diversion can be very meaningful.

WORKING WITH VOICES

Vocal demonstrations reflect the conductor's understanding of the human instrument. No choral conductor will ever know all that can be known about the human voice, but this fact should not deter him in seeking to enlarge his knowledge and understanding. His background must include private vocal study requiring of him the refinement of technical disciplines and the development of his own vocal potential regardless of its possibilities. It is additionally important that he understand the techniques of vocal production as they apply to different voices and not only as he has learned to apply them to his own instrument. The material covered in Chapter 1 should be recalled at this point.

In every rehearsal, a choral conductor must remember that he will provide the only vocal training most of the singers will receive—a tremendous responsibility which cannot be treated lightly. He must help these singers learn to use their voices correctly, to eliminate bad habits, to breathe, and so on. Although the fact that he is actually giving voice lessons when he rehearses should not be obvious to the chorus, the latter will appreciate what is taking place in their own personal vocal development. By the same token, when there is an absence of vocal instruction or an employment of a type of vocal guidance which asks for a production alien to sound vocal pedagogy, again the singers may not be aware of what is happening to their voices but will assume that such affectation and bad singing are normal. The absence of competent vocal pedagogy is usually the result of limited choral experience, no private lessons in voice, a solely instrumental background, or a generally weak vocal and choral background.

When there are chorus members who are studying voice privately, they should be able to recognize that the choral conductor thinks like a singer, that he is empathetic with what is involved in voice production, that he attempts to assist and augment the vocal training received in the private studio, and that he desires to help and not inhibit the singer. The conductor's explanations, demonstrations, and vocal demands should always be consistent with what the voice student encounters in a competent private studio. To do otherwise is to add weight to the argument that there is a radical difference between solo and choral singing. Most certainly, a choral conductor can help or hurt the human instrument in a choral rehearsal, but so can the voice teacher in a private lesson. The choral rehearsal is not inherently bad for the singers and their vocal development. How much a choral conductor understands about the voice, however, and how he works with that understanding is of ultimate consequence and concern. He must, therefore, constantly seek to expand his knowledge through continued study.

Singers as a group have less musical training and technical proficiency than instrumentalists because it is possible to begin the study of an instrument many years before it is advisable to study voice privately. Unfortunately, it is not possible to compensate for this difference. This does not mean that singers are less musical, less intelligent, less sensitive to musical stimuli, or less capable of artistic performance; rather, good choral performances simply take more rehearsal time than their instrumental counterparts. In addition, instrumental conductors can rely on preparatory instruction and private practice outside the rehearsals. This advantage, added to the opportunity of beginning technical instruction at an earlier age saves much instrumental rehearsal time. By contrast, singers even without this early training receive little or no technical guidance outside the rehearsal. Therefore, because the human voice is the most complicated of all instruments, time must be allotted in each choral rehearsal for vocal training and development which the conductor must provide.

The choral conductor must never forget that the human voice is more easily strained and fatigued than the lips, fingers, and arms used in instrumental performance. Excessive repetitions and drilling in rehearsals can be dangerous. The choral conductor must be most careful about demanding too much volume too soon, especially when the drill involves cleaning up rhythmic problems or inaccuracies in the parts. Drills can be developed which accomplish the desired results without taxing the voice. For example, when working on the parts, the chorus can sing on *loo, lah, tah*, or any other contrived syllable, and master intervals without using their full voice and without the complications of singing the text. This procedure not only provides a welcome contrast in tone production, but it also allows the singers to concentrate on the specific problems to be overcome; that is, they do not have to divide their attention by reading notes and words at the same time. As another example, a choral conductor can provide relief from singing when working on rhythm by having the singers speak the words in relation to the note values in the music. Good singing is always more of a mental than a physical effort. A chorus member should be taught to think before he sings and then to listen critically to his singing. This process must not, of course, be stressed to the point that he becomes self-conscious about vocal production; rather, the emphasis should be on concern for self-improvement, for as the individual singer improves, so does the whole group.

USE OF THE CONDUCTOR'S VOICE

A few final words about the conductor's use of his own voice should be added at this point. It has been previously stated that vocal demonstration by the conductor is important and that he can use his own voice effectively regardless of his native endowment. He should never forget, however, that the singers in a chorus will have a tendency to imitate the sound of his voice whether that sound be good or bad. Many conductors sing with the chorus so much of the time that they cannot concentrate on a critical appraisal of the chorus; that is, they cannot possibly hear their singers as they should. However, a choral conductor can often help his singers mold a phrase more quickly by providing the model as he sings along with them—so long as he does not overdo it.

Many of the rehearsal procedures which a choral conductor uses to work on the development of good vocal technique involve diction. A choral conductor can use various ways of establishing correct vowel formations and precise consonant articulation. In most choral literature the variety of sounds produced by the human voice emanate from the phonation of the text on pitches prescribed by the composer. The duration and range of these pitches are more varied and extensive than those used in normal speech. Thus, the words must be sung with great emphasis on clarity and precision so that the listener can understand them easily and so that the relationship between text and musical setting can be enhanced. Through explanations, demonstrations, and conducting techniques, the choral conductor can guide the singers to a common delivery of syllabic stress and duration. He will need to explain to the group that it is necessary for every singer to contribute uniform vowel sounds, carefully articulated consonants, and well-modulated verbal and melodic nuances. Only then will the chorus be able to sing a musical phrase with correct vocal technique and to mold and shape the contour of the melodic lines with verbal nuances and dynamic graduations, in keeping with the style of music being presented. The success of this process depends on how the singers respond to the stimulus and guidance of the score and the stimulus, guidance, sensitivity, and imagination of the conductor. Quite frequently, the singers add their own dimension to that of the score and the conductor, and this in turn arouses in the conductor an expanded imagination. This reciprocal stimulation must not be overlooked. Finally, his conducting gestures must clearly indicate the interpretation of the text and music so that there will be uniformity and precision in the singing.

There are a host of choral conductors who will argue that there is much choral music in which the text is inconsequential and the musical ingredients paramount. This may sometimes be true, but vocal and choral music are a consequence of the text (unless a text has been added to music which was previously written without words), so that, in addition to the appeal of the music itself, there is an added essential dimension when the text is heard. Dynamics of music should be understood as complementary and not supplementary concerns, and, thus, the rhythmic features must be understood not as ends in themselves but as essential parts of the whole mosaic of syllabic sounds related to note values. In many instances, the rhythmic problems are primarily related to faulty articulation of consonants. Exploitation of Dalcroze eurhythmic principles can be of great assistance in establishing rhythmic accuracy. Talking and singing while walking relates the kinesthetic experience to sound duration within a specific rhythmic framework. Snapping fingers, clapping hands, patting of the hands, and bodily movement can also be incorporated in rehearsal procedures which seek to secure accurate rhythm by correlating the syllabic sounds with the note values.

It is dangerous, however, to use the text constantly in any rehearsal, especially when working on refinements which are not related to diction. Continuous use of the text leads to a sense of familiarity which can weaken the crispness and precision in articulation of consonants and accuracy in formation of vowels. Singers often think that they are delivering a text with clarity and sensitivity when they are actually obscuring it. The choral conductor must be a severe critic, but the longer he rehearses the same text the more he runs the danger of imagining that he hears it distinctly, even when in actuality it may be diffused. He must respond to the diction of his chorus like an objective listener in an audience who is hearing the text for the first time.

INTONATION

The text can also be used to assist good intonation. Naturally, there are other factors, such as posture, fatigue, weather, humidity, atmospheric pressure, acoustical environment, and poor ventilation, which also affect pitch. Strict reliance on the piano accompaniment can also lead to faulty intonation. A slow tempo makes great demands on breath support to secure and sustain pitch, while a fast tempo requires quick and accurate shifts from one pitch to another. It is also exceedingly difficult for a choir to sing a succession of notes on the same pitch, especially when there is great variety in the sequence of vowel sounds. Pitch problems are often the result of poorly or incorrectly produced vowel sounds. Thus, the choral conductor will need to stress correct vowel formations not only for the sake of clarity but also to help intonation. Good intonation can also be assisted by careful attention to ascending and descending intervals. Singers should be taught to think wider intervals on ascending intervals and to sing shorter intervals when descending. They must be trained to listen carefully, to hear augmented and diminished intervals, and to hear their own part in relation to the others. They should be made aware of chordal progressions, where the parts are going, and how they move. Rehearsal techniques can help the chorus hear ahead of time the next sound they are to produce. Homophonic music is best used in developing this ability. The music should not be sung in strict time, but each chord progression should be sustained until the singers have time to think ahead to the next chord. Eventually the chord progression can be taken at the regular tempo, and the intonation should be improved.

Other procedures can be used to combat and correct faulty intonation. For example, the conductor can change the key of the choral work by raising the pitch a half or whole step. This, for some strange acoustical reason, frequently produces a more secure intonation. Some choruses find it easier to sing with more secure intonation in certain keys. Radical changes in tempo can also assist better intonation by keeping the mind and body alert and thus curtailing nonchalance. This also forces the body to react with immediacy in order to produce the vocal sounds within the changing tempi. Having a chorus stand often helps, especially if they have been seated for a long period of time. (The conductor should, in general, require frequent changes in body position with special emphasis on good posture when seated.) Occasionally, poor intonation becomes a fixation and the longer a conductor struggles to correct the pitch problems, the more he compounds the difficulties or confuses the singers. In such instances, it is often helpful to turn to another choral work, one that is quite familiar and easy for the chorus to sing or one that requires drills which do not involve intonation as a major concern. This period of contrast, by concentration on another choral work providing other problems, can then be followed by a return to the previous work with the frequent result that former problems of intonation have disappeared.

RHYTHM

Rhythmic problems are often diction problems and as such are related to poor consonant articulation, to incorrect duration of vowel sound, and to rushed diphthongs. Musical ideas are framed within organized time; there is a sequential movement of these ideas in sound which connects the sounds of previous moments to those of the future. This sequence has been ordered by the composer, and the conductor must see to it that the sequence is orderly. He provides the control, and the chorus must accept the rigorous discipline he demands during a rehearsal while he seeks to obtain the proper length of vowel sounds, the proper duration and precision of consonant sounds, the subtle nuances of a syllabic sequence, and the reproduction of melodic lines with the contours prescribed by the composer. Repeated drills stressing vowel duration, precise articulation of consonants, and the cadence of diphthongs should always relate the note values and the syllables with the note values to which they are assigned. The choral conductor must never forget that even experienced and well-trained singers will need surveillance. They often think that they are producing clear diction when they are not, and they also forget that the possibilities for inaccuracies are multiplied by the number of singers making up any chorus.

BLEND AND BALANCE

The choral attributes of blend and balance must also be developed in the rehearsal. In a select group, the choral conductor can almost predetermine the results through his choice of personnel who complement each other. All other groups will confront the conductor with myriad complications. Some voices are loud while others are soft, some are penetrating while others are subdued, some have a pleasing quality while others are harsh, some are flexible while others are restive, some are well modulated while others are raucous, some have a wide range while others have a limited range, and some are musical while others are not. The choral conductor must know how to take this "raw material" and mold it into a choral ensemble. He should use his knowledge of vocal and rehearsal techniques to achieve blend and balance. Blend will primarily be the result of refined vocal production. As the singers learn how to produce vowels correctly they will present a more homogeneous section sound. Any deviation from correct vowel formation and production will distort the section sound and inhibit blend. The demands of range and tessitura are also factors which help or hinder blend. The choral conductor should know how to work the singers at the extremeties of their range so that they are not overly taxed, and learn what adjustments are needed in order to maintain blend. He must also know that problems of range and tessitura affect balance. Thus he will need to dictate what must be done to produce a balanced relationship of parts by changing gradations of dynamic intensity. This can be done by altering the dynamics of each section, by deleting voices from the dominating sections, or by shifting voices from one section to another to increase the dynamic potential of the weaker section. If the bass part is primarily above the staff and marked *piano*, the basses can drop out and leave the baritones to carry the part. If the entire soprano section is too dominant, only the lighter first sopranos should sing. In contrast, second sopranos can help first altos, second altos can help first tenors, baritones can help second tenors, and first tenors can help second altos when sections require louder dynamic levels to balance with the rest of the chorus. It will be important to experiment in order to know how much to add and also how much can be withdrawn from a section without hampering its sound. Without such experimentation, the conductor may be creating new problems in balance.

The choral conductor should also understand that chord structure affects balance of parts. The relationship of intervals making up a chord helps or hinders balance. For example, what is doubled? Where is the third or fifth located and at what part of the range for that particular voice part? Are the altos below the tenors? Is the relationship of the outer voices close or distant? Or, what vowel sound is assigned to each section and how will these differences affect balance?

These questions will have to be answered by the choral conductor. His study of the score prior to the rehearsal should help determine what must be done to achieve balance; yet often the peculiar makeup of a particular chorus will require special adjustments to take care of unique complications. For example, the immaturity of basses will be more pronounced in some choral works, while it will be obscured in others. The choral conductor should share these concerns with his singers so that they will understand why he employs certain routines aimed at achieving a balance of parts and also so that the singers themselves will develop on their own a sensitivity toward the achievement of balance.

The singers should also be aware of the variable importance of vocal lines so that they will make the necessary adjustments in dynamics to allow important lines to dominate and thereby achieve proper balance with the other parts. This is especially important in nineteenth-century contrapuntal choral music. Again, it will be important to stress that each singer must listen to himself, to his section, to other sections, and to the accompaniment. The instrumental accompaniment must ultimately be balanced with the choral sound, and each of the following present different problems of balance: piano, woodwind ensemble, brass ensemble, string ensemble, percussion instruments, chamber orchestra, full orchestra, and full band. The choral conductor must prepare the chorus to sing with varying degrees of intensity which are related to the particular type of accompaniment; for example, there will be a difference between the choral tone required for a work with brass and that required for a work with a small consort of strings. When an instrumental conductor is to conduct the performance, the choral conductor should not make his singers fully dependent on him and his conducting but rather make it possible for the singers to respond to another conductor by training them in such a way that they are able to make necessary adjustments with ease and immediacy. When the choral conductor does conduct the performance, he can prepare his singers in accordance with his plans for orchestra-choral balance.

CONDUCTING TECHNIQUES

Reference has been made several times to the importance of conducting technique. It has been suggested that much of what is done in a rehearsal is ultimately dependent on how expressive the conductor is with his conducting gestures. Conductors are known for their personal idiosyncracies which often defy analysis and suggest hypnotic control. Some choruses seem to be able to sing in spite of what the conductor is doing on the podium, and yet there is always a relationship of choral sound to the physical movements by the conductor. Whatever he does, however, the conducting gestures must be functional. They should be a sign language which conveys to the group what the conductor expects from them.

The conventional beat patterns which are generally used by conductors should be employed. There is no reason why a choral conductor should not use them; there are many reasons why he should—one of the most important being that they will help secure the rhythmic pulse. He should also know how to control cues and cutoffs, but he must understand that much more is involved than just the movement or gesture. Here is a list of what should be involved in a cue:

1. The cue must include an alerting motion which signals to the chorus that they should get ready to sing.
2. The cue must tell the chorus when to breathe and help them to do so rhythmically.
3. The cueing gesture must be related to the rhythmic pace of the choral work being sung.
4. The cue must provide a *point of reference* to which the singers react, and the conductor should time his arrival at that point so that when the singers react they will begin singing precisely on the beat. The conductor's movement to the point of reference will actually be ahead of the beat so that the singers will respond at the correct time.
5. The cue should indicate at what dynamic level the chorus is to start singing.
6. The point of reference should help the chorus begin singing on either a vowel or a consonant. Many so called *glottal attacks* are the result of the singers' response to a poor gesture used by the conductor at the entrance cue.
7. If the entrance begins on a consonant, the point of reference should help the singers differentiate between voiced and unvoiced consonants.
8. All of the above must be related to the style of the music.

During the rehearsal, the choral conductor establishes the effectiveness of his gestures for important cues.

When considering the responsibilities involved in a cutoff or release, most of the above can be applied with the following modifications:

(2). There is obviously no need to indicate when to breathe.
(4). There must be a point of reference to which the singers respond by *stopping* the sound.
(5). The cutoff or release gesture must be consistent with the dynamic level of the vowel sound in the final syllable so that when released the final consonant is not produced too loudly or too softly.

Points (1), (3), (6), and (7) are applicable except that the gesture finishes the sound in contrast to beginning the sound. The magnitude of the gestures involved in cues and cutoffs should be fairly large at first in rehearsals so that they will attract attention. As a chorus becomes more familiar with and responsive to the conductor's movements, the movements should become smaller and smaller so that the slightest movement will elicit the response desired by the conductor. This rapport must be established during the beginning rehearsals.

The choral conductor must also learn to use his left arm in various ways to aid his communication with the chorus. It can mirror, supplant, supplement, or complement the right arm. It can be used for cues and cutoffs, for control of dynamics, and for molding or shaping of phrases. It must always be used purposefully and never call attention to itself through movements which are incongruous with either the music or the gestures generally associated with conducting. The choral conductor must use the rehearsal to practice this part of his craft because without the response of the singers he will never understand how his movements must be adapted to a wide range of variations in order to guide and control the singers, and he will never acquire the highly refined sense of timing which is required for the movements to be effective.

SECTIONAL REHEARSALS

The rehearsal experience sometimes calls for a section to rehearse by itself. There are many choral conductors who consider sectional rehearsals a necessity and include them as a regular part of the rehearsal schedule. They believe that a sectional rehearsal will save time in full rehearsals because each section will have used such a rehearsal to help solve such problems as technical difficulties, note accuracy, intonation, and rhythm. Some choral conductors maintain that the sectional rehearsal helps group identity, esprit, and élan. There are other conductors, however, who do not consider the sectional rehearsal a necessity but maintain that it is a waste of time; they contend that it is best for the parts to be learned in relation to each other because intonation is primarily a chordal rather than a linear-intervallic problem. They also believe that rhythmic problems are frequently the result of an interaction between parts so that the singers need to stabilize their own part within the complex diversity of the whole; that since they are often related to consonant articulation, the conductor can more effectively correct the whole chorus in full rehearsal. The latter course of action saves time when the conductor supervises the sectionals (if any are held) and assures a uniformity of correcting procedures when he does not. If he does not supervise all sectional rehearsals, however, how can he be assured that everything he would want to do will be done and that it would have the same level of achievement he could obtain?

Every choral conductor will have to answer the following questions concerning sectional rehearsals. Will they be used regularly or only occasionally? Will they be routine or timely? Is there sufficient rehearsal time to justify using some of it for sectional rehearsals? Is enough space available? Will the conductor be able to indicate precisely what the sectional rehearsal is to accomplish? Will the sectional rehearsal save time for the full rehearsal? Is the conductor merely following a procedure he came to know when he was a singer in a chorus? Is the conductor scheduling sectional rehearsals because he thinks that the chorus in which he sang could have benefited from sectional rehearsals?

VISITORS

The choral conductor will also have to decide whether or not visitors are to be allowed to observe rehearsals. They may consist of parents and friends or other choral conductors who like to watch another conductor rehearse or who feel that a visit by their chorus to a rehearsal of another choral group has great educational value. If no visitors are allowed, the conductor must examine his reasons. Would visitors make him self-conscious? Will they embarrass the chorus? Will they upset his routine? Will they inhibit him and the singers? Will he and the singers have to worry about the impression they will make? Will the visitors understand why certain things are done and said? Will the visitors know how to conduct themselves during the rehearsal? Will they provide added motivation or distraction? Will the chorus be able to accomplish as much as it could without the visitors? Will the visitors hear the chorus and watch the conductor work at a time when both can be observed to their advantage or disadvantage? If he permits visitors, the choral conductor might find them more helpful than embarrassing. He must learn to go about his work as if the visitors were not there. His tactics should be the same, although he may feel somewhat restrained when disciplinary action is necessary. He may find, however, that group response is greater and the quality of performance much higher when visitors are present.

Visitors can also help a choral conductor view himself more objectively. Every choral conductor needs to do this periodically even without the stimulus visitors can provide. The tape recorder, as was mentioned earlier, can be used to help the conductor listen to his chorus more objectively. He can concentrate on what he hears—without the distractions of conducting. It will show him how he uses rehearsal time and how he sounds to the chorus when he speaks to them, demonstrates for them, criticizes them, corrects them, and compliments them. Videotapes can also be used by the choral conductor, which adds the opportunity to see himself—his movements, stance, conducting gestures and facial expressions, his reactions to the chorus and their reactions to him. Through this medium, a choral conductor can visit his own rehearsal; he can hear and see what the visitor hears and sees. He will be able to see himself objectively, and, by analyzing his procedures, he can help himself become a better choral conductor and a more efficient rehearsal technician. Constant self-appraisal by a choral conductor is essential, but few conductors are able to do this without the assistance of tape recorders, for they provide an added dimension of critical appraisal by means of which the conductor can see and hear himself objectively.

POSTREHEARSAL REVIEW

After a rehearsal, every choral conductor should review what has transpired. He should examine what he had planned to accomplish and then objectively appraise what was actually accomplished. He must be honest in his evaluation of failures, which may seem to outnumber accomplishments on certain days. He must be ready to analyze those procedures which proved to be ineffective, why the chorus reacted as it did both positively and negatively, what procedures showed promise and why, and how effectively the rehearsal time was used. A conductor who does not do this never learns from his own experience, he rarely changes his rehearsal methods, and he wastes rehearsal time. Most conductors would be surprised or embarrassed if they saw and heard themselves waste time, give incompetent demonstrations, use wrong procedures, overlook glaring mistakes, or fail to recognize significant refinements. When these have all been recorded on tape, the conductor will find it hard to believe what he sees and hears. Yet, he will profit from observing himself. Because of his total involvement in a rehearsal, a choral conductor is often oblivious to what in retrospect seems so obvious. Finally, a postrehearsal review, whether it be a videotape or purely reflective, should always include an inventory of what took place, but emphasis should be placed on matching accomplishment or failure with what any conductor would have the right to expect from a chorus at its particular level of choral experience and potential.

DRESS REHEARSAL

All rehearsals culminate in what is referred to as a *dress rehearsal*. On this occasion, the chorus has the opportunity to hear itself in the acoustical environment of the concert hall. The choral conductor will need to be sensitive to the subtle changes that occur naturally and to those which he will need to effect. Final adjustments of balance, refinements of phrasing, or changes in dynamics and tempo will be necessary in relation to the acoustical environment. These alterations must be minor, however, and must not represent a major deviation from what has been carefully developed and made routine during the weeks of previous rehearsal. Radical changes are dangerous, and the choral conductor must realize that he is taking a calculated risk if he asks for them.

The dress rehearsal is not like previous rehearsals. If it is, the conductor has been ineffectual and has not carried out his responsibilities in thoroughly preparing the chorus. At the start of a dress rehearsal, the chorus is either ready for a concert or it is not. Thus, this final rehearsal should be a time for reviewing what the conductor and chorus are capable of sharing together with an audience. It should be a time of both reaffirmation and confirmation. The rigorous disciplines of preparatory rehearsals should show their significance for the public concert, and the security of performance should attest to the validity of previous rehearsals. The chorus should not be overwhelmed mentally, vocally, or physically at the dress rehearsal, and there should be a minimum of starting and stopping, of preoccupation with details, of picayunish criticism, and of added directions. This final rehearsal should stimulate confidence and not destroy it.

It has been said that a poor final rehearsal means a good concert, the rationale being that the chorus, realizing that it has done poorly in the dress rehearsal, will be more alert and responsible during the concert. It has also been said that a good dress rehearsal can lead to a poor performance because the chorus will let down or will be too casual. Any chorus can be *underrehearsed* so that the concert performance sounds tentative and lacks security in technical details. The concert may not provide that final spark which brings off a polished performance; indeed, it may provide a spark that leads to disaster if the chorus has not been carefully rehearsed. A chorus can also be *overrehearsed* so that a concert performance lacks freshness, spontaneity, and enthusiasm. The chorus may have been drilled to the point where they react like zombies. If the conductor has planned his rehearsals carefully and has had a timetable for progress and refinement, the dress rehearsal should be the last step in the movement toward the climax achieved during the concert.

This final rehearsal is the time when the chorus realizes its capabilities and experiences an added or heightened sense of involvement. If they are ready for this realization and experience, then they have been well prepared during all other rehearsals. If they are not ready, then it is too late for the conductor to recoup the time that has been lost.

In addition to musical concerns during the dress rehearsal, the choral conductor will need to attend to such matters as the use of risers and their placement, the use of chairs and their placement, the use of stands and their location if an instrumental ensemble is involved, the location of a piano, the type and variety of lighting, the access and egress of the chorus, and their attire and deportment during the concert. He should make a complete list of all that has to be done during the final rehearsal, and, although much can be delegated to officers, committees, and work crews, he will need to supervise and double-check these details since he will be held responsible for any obvious omissions. He should also prepare a list of final directions which have to do with concert arrangements, such as starting time, meeting time, attire, and so on. He should not leave anything to chance and should welcome questions from the chorus if his directions have not been complete or clear.

The dress rehearsal must be carefully organized so that the time available is fully utilized, all the repertoire is covered, and sufficient time is allowed for the nonmusical details. To do otherwise not only wastes time and produces chaos, it also shows disrespect for the time and energy which the performers are contributing. When instrumental forces are being used, the rehearsal sequence should be organized so that they may be called and used without much waste of their time. For example, if the brasses are used in only three choral works, these should be rehearsed first even though it may not be in the sequence of the concert. Instrumentalists should not be kept idle while the chorus rehearses unaccompanied choral works. This will be especially important when union instrumentalists are being used, for the conductor will need to schedule the sequence of a dress rehearsal most carefully in such instances so that money is

not wasted in addition to time. A well-organized dress rehearsal that is conducted with efficiency and thoroughness will have tremendous psychological
value on all performers as they move on toward the concert.

THE STIMULUS OF PERFORMANCE

As mentioned earlier, the concert appearance is generally considered to be the
chief source of motivation for the chorus as for other performing groups. Every
rehearsal is related to that peak of achievement which a chorus discloses during a
concert performance; thus, every choral group needs the stimulus of public
performance. It is important that the singers have the satisfaction of completing
the process of technical preparation; in doing so, they can bear witness to the
quality of preparation and to their growth as a choral group. In this way, as was
also stated earlier, concert performances are like periodic reports on the status of
choral artistry by both the chorus and its conductor. These appearances will also
provide opportunities for the chorus and its conductor to demonstrate their
ability to perform a variety of choral literature with stylistic sensitivity and
accuracy. Every concert should verify that the chorus and its conductor are
striving for continued development and refinement of technique, style, and
musical knowledge.

A NEVER-ENDING PROCESS

A choral concert is a report of the progress made in rehearsals, and after its
completion the chorus and conductor should evaluate this *report* to the audience
and ascertain if that *report* measured up to their expectations, if it proved to be
an accurate summation of their preparatory efforts, and if there was evidence of
achievement or failure. The concert is not an *end in itself*, for the chorus and the
conductor must profit from this analysis and continue to learn together more
and more about the choral art. Thus, though the concert may be a goal which
serves as an incentive, it is even more importantly one of a series of events in the
total choral experience. The concert is a phase of a cyclical process: after the
concert the chorus and its conductor return to the rehearsal room and continue
this never-ending process of choral education, musical development, and artistic
refinement.

ᴄɧʀᴇᴇ

THE CHORAL CONDUCTOR
AND THE MUSICOLOGIST

Walter S. Collins

Not long ago, I had occasion to attend a stunning performance of Handel's *Messiah* directed by one of our most distinguished conductors. Not only was the technique faultless, but a sweep and grandeur seldom heard in this much-abused work were restored with overwhelming effect. Wishing to renew an old friendship and to express my congratulations to the conductor, I sought him out backstage. When I finally found him, he was closeted away from well-wishers deep in discussion with a noted musicologist on the appropriateness and authenticity of the ornamentation which had been used in the performance.

The incident left a strong impression on me because it so typified the new attitude between scholar and performer which has developed since World War II. As the generation of musicians trained in the forties and fifties has begun to make its influence felt, a healthy trend toward cooperation instead of disregard or even hostility has arisen. We have at last begun to listen to rather than ignore each other. As a well-known piano pedagogue recently said, "the contributions of musicology have by now gained recognition by all up-to-date performers," and the teacher "at least feels that he should 'look it up' . . . and no longer proclaims that his instinct is infallible and his sole guide."* In fact, the musicolo-

*Walter Robert, "Musicology and Piano Playing," *The Piano Teacher*, VI, No. 5 (June, 1964), 9.

gist and the performer have even become one and the same person in many cases. It is no longer unusual, for example, to find a musical scholar performing successfully in public, or a professional performer conducting research and publishing his findings. Professional ensembles are thriving on repertoire which not long ago was solely the province of the classroom and the library. University curricula are being broadened and new degrees instituted in recognition of the need to train this new breed of scholar-executant.

The associations of the performer and musicologist have not always been as healthy as they are becoming today. In the past, musicologists have often criticized some of our finest virtuoso soloists and conductors for relying entirely on their musical instincts while neglecting historical fact about performance. And, indeed, many performers, including some very distinguished ones, have at times used scores and styles of performance which seriously abuse the composer's intentions. In addition, they have too often ignored the vast body of new repertoire which musicology has brought to light in the last two or three generations.

On the other side, performers have charged musicologists with being divorced from the daily practicalities of performing live music before live audiences. They have been fond of such witticisms as those which reproach the scholar for producing "words without music" or "books about books about music." Even the general musical public has been persuaded that the typical musicologist is an eccentric who takes all the joy out of music by talking it to death. A certain amount of this criticism is justified. Some musicologists, again including some very distinguished ones, have failed to make the results of their research meaningful to the performer. They have too often written only for each other, analyzed without making the implications of their analyses clear, and forgotten that the end of all their labors must ultimately be the sound itself.

Despite past faults on both sides, this divisiveness is no longer worthy of serious musicians of any kind. Scholars need to have their books read and their editions performed; performers need new repertoire and informed advice on performing it in order to improve their programs and to satisfy a growing public interest in less familiar music. Communication and cooperation must be encouraged by all possible means.

It seems appropriate, therefore, that a book on choral music such as this one should investigate the relationship between the choral performer and the musicologist and try to stimulate its improvement. This chapter, written by a choral conductor who is also a musicologist, is an attempt to inspire wider cooperation by discussing how these two groups have served each other in the past and by pointing out the possibilities for greater service between them in the future. While it is addressed primarily to the choral conductor, the musicologist may also read it with profit; cooperation is by definition two-sided, and much remains for both to achieve.

The role of the choral conductor is considerably clearer than that of the musicologist. What, in truth, is a musicologist? Or more properly, what is musicology? Arriving at a definition is no easy task. Musicology, not yet a century old, is a much younger field of choral conducting, and even musicologists themselves do not agree on the contents and limits of their discipline. Every year in books, articles, and speeches they try to agree on a precise definition of musicology and have yet to reach a satisfactory consensus. In a chapter such as this one, therefore, it is neither practical nor possible to develop a new or meaningful definition of musicology. It can only summarize commonly held positions briefly, refer the interested reader to more detailed discussions,* and try to point out to the choral conductor what aspects of musicology have been and are directly relevant to his interests.

Definitions of musicology usually encompass the methods as well as the contents of the discipline. The earliest definitions, in the late nineteenth century, emphasized musicology's use of the "scientific" research method, hoping perhaps to share in the new eminence of science which was developing at the time. This emphasis is reflected as late as 1941 in Glen Haydon's standard definition: "Musicology is that branch of learning which concerns the discovery and systematization of knowledge concerning music."† This is the attitude which looks upon musicology as pure research, its responsibility as the uncovering, organizing, and recording of information pursued for its own sake—which is exactly what most musicologists do and what has led to some of their difficulties with performers.

More recently a new attitude has been growing which emphasizes the humanistic method of research in contrast to the scientific. This point of view holds that the musicologist should be not only a seeker after and systematizer of musical information, but also the evaluator of it. "The true scholar knows that history consists not merely of facts but also in the values set upon them."‡ This school maintains that critical evaluation is the highest rung on the ladder of musicological activities, an attitude which is more sympathetic to the views and needs of the performer.

As for the subject matter of musicology, the early definitions were very broad, encompassing knowledge about any phase of music—its history, its composition, its science, its physiology and psychology, its sociology, its teaching, its practice, and so on. But the science of music outgrew musicology in its headlong advance into technical complexity, only to reappear recently in electronic music as the domain of the composer. Occasional bows are made to the

---

*Frank Ll. Harrison, Mantel Hood, and Claude V. Palisca, *Musicology* (Englewood Cliffs, N.J.: Prentice-Hall, 1963); Joseph Kerman, "A Profile for American Musicology," *Journal of the American Musicological Society*, XVIII, No. 1 (Spring, 1965), 61-69; Edward Lowinsky, "Character and Purposes of American Musicology; A Reply to Joseph Kerman," *Journal of the American Musicological Society*, XVIII, No. 2 (Summer, 1965), 222-34.

†Glen Haydon, *Introduction to Musicology* (New York: Prentice-Hall, 1941), p. 1.

‡Paul Henry Lang, Letter to the editor of *Music & Letters*, 43, No. 4 (October, 1962), 396.

sociological implications of music, but the physiology and psychology of music have also become too technical in their methodology for most musicologists.

In practice, therefore, despite what he may say about himself and his role, the musicologist has become primarily a historian of music, and the vast majority are historians of Renaissance and Baroque music in Europe. Recently, there has been a gratifying trend toward activity in the music of the Classic, Contemporary, and even the Romantic eras. Even more important, musicology has expanded its borders outside Western Europe to include music not only of the Western Hemisphere but the music of all cultures and times. Comparative musicology, or ethnomusicology as it is now most frequently termed, is having the effect of extending the scholar's and performer's legitimate concern to the music of all men, not only to that of the civilized Westerner. The day may soon be coming when choral programs will as logically include an African hunting chorus as a Renaissance Christmas motet.

It should be noted that the popular writer on music, the radio announcer, the recorder player, the analyst, the newspaper critic, the conductor who specializes in early music, or even the teacher of music history are not necessarily musicologists, despite everyday usage which often bestows that title upon them. Such people may or may not be musicologists, but they are not so by virtue of activities which lack the required breadth of purview and commitment to research.

Not all the musicologist's activities are equally important to the performer. The remainder of this chapter, therefore, will limit itself to those areas of musicology which are the most directly relevant to the performer: the provision of accurate scores; information on how to perform them according to the composer's expectations; and the production of reference and literary publications which will assist the performer to find and understand the music.

MAKING SCORES AVAILABLE

Past Achievements

The musicologist's chief service to the performer has always been to provide him with music which would not otherwise be available for performance. Compare the situation today with that of the choral conductor of little more than a century ago before the musicologist began this service. The director of the town choir could not ask his local music store to order fifty copies of a Byrd anthem for him because such copies simply did not exist. If he wished to perform a Handel chorus, a Victoria motet, or even a Beethoven mass, he would have had to locate an early printed copy or a manuscript of the work, decipher the notation, and produce sufficient copies for his singers. The deciphering and copying would have been troublesome enough, but the difficulties of locating a copy of the music would often have been insurmountable. The earlier in history a composer had lived, the less likely it was that a printed copy of his music had ever been published at all. Even if it had been, most copies had long since been destroyed, lost, or scattered. Manuscript copies of earlier music were even more rare. Not only would there have been few copies made originally, but since musicians had never before been interested in performing music of any time but their own, they had rarely seen any need to save manuscript copies of a dead composer's music. Indeed, only the merest chance made it possible for many priceless masterpieces of earlier eras to find their way to hidden shelves in secluded libraries where they rested uncatalogued, unseen, and unperformed.

Mendelssohn's revivals of the large choral works of Bach in the 1820s and 1830s accelerated the awakening interest in music which was written before one's own time. It is indicative that the earliest efforts at revival were often those of performers rather than scholars. More and more during the nineteenth century, the performer and the student of music history began to demand copies of music by composers no longer living, and the new profession of musicology began to respond. Among the earliest attempts at collecting and publishing earlier music in a systematic way was the momentous *Bach-Gesellschaft* edition of the collected works of J. S. Bach. Since that time, nearly every major composer of the last five centuries has had at least a start made on a collected edition of his works. What started with major composers spread to a host of lesser ones. Not only collected editions of single composers, but anthologies of many composers and great national series such as Austria's *Denkmäler der Tonkunst in Österreich*, Germany's *Denkmäler deutscher Tonkunst*, and Britain's *Musica Britannica* gradually became available. Even today, these and a number of similar series continue to rescue music which otherwise would remain unstudied and unheard.

These massive editions, which are to be found in most major music libraries, have become the standard sources of most early music. They are indispensable tools for any serious choral conductor, not only for the repertoire contained therein but also as standards against which to check modern editions of particular works. That many of the early editions are being superseded today by newer editions—including the *Bach-Gesellschaft* edition by the superb *Neue Bach Ausgabe*—is only because editing standards have to be redefined by each generation in its own terms. This fact and the continued discovery of new sources of information will undoubtedly result in further editions which must also be consulted by the performer seeking an accurate score. However, the debt owed by today's scholar and performer to these early pioneers is still immense even though increased knowledge and changing fashions are making many of their efforts obsolete.

As pathbreaking as most of the best early editions were, they were often more useful for the scholar than for the performer. Because the editor was attempting to be "scientific," to provide a version of the music exactly as the composer wrote it, he reproduced clefs no longer convenient to the performer and long note values which implied to the performer slower tempi than were correct. Bar lines, without which modern musicians could hardly function, were often omitted as in the original sources. Suggestions for performance—such as dynamic or tempo indications—were not offered, nor were translations of texts or reductions to piano-vocal score provided. Extended critical justifications filled many pages unneeded by the performer, and the volumes were usually too large for the music stand, not to mention prohibitively expensive. Thus, these early examples of scholarship too frequently followed the original music to the library shelf, and one of the major divisive factors between musicologist and performer had been formed. More and more, performers were demanding music of earlier times, but musicologists were not providing it in a form which they could use.

The Practical Edition

This discrepancy between supply and demand brought about a misfortune from which choral music has not yet recovered—the "practical" edition. Some performers, more conscientious than their fellows but insufficiently trained in scholarly or historical matters, began dipping into the rich storehouse of the great editions in order to extract the gems. Finding an attractive nugget which should be brought to his listening public, the enterprising performer made a copy for his own use and began performing the piece. When it had a good reception, he was naturally moved to publish his version for the use of other performers, and the practical edition was born. Not only did this "editor" or "arranger" use modern clefs and note values, bar lines, and a format practical for the performer, but under the guidance of his musical instinct, he usually included his ideas on how the piece ought to be performed. He supplied tempo markings, dynamic indications, and phrase marks; he provided translations of texts, often omitting the original text as unusable to his purchasers. He arbitrarily removed sections which did not appeal to him (as in Vivaldi's *Gloria*) and corrected "wrong" notes (as in the famous augmented fifths in Gibbons's *The Silver Swan*). Furthermore, mistakes in copying and even ascriptions to incorrect composers crept in and became frozen into the pieces as editor after editor would offer *his* version of the best seller based on the first one.

The process did not stop there. Simple music sold better than difficult music, so complex passages were simplified, long pieces were shortened, high passages were lowered, and the "arrangement" was born. Now the composer's original concept of the piece was so covered over with accretions as to be virtually indiscernible.

The result of this process in choral music today is that there may be as many as a dozen or more "editions" or "arrangements" of many popular early choral works, none of which satisfies the requirements of scientific scholarship or even makes clear whose music is whose. Some choral conductors, trained to believe what they see on the printed page, may buy an edition in the hope that their performances will resemble that of the famous conductor who has marked it up, or simply because it is less expensive, has an attractive cover, or comes from a publisher who gives fast service. The many fine editions which are available are thus passed over. Many conductors who would be mortified if their singers performed a wrong note in public accept editions full of them. Even some of our best conductors, who would not consider using anything but an *Urtext* edition of the Bach *Well-Tempered Clavier* to study at the keyboard, continue to perform from serious distortions of Bach's choral music. Universities which would be outraged at any tampering with *Hamlet* or even Beethoven's *Fifth Symphony* unknowingly subsidize their choir's annual misrepresentation of the *Messiah*.

The blame for the situation must be shared by all parties to the process. Many editors are not even conscious that a problem exists, and a number of those who are have no desire to tamper with success. Many publishers of music who conduct their business affairs with impeccable ethics remain either unconvinced or ignorant of the serious distortions and plagiarism that appear in their publications. Suggestions for change to either group meet with little or no success because even very fine performers continue to buy these faulty editions. Here is where the musicologist must also share the blame. He has somehow failed to convey to the performer what he needs to know to be an intelligent buyer, to persuade him that a performance of a composition based upon a poor edition cannot be anything but a poor performance.

Perhaps the following pages can break this unhappy chain by pointing out to the editor and publisher some of the abuses which they have allowed to creep in, and by teaching the choral performer how to choose an edition.* Then perhaps the musicologist-editor will begin to provide more of the accurate and also practical editions of choral music than he has in the past, and the spiral will turn upward.

An Example of Choral Editing

As an example of a composition which is available in a number of different editions, I should like to offer an actual case from my own research experience. Although it is an extreme case and involves a piece that is not in itself that important, it is by no means atypical of the editorial abuses that have been heaped upon much more important early works which have achieved any measure of popularity. Describing its publishing history in some detail will hopefully lead to an increased understanding of editing problems. Upon this understanding can then be built the basis for a rational choice among editions of other choral music.

For a number of years I conducted research into the sacred music of

---

*See also Walter Collins, "What Is a Good Edition?" *The Choral Journal*, XII, No. 3 (November, 1971), 15-18.

Thomas Weelkes (c. 1576-1623), one of the greatest of the Elizabethan composers. Although most of his secular music had been available in print since Edmund Fellowes's monumental *English Madrigal School* editions appeared early in the twentieth century, very few of Weelkes's many pieces of sacred choral music had been brought to light. Even now, there are several important works still awaiting publication.

One day I found reference to a piece by Weelkes entitled "O sacrum convivium." My curiosity was instantly aroused, because in ten years of searching I had uncovered only one other piece by Weelkes with a Latin text. I awaited the filling of my order for the composition with considerable excitement. When it finally did arrive, my disappointment was keen, because it was immediately recognizable as a version of an anthem long since published under Weelkes's name with the title "Let Thy Merciful Ears, O Lord."

The story does not end there, however, because the latter version already had a fascinating history of publication. It all began when Edmund Fellowes, one of the finest English editors of the early part of this century, found three parts for this composition in some part books at Peterhouse College, Cambridge. (It was common practice in Weelkes's time to copy polyphonic music in single-voice part books, one for the soprano, one for the alto, etc.) Only the soprano, tenor, and bass part books survived (Figure 3-1). No composer was

Figure 3-1 Beginnings of Peterhouse College (Cambridge) Music Manuscripts 45, 43, and 36

identified, but since the piece immediately followed a service by Weelkes in the part books and was not too unlike other Weelkes pieces in style, Fellowes assumed that it was by Weelkes and published it that way. He did not feel it necessary, by the standards of "practical" editions of his time, to mention that he had added an organ reduction of the voice parts and marked it "for practice only," an assumption, we shall see later, that is dangerous for Renaissance music, where unaccompanied singing was more the exception than the rule. Fellowes also did not reveal where he had found the music nor give an indication of what he, as editor, had added, either in the way of performance markings or anything else. Nor did he explain that he had changed the original clefs, the time signature, much of the text underlay, some notes, and reduced the note values by half (Figure 3-2). He did, at least, indicate that he had raised the composition by a major second and had added an alto part of his own composition, a courtesy not usually followed by the later editors who so frequently plagiarized this edition.

Figure 3-2 From Tudor Church Music, No. 35, 1926; by permission of Oxford University Press, London

The piece's simple charm made it an immediate best seller, and the usual process of dispersion to other publishers began. The first reedition, which appeared in this country, was essentially a copy of Fellowes's.* Unusually, it had the permission of the original publisher to reproduce it and identified Fellowes as the editor.

Sometime during the 1930s, Fellowes discovered the missing alto part and in later editions quietly changed most—but not all—of the few notes of his own alto where he had guessed wrong. (These are largely toward the end of the piece and thus do not appear in the accompanying examples.) However, the ascription to Weelkes, the organ part, and his other alterations remained.

Over the years many other editions have appeared, most of which imply that they were originally edited or arranged by someone else. One recent American edition even claims that the editor had "made reference to the microfilm of the original manuscript." The most extreme departure was for a long time the Latin version, "O sacrum convivium,"† but recently this has even

*(Boston: E. C. Schirmer, #1018).
†Ed. R. Mills Silby (Dover, N.J.: George T. Carthage, 1954).

been translated back into English twice and published under the titles "O Holy Banquet"* and "Early will I seek Thee."† The source of all these other versions, however, is always betrayed by the appearance of Fellowes's changes, his organ part, and his ascription to Weelkes.

The completion of the story had to wait until the 1950s, when, during several trips to England seeking Weelkes manuscripts, I happened upon more sources for this piece in some seventeenth-century part books in the British Museum, Durham Cathedral, and York Minster. Their discovery was accidental because the piece was not attributed to Weelkes at all but to a composer named Mudd (Mudds, Muds), without specifying which one it was of several seventeenth-century English composers of that name. Besides supplying verification of the Peterhouse parts and identifying the correct composer, these parts also happily contained the missing alto (Figure 3-3) and an organ part (Figure 3-4).

Figure 3-3 Beginning of p. 318, Durham Cathedral MS C.7

Figure 3-4 Beginning of p. 16, Durham Cathedral MS A.3

Now for the first time it was possible to make the piece available to the performer under the name of its true composer, in the form in which he composed it, and with all the notes which he had composed‡ (Figure 3-5).

The comparison of this version and the Latin version (or its retranslations) can serve as a classic example of the barriers which can grow up between composer and performer by the indifference, carelessness, or ignorance of editors. Without some notice to the contrary by the editor, the purchasers of this piece in its Latin form bought and performed it with the belief that it was by Thomas Weelkes, that it was an unaccompanied choral work in e minor with all four voices written by Weelkes, that it had a Latin text, that it had note

---

*Ten Rennaissance Motets, ed. and adapted by Eugene Lindusky (Cincinnati, Ohio: World Library of Sacred Music, 1964).

†Ed. and arr. by John A. Richardson (Waco, Texas: Sacred Songs CS-316, 1967).

‡Ed. Walter Collins (New York: Lawson-Gould #895, 1960). An editorial note explains editorial procedures and the former ascription to Weelkes.

values in quarter notes, a time signature of 4/4, and tempo, dynamic, and phrase marks which must be followed. A performance which realized Mudd's concept of his little anthem was clearly impossible under these circumstances.

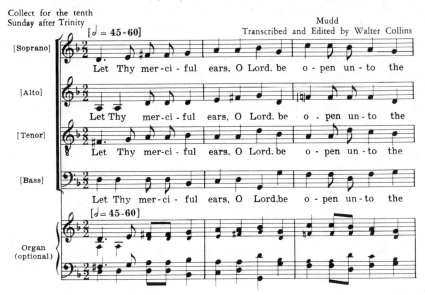

Figure 3-5 Copyright 1960 by Lawson-Gould Music Publishers, Inc; reprinted by permission

ARRANGEMENTS, TRANSCRIPTIONS, AND *URTEXTS*

Before discussing what an edition should ideally be, let us pause to clean up some terminological underbrush by discussing what it is not. An *edition* is not an *arrangement* and it is not a *transcription*. These three words have been used ambiguously and interchangeably for too long in choral publications. Attempts are at last under way to arrive at some standardization of meaning in their everyday usage; until there is such an agreement, both for choral music and other media, the purchaser of music can be no more sure of what he is buying than he could be in a grocery store which pasted labels on cans with no regard for their contents.

Arrangements

An arrangement is properly a deliberate alteration of the composer's original intent and is identified as such. In choral music this most commonly occurs in the rewriting for chorus of a solo song or an instrumental piece, the reworking of a mixed chorus for some other choral combination, the adapting of an entirely new text to the music, or the harmonization for chorus of a preexistent melody such as a folk or popular song. Ideally, each of these procedures should have its own descriptive term rather than all being lumped under "arrangement." Arranging also encompasses the unfortunate practice of simplifying or otherwise altering a piece for some reason or other—usually apparent only to the arranger—without changing the performing forces involved.

An arrangement should not absolve the producer of the responsibility of revealing the composer's original intent, however. A conscientious publisher will provide some information concerning the original title, text, opus number, and performing forces of the composition, as well as the source of the music used by the arranger.

Note that an arrangement is not simply a reprinting of a piece for the same performing forces as the original with someone's unidentified ideas of interpretation and/or a translation of the text imposed. Such "arrangements" are published by the hundreds each year, and the practice of calling them such should be discouraged by all possible means. They should more properly be called "editions," but then they must subject themselves to the restrictions implicit in that term as described below. Either they should be made full-fledged editions—

Figure 3-6

the best alternative—or they should not be published. The poorest alternative, if the practice must continue, is a new term for the process. Perhaps "interpreted by" would serve.

Transcriptions

A transcription is properly the literal reproduction of an original source in a new notation. This is normally applied to pre-Baroque music and is useful to the scholar only. Standardizing its modern usage in choral music, where it does not appear frequently, should not be difficult. The practice of calling a piano piece rewritten for orchestra a "transcription" will be harder to change, although such adaptations should more properly be called "arrangements."

Figure 3-6 shows how the beginning of "Let Thy Merciful Ears, O Lord" would appear as a transcription (without the complicating factors of accounting for variant readings among the several sources or of providing the usual critical notes). This is a much simpler case than most early pieces provide, yet it is clear that an attempt to perform effectively from such a transcription would meet with failure.

Furthermore, it is questionable whether a true transcription without any intrusion by the transcriber is possible at all. "Any such translation from one set of symbols to another is an act of interpretation."* Even the simple little Mudd piece above demanded decisions concerning the primacy of various sources, the meaning of the notation, the underlay of the text, and so on. It becomes apparent why many scholars today feel that the word "transcription" should not be used at all. "We had better abandon the noble but unrealistic idea of an exact science of transcription, guarding on the other hand against the silly notion (of which the results one sees in much 'sheet-music' editions of polyphonic music) that transcribing is merely a matter of personal taste—or the lack of it."†

Urtexts

Even wider problems exist with the *Urtext*, or original text, a term related to transcription but applied more often to post-Renaissance music, where strictly notational problems are less complex. Commonly, the purchaser of an *Urtext* believes that he is receiving an unencumbered view of what the composer wrote. As the *Musical Times* has said, "Gone, thank heaven, are the days when editors felt it their duty to fill out the text according to their personal inclinations. We live in an Urtext age, and we desire first and foremost to know what the composer actually wrote."‡

Let us examine the possibility of discovering "what the composer actually wrote." In the strictest sense, we can be satisfied only if we have a clear, readable, and verifiable version of the work in the composer's own handwriting. Such sources are extremely rare until a very recent period in music history. Even when they do exist, there also may be other copies in the composer's hand, or printed versions which he supervised, all of which vary from each other. What most frequently survive are copies of a piece in someone else's handwriting, perhaps copied from the composer's original or perhaps from another copy. Worse yet, there are often several of these which disagree with each other. This problem was already recognized in the sixteenth century. In 1597 for example, Thomas Morley, speaking of musical errors found in manuscripts, said ". . . for, copies passing from hand to hand, a small oversight committed by the first writer by the second will be made worse which will give occasion for the third to alter much, both in the words and notes according as shall seem best to his own judgement, though (God knows) it will be far enough from the meaning of the author; so that errors passing from hand to hand in written copies be easily augmented, but for such of their works as be in print I dare be bold to affirm that in them no such thing is found."§

*Arthur Mendel, "The Services of Musicology to the Practical Musician," *Some Aspects of Musicology* (New York: Bobbs-Merrill, 1957), p. 4.

†Arman Carapetyan, "Editorial," *Musica Disciplina*, V (1951), 5.

‡Quoted without other ascription in Guenter Henle, "Editing Urtext Editions," *The Canon*, 7, No. 10 (May, 1954), 414.

§Thomas Morley, *A Plain and Easy Introduction to Practical Music*, ed. R. Alec Harman (London: J. M. Dent, 1952), p. 255.

Few important composers, especially earlier ones, saw much of their music in print during their lifetimes, and even printed versions made under the composer's supervision present problems. Composers change their minds and engravers make mistakes. Publishers distribute prints without the composer having seen the proofs. Composers themselves miss errors while proofreading, and printers fail to alter proofs correctly even after the composer has marked them. "Mistakes—mistakes," wrote Beethoven to his publisher Breitkopf and Härtel on May 6, 1811;

> you yourself are a unique mistake— Well, I shall have to send my copyist to Leipzig or go there myself, unless I am prepared to let my works appear as nothing but a mass of mistakes— Apparently the tribunal of music at Leipzig can't produce one single efficient proofreader; and to make matters worse, you send out the works before you receive the corrected proofs—*

Only in the most unusual cases is it possible to discover without ambiguity "what the composer actually wrote." An editor's most important task, therefore, is to do the detective work which is necessary to arrive as closely as possible at the most authentic version.

THE NEED FOR EDITING

The necessity for an editor only begins at this point. Even assuming that one can uncover what the composer actually wrote, the infinitely more complex problem of what he *meant* by what he wrote presents itself. Take again the case of "Let Thy Merciful Ears, O Lord." From the manuscript sources, how does one know what forces are to perform? How fast does Mudd expect it to go? How is it to be accented metrically, if at all? How loud and at what pitch level should it be sung? Which words go with which notes? What did Mudd omit from the notation that he would have expected the performers to supply? Should the simple melodies be ornamented? Are the rhythms and accidentals to be sung exactly as written, or did he expect them to be altered?

None of these questions is answered by knowing "what the composer actually wrote." In the first place, notation changes. As simple a marking as "trill" or "adagio" has meant something different to the performer in each of the last four centuries. Second, notation never says everything necessary. The earlier in history a composer lived, the less likely would the notation he used indicate how the piece actually would have sounded—that is, the more it was simply a skeleton for the performance. Not only were there commonly accepted traditions of adding to and altering in performance what was written on the page, but in most cases the composer expected to supervise the performance himself, so there was no need for detailed interpretive indications on the score. Even today, our tenors sing the treble clef an octave lower than it is written, or

The Letters of Beethoven, coll. and ed. by Emily Anderson (London, Macmillan, 1961), p. 320.

we impose unwritten triplets on uneven divisions of the beat in jazz style. In both cases, of course, everyone "knows" how it should go, so there is no need to write it correctly. This is exactly parallel to the notational situation throughout most of music history. The modern musician must, therefore, learn to regard what Palestrina or Bach put on the page with what John White, former Director of the New York Pro Musica, calls a "suspicious delight." An *Urtext* is not enough. As Arthur Mendel puts it, "Western musicians of today have such strong habits of associating a piece of music with its graphic notation that they need constant reminding, by every possible means, of the limitations of notation as applied to either old or exotic music."*

Since most performers have neither the interest nor the knowledge to become experts on notation and performance practices, it is obvious that an expert editor is needed who can answer questions similar to those posed above—as much as they *can* be answered. "The fact is," Walter Emery states, "that until an editor has done his work, and done it properly, no performer can safely play old music, no analyst can safely analyse it, and no historian or critic can safely assess it. The editor's work is the foundation on which all other musical and musicological activities are based."†

THE PRINCIPLES OF EDITING

Having seen the distortions which can and do evolve, as well as the need for editing, the performer may more easily accept the two axioms that underlie the best editions and, for that matter, the best performances. The first of these is as follows:

> The ideal performance of a piece is that one which most closely approaches the composer's expectations for its performance.

Accept this for the moment on faith, or at least as an hypothesis; we shall defend it later while discussing authenticity of performance practice. One can even totally reject this first axiom, however, and still subscribe with comfort to the second, without which the first is unattainable:

> The ideal edition of a piece is that one which most accurately reveals the composer's expectations for its performance.

The doubter of the first axiom is still able to interpret a piece edited in accordance with the second in any manner he pleases, but the *composer's* intent is at least available to him as one possibility. This point needs emphasis because some publishers deny it: the accurate edition need be no distraction to the

---

*Arthur Mendel, *op. cit.*, p. 10.
†Walter Emery, *Editions and Musicians* (London: Novello, 1957), p. 14.

performer who does not care about authenticity—he can continue to impose his own interpretation without regard for the composer's desires—but the performer who *does* care about what the composer expected has the information necessary to make an intelligent choice. In a poor edition the composer's intent is not an available option.

Nor should this axiom be construed as preventing what may be the very valuable preservation on paper of a great performer's interpretation so long as it is made clear which is the performer's expectation and which is the composer's.

THE PRACTICE OF EDITING

Original versus Editorial Material

Providing the ideal edition described in the above axiom requires two basic procedures before anything else. First, *the editor must include everything which survives directly from the composer or from as close to the composer as possible.* This sounds obvious, but such simple matters as the original title and text of the piece, opus or other identifying numbers, the original performing forces (including descriptions of the instrumentation in vocal scores), even correct pitches, rhythms, and performance indications are frequently omitted from editions, especially choral editions. Even the identity of the sources used by the editor is usually lacking. Second, *the editor must distinguish with absolute clarity between what survives from the composer and what he has added himself.* It is only ethical to make clear whose music is whose, not to mention the importance to the performer of knowing what is fact and what is opinion.

An edition which does not observe these two basic rules is open to such immediate suspicion that it is nearly useless; yet in choral editions today not one in five does so.

The Methods of Separating Editorial Material

Several techniques are available for satisfying these rules. The most complete method is to provide an editorial note which describes in detail what the editor has done. For instance, an editorial note for a typical Renaissance piece might contain some statement such as, "All marks of interpretation and the bar lines have been added by the editor. The note values have been reduced by half and the pitch raised by a major second. Spelling and punctuation have been modernized, and missing portions of the text filled in without notice." The trouble with such statements is that they can, and often do in complex cases, become so lengthy and detailed that they take up more room than the music itself. Some shortening can be effected by providing an *incipit* at the beginning of the piece. This is a device which transcribes exactly the first few notes of the source with the original note values, original key and time signatures, original clefs and performing forces, and any initial interpretive marks. The incipit is very simple to print, and it can communicate quickly a large amount of information about the editing. Figure 3-7 presents again the opening of "Let Thy Merciful Ears, O Lord" with an incipit based upon the manuscript sources given in Figures 3-1, 3-3, and 3-4.

Figure 3-7

Other practices, such as surrounding editorial additions to the score with square brackets, crossing editorial slurs, and placing editorial accidentals above the staff, can also reduce the length of critical prefaces. Such markings have the added advantage of making, on the score itself, the distinction between what is original and what is editorial.

There are other ways of accomplishing the same end, but the method is less important than the accomplishment. This is not the place, moreover, to go into details of method which have been dealt with thoroughly elsewhere.* Nor is it appropriate here to relate the musicological arguments which still rage over such matters as whether to modernize clefs, reduce note values, transpose keys, or how to resolve doubts in text underlay. This clearly is the place, however, to express support for the school of thought which maintains that an edition should be made as useful to the performer as possible by utilizing notation familiar to the modern musician, by abstaining from complexity for complexity's sake, and by not attempting to create a pseudofacsimile of the original. Few performers would disagree with the musicologist Willi Apel when he says, "There are only two sensible ways of presenting old music: either in a facsimile reproduction or in a readable modern score."†

Editing for Both Scholar and Performer

Apel's statement is representative of an even wider and more important conclusion—being adopted at last by most scholars and serious performers—that an edition must satisfy both performer and scholar simultaneously. The difficulties of getting much old music published at all do not permit the luxury of offering two different editions, one for the scholar and one for the performer. No longer should we distinguish between "critical," "scientific," "original," "*Urtext*," and "scholarly" editions on one side, and "performing," "practical," and "artistic" on the other. No more do we need to tolerate the relegation of the completely scholarly edition to the library shelf unperformed nor the inaccuracy and basic dishonesty of the worst of our performing editions. The editor who follows the principles and practices of editing as outlined above, taking into account the special needs of the scholar and the performer, can accomplish the desired end of the combined edition, even though it will not always be easy. When he succeeds, he is building another important bridge between the two groups.

Once the cardinal rules of providing all original material and separating it from editorial material are observed, there are various other ways in which the scholar and performer can each be served. The scientific scholar must by definition be a doubter. He is devoted to the basic principle of all scientific research—that results have to be reproducible to be valid. He must therefore be able to follow the editor's steps and to reconstruct what has been done. He has

*Thurston Dart, Walter Emery, and Christopher Morris, *Editing Early Music* (London: Novello, Oxford University Press, Stainer & Bell, 1963).
†*French Secular Music of the Late Fourteenth Century*, ed. Willi Apel (Cambridge, Mass.: Mediaeval Academy of America, 1950), p. 20.

to know what the original notation looked like because it can tell him a great deal. He is partially satisfied by the incipit which shows him much he needs to know, but he may feel that he has to return to the original source in order to satisfy himself completely. Consequently, he must have full information concerning the sources of the music which the editor used for the edition. Unfortunately, this usually involves forbidding-looking lists of manuscript numbers and bibliographic references, but simple honesty demands it, and they can be hidden in small type at the end of an editorial note so as not to disturb the timid. The practice of listing the editor's sources, by the way, would eliminate the shocking amount of plagiarism rampant in choral publishing today. Few editors would have the nerve to admit in print to the common practice of simply reproducing someone else's edition with a few of their own interpretive markings added. Even though the music is usually in the public domain where such reediting is legally permissible, it cannot be considered ethically permissible.

The most impeccable editor will also list *all* sources for a piece as well as those he used, and he will discuss their validity and even their geneology.* However, since such a thorough presentation can become exceedingly complex, it may be more appropriately relegated to scholarly articles in journals with cross referencing in the edition itself.

The scholar, and to some degree the performer as well, must know when two sources disagree. Some simple method of showing variant readings between sources must be used, although such lists sometimes become very cumbersome to print with an edition. In such cases, a system of eliminating the less important variants from the list should be devised. In any case, the editor always has to make the painful choice between the variants by printing one and not the other in the music itself. In these choices he has to be a detective, not a musician. The important question to be answered in variant readings is "Which note is the composer's?" not "Which is the best?" The editor is not allowed the luxury of aesthetic judgement because modern judgement may be wrong. Needless to say, he can always record his own preference in some way, once the composer's preference has been indicated.

The editor must also assist the performer. In addition to making the notation as clear and usable as possible, the editor should record his opinions on how the composer would have expected the piece to be performed. Marks of interpretation, description of original performing forces with suggested ways to duplicate them today, and suggestions about ornamentation and alteration of notation are all helpful and necessary. This kind of advice is not to be confused with the usual doctoring of early pieces in popular editions. If the editor's opinions are not firmly based on the most thorough possible knowledge of the performance practices of the time, they are not worth printing, and he should not be editing. The editor's opinions should at least be more informed historically than those of the performer, no matter how illustrious, who depends only

---

*For discussion of this problem see Walter Emery, *op. cit.,* pp. 23-24.

on his musical instinct and tradition. No restriction of the editor's opinion is implied, however. His performance indications may be as numerous and detailed as he wishes, so long as they can be recognized as editorial and not original. As a matter of fact, conscientious performers have been begging the musicologist to offer more guidance about thorny issues of performing forces, ornamentation, and other matters of performance.* Also helpful is some brief and relevant information about the piece itself, its history, its place in the composer's work, perhaps even an analysis. Not necessary is extensive biographical information on the composer, which is nearly always available today in reference books on music. On the other hand, the date of the piece's composition and the composer's birth and death dates can help to establish a historical context for the singer and the audience.

The performer of vocal music is usually grateful for a translation of the text fitted to the music so that if he chooses he can perform the piece in the language of his audience; at the same time, the performer who wishes to perform it in its original form should not be neglected. The ideal solution is to underlay the original language, being as faithful to the source as possible, and to provide as well a singable translation. In addition, many performers also appreciate a printing of the text straight through in easily readable form at the beginning in order that it may be read and understood as a whole.

Several other simple devices can show the editor's concern for the performer's needs. Many choral conductors, for instance, appreciate having an indication of the range of the voices at the beginning of a piece. Others like to have an estimated time of performance for planning purposes. Many editors forget the simple courtesy of providing measure numbers or rehearsal marks. Such numbers should best be placed at musical divisions of the piece, rather than by some arbitrary system such as every five measures or the beginning of each staff, provided that there is at least one number per page. This would help to eliminate that most unmusical of choral rehearsal practices of beginning in midphrase "at the top of page 5."

CHOOSING THE EDITION

Faced with the choice of several different editions of the same piece—or even one—the performer should now be more able to ask most of the questions necessary for deciding which one to purchase. Stated most simply:

---

*Excellent and practical examples of such directions in choral scores are contained in Arthur Mendel's brilliant forewards to his editions of Schütz's *A German Requiem*, *The Christmas Oratorio*, Bach's *Passion According to St. John*, and Mozart's *Missa Brevis* (K. 192), all published by G. Schirmer of New York. Also not to be omitted is that excellent collaboration between a fine performer and a fine editor, *The St. Matthew Passion, Its Preparation and Performance* by Adrian Boult and Walter Emery (London: Novello, 1949).

1. Does the edition appear to provide all available original information?
2. Is the original material clearly distinguishable from editorial material?
3. Has the edition been made useful and convenient for both scholar and performer?
4. Does the edition provide intelligent and informed opinion about the composer's expectations for the performance of the piece?

The final question demands further discussion. Are the editor's opinions intelligent and informed? To determine the answer, there are two courses open to the practicing conductor. First, he must know the editor and publisher and their previous work well enough to trust them. Editors of practical editions like Thurston Dart, Arthur Mendel, Franklin Zimmerman, Wilhelm Ehmann, Denis Stevens, and others have earned that trust. The safer and ultimately more practical course, since there are so many editors and publishers of varying quality, is for the choral conductor himself to know enough about the performance practices of the piece under consideration that he is able to evaluate the editor's opinions.

Doing some editing from original sources himself is the conductor's quickest way to gain insight into the problems involved. With knowledge and some experience, he will be in a better position to see how close to the ideal of revealing the composer's expectations any edition comes. Only when he is satisfied that he has a good edition can he begin the intensive preparation of the score itself, as described by Julius Herford elsewhere in this book.

PERFORMANCE PRACTICE

Introduction

Once the performer has a reliable version of what the composer wrote, a good editor's opinion of what was meant by it, and trained opinions of his own, he must finally turn the piece into sound. He alone has to answer the final question of how the work actually should be performed. Here again, the musicologist can be of vital assistance to the performer. Performance practice (*Aufführungspraxis*) is that branch of musicology which studies the evidence of what the actual sound would have been. It is intertwined inseparably with editing but is more involved with matters such as tone quality, performing techniques, improvised ornamentation, and so forth, which do not show in even the best edition. As practitioners of the youngest branch of musicology, scholars of performance practice have only just begun compiling a body of information. There is still much work to be done, especially in choral music, since it has received less attention than most other musical media.*

Now the time has come to discuss the axiom stated earlier concerning the performance of early music: *the ideal performance of a piece is that one which most closely approaches the composer's expectations for its performance.* Can we accept this as true or not? Not all musicians do. One, for instance, recently wrote the *New York Times* that "any fine performer who grasps the spirit of the music does, in the last analysis, have the right to decide what sounds best to him."† A great deal of argument occurs every day on this very question of authenticity of performance. Indeed, a distinguished panel of musicians and scholars not long ago spent the better part of an all-day conference session discussing the topic, "How Far is an Exact Reconstruction of the Original Conditions of Performance (a) Possible (b) Desirable?"‡

Those opposed to the concept of authentic performance often maintain that the "exact reconstruction" of any historical composition is impossible, no matter how desirable it may be. Either there is insufficient information to allow us to recreate a performance exactly, or there is too much contradictory information, and such information may apply at one time and place but not another. We can never know the sound of the singing voice because no instrument or recording survives. Even where early instruments survive, it is impossible to use them in the original way because no player can have the training which led to the original technique. One can never reproduce the conditions, the acoustics, and traditions of a performance. Furthermore, even if one *could* do so, he *should* not because the audience which heard the original performance can never be reassembled. We cannot listen in any way but in modern terms, so a truly authentic performance would be completely unsatisfying to a contemporary audience.

The opposite view holds that "there is little hope of this music being appreciated at its true value until it is played exactly as it was originally intended to be played."§ Proponents of this position feel that the imposition of modern performance practices on a piece which was not written with them in mind is incongruous. They would argue that the most satisfying performance from a

---

*The best bibliography of research in the field of performance practice is *Performance Practice: A Bibliography*, ed. Mary Vinquist and Neal Zaslaw (New York: W. W. Norton, 1971). Another fine bibliography is contained in Robert Donington, *The Interpretation of Early Music* (London: Faber and Faber, 1963). This book is itself a major source of information on the subject. An expanded version has been announced.

†Eleanor Vail, Communication to *The New York Times*, June 4, 1961, Section II, p. 9.

‡International Musicological Society, *Report of the Eighth Congress* (Kassel: Bärenreiter, 1961), II, 122-24.

§Gerald R. Hayes, *Musical Instruments and Their Music, 1500-1750* (London: Oxford University Press, 1928), p. 3.

musical standpoint is the one for which the piece was written, that the original performance expectations are an inseparable part of the piece itself.

Our axiom sides more with the positive side of the argument, though by using the word "ideal" performance it implies that exact reproduction of a composer's expectations may not be possible. The reason for this one-sided stand here is that the American choral conductor, to whom this book is addressed, rarely pays much attention to the original conditions of performance. He needs to hear the other side. Furthermore, the antiauthentic attitude leads to abuses which no serious musician can tolerate. It encourages the philosophy that if the composer had had modern instruments and choirs he would have written for them, which in turn results in performances of Bach organ fugues by marching bands, and in the singing of simple little madrigals by elephantine choirs of 300. Had the symphony orchestra been available to Bach, of course he would have written for it. But the point is that he did *not* have it, that he had to write within the limitations of what was available to him. The limitations of the medium, and the artist's solution of the problems these limitations impose, are an integral part of any work of art. Remove the limits, and you have removed part of the artistic creation itself.

Carried to its logical conclusion, the negative argument on historical authenticity permits the performer total liberty in performing any piece of music. It gives encouragement to those performers who neither know nor care what the composer wanted for his piece, performers who without restraint impose their own personalities upon what is written on the page, or, even worse, pay little attention to the page at all. Ultimately the composer gets removed entirely, as evidenced by the attitude—especially prevalent among opera buffs— which expresses itself in terms of "Tebaldi's *Bohème*," or "Shaw's *B minor Mass*."

An Example of Authentic Performance Practice

Let us test the idea that the most convincing and musical performance is the one which most closely approaches the composer's by comparing a typical modern performance of a Renaissance choral work—one inspired by tradition and uninformed musical instinct—with one influenced by what we know of an authentic performance. It soon becomes apparent that if this music had received in its own time the monotonous and insipid performances it so often gets today, it never would have survived.

Tempo Consider the tempo of the typical modern performance. The long white notes of Renaissance notation (and the reverence with which one should properly approach such ancient and august matters) obviously must call for a slow and dignified tempo at all times. To the contrary, however—though it is always difficult to be sure about tempo in any era—it appears that tempi were often as vigorous and fast in the Renaissance as they are today.* The composers

*Curt Sachs, *Rhythm and Tempo* (New York: W. W. Norton, 1953).

were vital, spirited, and energetic men—sometimes too much so, considering the number who were constantly in trouble with ecclesiastical and political authorities. When they wrote "alleluia" or "hosanna," they must have intended them to be sung with just as much spirit as would a twentieth-century composer. Yet, one too often hears a Renaissance "Gloria in excelsis" sung as if it were a "Lacrymosa." Performance by half-note beats (after reduction) rather than quarter-note beats—in contradiction to the incorrect quarter-note time signatures given in many editions—would both improve tempos and be much closer to the Renaissance *tactus* feeling.

Tone Color Consider the tone color of the typical modern performance. Tradition, instinct, and—to the uninitiated—the score, indicate that a Renaissance motet or madrigal should be performed "a cappella." The fact is, however, that "a cappella" does not necessarily mean unaccompanied when applied to Renaissance music, no matter how the score looks in the modern sense. The unaccompanied chorus was only one of many possible alternative methods of performance and one which was probably used less than most others. The evidence continues to grow that most of the time, instruments—if only the organ—played along with most Renaissance choirs.* Furthermore, sacred polyphonic vocal music may have been performed by soloists and instruments as often as it was by choral groups; secular music, and all polyphonic vocal music before the early fifteenth century was probably performed in this manner exclusively.† The Machaut *Mass*, for example, should not even be included in histories of *choral* music. Some of our most exciting performances of Renaissance music today continuously change color during the course of an extended piece, using different combinations of soloists, choruses, and instruments. Because of this freedom, almost *any* choir, no matter how small or inept, can perform Renaissance works in a satisfying way. If it is weak on tenors, an instrument can play the part instead; if there are pitch problems, the organ can double the voices throughout; if certain passages are too difficult, soloists can be used. The result can be far more interesting to the listener and is more authentic than the tutti unaccompanied performance one usually hears.

Phrasing Consider the phrasing of the typical modern performance. The vertical orientation of so much of our choral music has too frequently led to stilted and wooden phrasing in the performance of Renaissance pieces, and in most choral music for that matter. Our tendency to think more in terms of the harmonic relationships among the voices than we do of their separate melodies has resulted in what is perhaps the weakest aspect of all modern American choral

---

*Denis Arnold, "Instruments in Church. Some Facts and Figures," *The Monthly Musical Record*, 85, No. 964 (February, 1955), 32-38; and J. Bunker Clark, "The A Cappella Myth!" *The American Organist*, 47, No. 4 (April, 1964), 16-21. Also reprinted in *The Choral Journal*, IX, No. 4 (January-February, 1969), 28-31.

†Manfred Bukofzer, "The Beginnings of Choral Polyphony," *Studies in Medieval and Renaissance Music* (New York: W. W. Norton, 1950), pp. 176-89.

performance. Too often we hear choral performances in this country which are flawless in tone, diction, balance, and pitch—in every technical aspect except the expression of a beautiful musical phrase. Such vertical concentration negates the very basis of the polyphony of Renaissance music. We must remember that Renaissance singers sang from separate part books which only indirectly allowed them to compare themselves to the other parts vertically as modern singers so often do. They were forced to think horizontally. In most carefully constructed Renaissance pieces, moreover, the polyphony creates a fascinating interplay of conversation of line and text which can survive only if each voice proceeds as if it had an almost independent melody, rising and subsiding according to the dictates of all melodic singing, expressing its particular text in the most musical way possible. Melodic imitations, of course, demand similar phrasing among the voices, but the similarities occur at different times. The true glory of polyphonic music lies in its emphasis on the independence of the lines rather than their interdependence.

Meter   Consider the metrical accentuation of the typical modern performance. Tradition and editorial bar lines lead to too many regularly accented readings of Renaissance works. Many choral conductors still do not realize that until the seventeenth century, very little music had bar lines at all, and that which did used the lines only as guides to the copyist and the eye, not as indicators for accenting. A more authentic performance today would result from printing the music with irregular barring based on the word accenting of each part as in the opening bars of Victoria's "O magnum mysterium," shown in Figure 3-8.

Figure 3-8

Unfortunately, however, the modern singer would be easily confused by such a score, and most modern conductors made uncomfortable. Other methods, such as placing the bar lines between the staffs or using regular, apostrophe-like marks above the staff to show the beats rather than the measures, have been proposed but rarely adopted.* Perhaps someday singers will again be able to perform from independent parts as orchestral musicians do, perhaps even parts with irregular barring, or, in the Renaissance manner, with no bar lines at all. However, modern performers are probably too thoroughly trained in the bar line to give it up, as are conductors too fond of their beat patterns. The conductor must see to it, therefore, that his singers understand that the bar line in Renaissance scores is not the same thing as a modern bar line, that his downbeat does not mean what it usually means.

Dynamics Consider the dynamics of the typical modern performance. The nineteenth-century tradition, still followed by many, dictates that Renaissance pieces be performed with numerous large *crescendos* and *diminuendos* in the nineteenth-century manner. A more recent tradition, taking literally the lack of markings in most critical editions, employs no dynamic change at all. Although we still have much to learn about Renaissance dynamics, the truth appears to lie between these two extremes. A reasonable statement might be that dynamics

*See, for example, Thomas Stoltzer, *Psalm 86*, ed. Otto Gombosi (St. Louis: Concordia Publishing House MS 1018, 1953). See also the "Varia-Bar" editions of the Mark Foster Music Co.

within sections should be governed by the natural rise and fall of the melodic lines, while overall dynamic levels between sections should vary according to the meaning of the text. The "Et resurrexit" section of a Renaissance mass, for example, should be sung with greater enthusiasm and volume than the "Crucifixus."

Ornamentation Consider the use of ornamentation in the typical modern performance. We perform Renaissance melodies exactly as they appear on the page. Although the research on Renaissance ornamentation is still in its rudimentary stages, especially as it concerns choral ornamentation in contrast to solo ornamentation, it may well be that the simple appearing, "pure" lines of Palestrina and others were ornamented almost beyond recognition by the singers of the time.* Adoption of this practice would no doubt result in a more highly colored sound than we are used to hearing in Renaissance choral music, but we must wait until more evidence is available.

Conclusion

In each of these cases, then, it is apparent that the manner of performance which is as authentic as our limited knowledge can make it, and which is guided by an *informed* musical instinct, is more interesting even to the present-day listener than is the typical performance given us under the dictates of our traditions and untutored musical instincts. Similar arguments could be constructed for any era of music history. As has been said, there is no need either to sugarcoat or bleach out Byrd and Bach, because they are more intriguing in their own garb.

THE MODERN PERFORMER AND PERFORMANCE PRACTICE

Defenders of both sides of the authenticity argument have been known to make the same mistake of assuming that there is a correct performance, that the composer would have expected one particular rendition and one only. The earlier a composer lived, the less likely it is that he expected any such thing. When he performed his music himself, he used the forces available to him and made the best of what was often a bad situation. He would have expected anyone else who performed his music under different circumstances to do exactly the same thing, even though the results might be quite different. Consequently, the only reasonable solution today is to take the first axiom

*Manfred Bukofzer, "On the Performance of Renaissance Music," *Proceedings of the Music Teachers National Association*, XXXVI (1941), 225-35. Imogene Horsley, "Improvised Embellishments in the Performance of Renaissance Polyphonic Music," *Journal of the American Musicological Society*, IV (Spring, 1951), 3-19. Gordon Flood, "Extemporaneous Ornamentation of Renaissance Polyphonic Music," *The Choral Journal*, XII, No. 6 (February, 1972), 12-18.

simply as a general goal when it speaks of an "ideal" performance. That such a performance can never be reached, and furthermore that the ideal may exist only as a set of boundaries beyond which one should not go, is admitted in advance. It still must be the goal, however, because the alternative of total freedom of interpretation is inadmissible, as we have seen. As Donald Grout says, "The problem with regard to most old music, then, is not to determine a single fixed, invariable practice but rather to determine the limits within which the several aspects of performance might have fluctuated without leading to results that the composers would have found unacceptable."*

How does the performer find these limits? Defining them is one of the musicologist's chief responsibilities to the performer. Unfortunately, he has not yet filled this role very successfully. The study of performance practice still has far to go, and several generations of research will have to be done before enough definitive answers are available to satisfy everyone. It is one of the last major frontiers in musicology's realm. Much work has already been accomplished in defining the limits, however, and it is the performer's responsibility to pay it heed even though it may be presented in a form which is difficult for non-experts. The performer must earn the right to interpret within the limits by making the effort to find out from the musicologist as much as there is to know about them.

BIBLIOGRAPHY

Introduction

The provision in print of literature about music and reference materials concerning music has always been an important function of the musicologist. Nearly every practicing scholar eventually publishes in some form or another the results of his research and his opinions on it, be it in general or limited histories of music, biographies, monographs on some specific aspect of music, periodical articles, or even critical editions of the music itself. Those with a different kind of interest produce reference works such as dictionaries and encyclopedias, or bibliographic tools such as systematized lists of books, manuscripts, periodical articles, recordings, music, and so on. Unhappily, however, only a small proportion of serious scholarly writing—or, for that matter, of the huge outpouring of popular literature on music—is devoted to assisting the performer, and that devoted to assisting the choral conductor is minuscule.

For example, what has the musicologist offered to the choral performer in the way of literature or reference works specifically on choral music? How many

*Donald Jay Grout, "On Historical Authenticity in The Performance of Old Music," *Essays on Music in Honor of Archibald Thompson Davison* (Cambridge, Mass.: Harvard University, 1957), p. 343.

bibliographies, analyses, or monographs have been published with the particular aim of serving the choral conductor? Considering the amount of repertoire, the potential market, and the pressing need, publications of this nature are distressingly rare. Tremendous amounts of work need yet to be done, and it is the intent here to point out to the musicologist, the bibliographer, and the research-oriented choral conductor some of the directions it should take. This chapter cannot contain an exhaustive bibliography of choral music (a task which in itself needs doing if only to expose the wide gaps in coverage); but it can call attention to some of the important works by musicologists, or which utilize a musicological approach, and plead for more of the same.

Several types of writings on music are not relevant to the present discussion. General and period histories of music, for instance, while indispensible to the choral performer, cannot be dealt with here because they are obviously not limited to choral music. We must exclude most biographies of musicians for the same reason, even though the best of them have important and frequently overlooked discussions of composers' choral music. Also outside our present boundaries is the one area where literature about choral music is extensive—choral conducting and techniques manuals—on the grounds that its intent is less musicological than pedagogical. Almost every important choral conductor eventually reaches print with a book describing the methods which have made him famous, but such publications are instruction books, not scholarly studies. "It is outside the scholar's sphere to theorize about the performer's digital, pharyngeal, or mental mechanics."* This restriction should not be taken to include, of course, historical studies of teaching methods, or other researches into performance practices which are so sorely needed in choral music.

Critical Editions

We have discussed earlier some of the technical considerations involved in providing critical editions of music. Once provided, such editions are the single most valuable bibliographic resource for performers. Many collected editions of the works of single composers and major editions of groups of works or composers have appeared over the last century. The conscientious choral conductor uses them almost daily for the purposes of comparison with performing editions or for seeking new repertoire. Some are still being produced, but the production is slower than most musicologists and performers would wish. Until most of the music of the past is available for study and performance, all other musicological activity is based on incomplete information. Who knows, for instance, whether the music of another Bach or Palestrina may lie hidden in some remote monastery library? And the discovery of even one or two major new works of Handel or Brahms could change the opinion of their entire output.

*Harrison, Hood, and Palisca, *op. cit.*, p. 109.

Collected and *Denkmäler* editions have seldom been devoted to choral music exclusively, even though many are filled with it. Although they are not strictly critical editions, among the best edited anthologies of choral music are *Das Chorwerk* (ed. F. Blume, Möseler, 1929-), which recently passed one hundred small volumes, and Feininger's *Documenta Polyphoniae Liturgiae* (St. Cecilia Society, 1947-), a series of Renaissance compositions for chorus. Scholarly editions of individual choral works or even separate volumes of choral works are far too numerous to list here, despite the need for such a list (see p. 126).

Monographs

The most useful kind of literary publication for the performer is the monograph, a shorter book which discusses in depth some particular aspect, form, medium, or genre of music. Writings of this kind on choral subjects have not been frequent, but there have at last been several recent attempts to fill the worst gap, a basic history of choral music. *Choral Music*, edited by Arthur Jacobs (Penguin Books, 1963), is a chronological series of essays by a number of fine musicologists on different eras of choral music. Several useful appendices include a bibliography, a discography, and a list of recommended editions. *The Choral Tradition* by Percy Young (Hutchinson, 1962) is a less scholarly but more unified attempt by one man to present "an historical and analytical survey" of choral music since the sixteenth century. More limited in its subject matter is the excellent *Choral Music of the Church* by Elwyn Wienandt (The Free Press, 1965), which contains one of the best bibliographies of choral music presently available (see p. 237). All three of these books hopefully indicate a growing awareness among musicologists of the pressing need for literature in the history of choral music.

A monograph may be written with emphasis on the history, analysis, bibliography, or on performance itself—or ideally on all four. Second, the subject matter can properly be all choral music—or one type of choral music, or even a single choral work—of a particular composer, an era, or a country. It may even concentrate on a single choral form or device. All sorts of titles of monographs which do not exist but which would be valuable contributions to the literature immediately suggest themselves from various combinations of the above aspects: "The Choral Music of Mozart"; "The Baroque Chorale Motet"; "Contemporary French Choral Music"; "The Cantata"; "A History of the Multiple Chorus Technique"; "Choral Music in Musical Comedy"; "The A Cappella Idea"; and so on. Such books exist for most other musical media, but they are very rare in choral music, though the number of unpublished doctoral dissertations on such subjects is growing. They would, of course, be especially useful to the performer if they were to include bibliographic information on available editions and recordings of the music under discussion. Even more important would be knowledgeable advice on proper performance practices. Consider, for example, how useful to the choral conductor would be a series of monographs on the choral music of individual composers which would not only discuss the music in its historical context and analyze it but which would gather together all possible information on how to perform it and where to find editions of it. There must be a dozen such books on the Mozart quartets or piano sonatas; there is not a single one on his choral music. There are several histories of the symphony in English, but none of the oratorio.

Strangely enough, a large number of monographs already exist among the hundreds of musicological dissertations and theses which have never been published. The results of thousands of expert man-hours of research lie unused in graduate school libraries or on microfilm because they have never been made easily available. The fault does not lie entirely with the oft-berated publisher; just as often such works stay in manuscript because the author is unwilling to put them into a form which would be useful to the reading public rather than his doctoral committee. The elimination or condensation of the usual introductory chapters which set the background and summarize the previous literature, the streamlining of the scholarly apparatus of footnote verification, and the curbing of mathematical computations, charts, and long appendices that are useful only to another scholar, could often result in a monograph of reasonable length which would be useful to both scholar and performer and thus of interest to the publisher.

Dictionaries and Encyclopedias

Lexicography constitutes an important part of musicology's publishing activity. Dictionaries and encyclopedias of music are indispensible sources of information to the choral conductor. For example, the lists of a composer's choral works—full of unknown gems—in the large general musical dictionaries are available nowhere else so conveniently. Again, however, there is not a single lexicon which concentrates on choral music, as there is for most other media. On the fringes are the various dictionaries of church music and hymnology, as well as the sections of Valentin's two-volume *Handbuch der Chormusik* (Bosse, 1953, 1958) which precede the lists (see p. 127); but the former are not primarily on choral music, and the latter are too brief and unsystematic, not to mention less useful to one who reads no German. Choral musicians should urge the musicologist to provide them with an organized and convenient encyclopedia of choral music which pulls together in one place the lexicographic information they need.

Periodicals

There are hundreds of periodicals on music, most of which at some time or another publish articles of specific interest to the choral conductor, not to mention articles of general interest to all musicians. Of those concerned solely with choral music, most are in languages other than English, making them of limited use to the average American choral conductor. Omitted for different reasons from the best list of periodicals* are the two most important American journals; *The Choral Journal* (P.O. Box 17736, Tampa, Florida 33612), the official publication of the American Choral Directors Association, and the *American Choral Review* (130 West 56th Street, New York, New York 10019), which is the journal of the American Choral Foundation, Inc. *The Choral Journal* is the less musicological of the two, consisting of association business, reviews of new music (largely octavo), articles on a wide variety of choral subjects with emphasis on techniques, organizing choruses, reports of the activities of members and their choruses, and so on. The *American Choral Review* becomes more important from a musicological standpoint with each issue while also succeeding in being of direct practical usage to the serious conductor. It contains important scholarly articles on choral music of all kinds, with more of an emphasis on historical and analytical subjects than on techniques and day-to-day problems. Reviews of new books, recordings, and music of interest to the choral conductor have been joined recently by journalistic reports on important choral events throughout the world. Although there are a number of journals devoted to church music with varying degrees of emphasis on the problems of the organist and the church choir, the only other journal in English on Campbell's list of choral periodicals is *The Texas Choirmaster* (P.O. Box 3428, McAllen, Texas 78501). He describes it as having "chatty articles *re* the problems of the choral director of all possible parts of the profession ... reports of meetings of the Association. Reviews of pertinent new books and music— although quite short, they seem quite well done." It has since ceased publication.

Bibliographies: Lists of Books and Articles

There is no published bibliography of books and articles on choral music other than a few brief lists appearing in periodicals.† Most systematized general bibliographies of music books, however, do contain sections on vocal music or church music if not specifically on choral music. There are also a number of lists in existence which were privately prepared for teaching purposes; they usually consist largely of books of importance to any performer and books on choral techniques, *RILM Abstracts* and *Music Index* are, of course, invaluable sources of information for literature about all kinds of music, and some books such as Wienandt's *Choral Music of the Church* contain useful if limited bibliographies.

*Frank C. Campbell, "A Critical Annotated Bibliography of Periodicals," *Research Memorandum No. 33* of the American Choral Foundation (New York, July, 1962).
†Among the best is Bruce D. Hoagland, "Materials for Choral Practices and Techniques," *The Choral Journal*, VI, No. 3 (January-February, 1966), 21-22, and continued in the next three issues.

There is a great need, then, for a classified, systematic bibliography of information on choral music, including articles from those periodicals which less frequently come to the attention of the choral conductor. This would seem to be a highly appropriate undertaking for a musicologist with a bibliographic bent.

Bibliographies: Lists of Recordings

There seem to be no lists of recordings of major importance. The better general discographies include sections on choral, or at least vocal, music. Choral periodicals also list and review new recordings. While a classified choral discography would be useful to the performer, his need for reference materials is perhaps greater in other areas.

Bibliographies: Lists of Music

Lists of choral music are so numerous that it will be possible to discuss only the more important ones here. Lists range all the way from those produced by music publishers to stimulate sales of certain pieces in their catalogs, through repertoire lists of individual choirs and groups of choirs and contest lists prepared by conductors' organizations or educational groups, to lists of the standard repertoire in choral-conducting textbooks and lists of new choral music in periodicals. It is not always easy to draw the line between musicological bibliographies with some claim to comprehensive coverage and lists which simply record someone's preferences or recommendations. (One very rough rule of thumb is whether the list is arranged by composer or merely by title.)

In any case, there have been only a handful of serious musicological efforts to provide systematic reference lists of choral music. Furthermore, those that do exist are not always designed to be of practical use to the performer. The list of Beethoven's choral music in *Grove's Dictionary*, for example, is very useful; but it is much less useful than Elliot Forbes's list* which includes information on performing editions, difficulty, cost, publishers, availability, and so on. Such lists are urgently needed in far greater numbers than they are presently being produced, especially since publishing activity changes them daily.

The whole problem of lists of choral publications is a classic one of information retrieval which cries out for computerization. Consider how helpful it would be, for instance, if a conductor could easily and quickly acquire a list of all editions in print of choral pieces which were written in the Romantic era, which were of no more than medium difficulty, whose tenor part did not go any higher than F, and whose text was appropriate for Easter; or another of all contemporary compositions for women's chorus and band with secular English texts; or another of all the choral music of Handel in print; or another of all the choral settings of "Yankee Doodle." Compiling such lists is exactly what computers are able to do most efficiently. Although entering the necessary

*American Choral Review, XI, No. 3 (1969).

information into the computer initially would be a massive task—and keeping it up-to-date also formidable—many projects of greater complexity are in progress daily. Once the initial insertion of information had been accomplished for choral music, the instantaneous production of any kind of organized list of compositions would be a simple matter. This is the kind of project that one of the conductors' or publishers' organizations should initiate and support, in the same way that the College Music Society has begun producing by computer its biennial directories of college and university music faculties.

The most comprehensive lists of choral music yet printed are those contained in Erich Valentin's two-volume *Handbuch der Chormusik* (Bosse, 1953, 1958). Although the book is in German, the user with only the most rudimentary knowledge of the language should have no trouble in using the lists. They are organized into the basic voice groupings, accompanied and unaccompanied works, and sacred and secular texts—for example, "Sacred Music for Unaccompanied Male Chorus" or "Secular Music for Mixed Chorus with Instruments." The length of compositions in minutes is usually given, as well as complete indexes by composers' names. Most useful is the information concerning the publishers of each piece. The American conductor should not be put off by the fact that most of the publishers listed are European. Not only does this open up major new sources of music to him, but European houses usually have American agents; if not, most enterprising music retailers order music directly from a foreign publisher. Many conductors even order directly themselves from mail-order retail dealers in Great Britain or on the Continent, usually at a considerable saving in price. Nevertheless, one hopes that Valentin's recently announced third volume will cover American publishers as well as more recent European publications.

Four American lists make some attempt at comprehensiveness although in limited areas. They are Merrill Knapp's *Selected List of Music for Men's Voices* (Princeton University Press, 1952); Kenneth Roberts's *A Checklist of Twentieth-Century Choral Music for Male Voices* (Detroit: Information Coordinators, 1970); Arthur Locke's and Charles Fassett's *Selected List of Choruses for Women's Voices* (Smith College, Third edition, 1964); and Charles C. Burnsworth's *Choral Music for Women's Voices: An Annotated Bibliography of Recommended Works* (Metuchen, N. J.: Scarecrow Press, 1968). These are indispensable reference tools for the conductor of a male or female chorus. Knapp's book badly needs an up-dated edition similar to that which Locke's first and second editions recently received.

The American Choral Foundation, Inc., since being founded in 1958, has done more than any other single agency to provide bibliographic materials for the choral conductor. Early in its history the Foundation produced a series of file cards, each containing not only the bibliographic information on a book of interest to the choral conductor but also a list of libraries throughout the United States which had that book in their collections. More important are the individual pamphlets which make up its *Research Memorandum* series, which have been published six to nine times a year since 1959. Most of these are important specialized lists of choral music, such as No. 13, *A Selective List of XV and XVI Century Netherlandish Choral Music Available in Practical Editions* by Noah Greenberg; or No. 24, *A Selective List of Choral Compositions from the Classical Period in Practical Editions* by Jan LaRue and John Vinton; or No. 46, *A List of Contemporary American Choral Music for Mixed Voices* by James Case. Many are also less specialized lists by well-known conductors of their preferences and recommendations in special choral areas, such as No. 35, *Select List of Choral Music for Festivals* by Helen Hosmer, or No. 41, *A Select List of Choral Music from Operas, Operettas, and Musical Shows* by Lehman Engel. These, and the many others in the series (which has passed ninety in number), are invaluable reference materials that are available nowhere else.

Also deserving mention are the *Catalog of Published American Choral Music* compiled by Crawford Gates (The National Federation of Music Clubs, 600 South Michigan Avenue, Chicago, Illinois 60605, 1969), the second edition of this valuable reference; *Major Choral Works by Contemporary Composers* (The American Music Center, 2109 Broadway, New York, New York 10023); and the choral portion of *Contemporary Music: A Recommended List for High Schools and Colleges*, compiled by a committee chaired by George Howerton (Music Educators National Conference, 1201 15th Street, NW, Washington, D.C. 20036, 1964).

A more general list of choral music and vocal solos has recently been published jointly by the Music Educators National Conference and the American Choral Directors Association with the title *Selective Music Lists 1968*. It represents the efforts of two committees under the chairmanship of Robert S. Hines. The music is listed under such categories as type of chorus, difficulty, sacred, or secular. While it is a fine effort which will be helpful to many conductors, it would be even more useful if it contained indices by composer and title. One would also like to know the basis on which the selections were made for the list other than simply that they are "recommended."

Publishers' catalogs, although rarely drawn up by musicological methods, will always be the primary source of what choral music is available. Some lists are more useful than others, and the purchaser usually has to do his own systematizing and organizing of the lists to derive maximum benefit from them; but he cannot do without them. Most disappointing are the huge classified lists published annually by several of the major retail dealers in choral music which not only list the music entirely by title, but which do not even offer indices by composer or title. A happy practice has been the recent one, by some publishers who have contemporary composers under exclusive contract, of offering attractive individual pamphlets which list a composer's published works.

Thematic catalogs of the complete works of most major composers are now available. Although they list all works, they are an important and frequently neglected source of information about choral pieces. They even contain listings of published editions, though rarely do they list recent octavo editions of smaller works, which is the kind of information the choral conductor needs most often.

SUMMARY

This chapter began with a description of the closing gap which has sometimes existed between musicologists and performers. It continued with an attempt to effect a further narrowing of this gap by discussing those areas, especially in choral music, where important services to each group by the other are both necessary and possible. It should properly end with an exhortatory appeal that something further be done, with a call to specific action which will complete the reconciliation.

Ignorance is always the major cause of misunderstanding between groups of people, and information has been offered here that would reduce the misunderstandings between the two groups. Besides understanding, however, there must also be concessions in attitude made by each side. No more should the musicologist complain that he cannot get his research published, and that when he does manage to do so, the performer will not use it. When he makes his publications more effectively serve the practical needs of what should be his largest market—the performer—his efforts will not go unrecognized. No more, on the other hand, should the performer complain that musicological research is impractical and irrelevant while at the same time failing to use the products of that research which have clearly been designed to serve him. He must give up the anti-intellectual bias which deprives him of the ability to be selective between practical and impractical musicology.

In specific terms, then, what must each group do? In each of the major areas of contact between musicology and choral performance which we have discussed—the provision of scores, performance practice, and bibliography—both the musicologist and the performer have obligations. First, the musicologist must provide more scores which will satisfy his fellow scholar but which at the same time are suitable for use in performance, that is, accurate scores in modern notation which include information and informed opinion on authentic performance. Second, in order that such opinion will have greater validity, the musicologist must increase the tempo of his work in performance practice, especially choral performance practice, and provide more concrete information than is now available on the actual problems of historical performance. The choral conductor does not ask to be told exactly how he should interpret a Bach cantata, but he needs to know more accurately the limitations within which he has the right to interpret each aspect of the music. Third, the musicologist must begin to provide a more extensive literature about music, especially choral music, which is intended for the performer. Hundreds of general and specific histories of choral music, monographs on various aspects of choral music, dictionaries, encyclopedias, and bibliographies are needed for the daily use of the choral performer. Surely there is an extensive market for the musicologist in this area. With the exception of pianists, there are probably more choral conductors today than any other variety of serious musician. If only one tenth of the choral conductors and half the music libraries in this country bought a monograph on the history of the part song, for example, its commercial success would be more than assured.

The performer also has responsibilities. He has ultimate control over the quality of editing of choral music through his power of purchase. Consequently, he is under a heavy obligation to learn how to discriminate between good and bad editing in choral music, so that he will no longer subsidize the careless editing that pours from the choral presses today. Furthermore, the choral performer must begin to take greater cognizance of what musicology has learned and is learning about the performance practices of earlier music. He must also adopt a more modest estimate of his musical instincts as they are applied to the interpretation of this music. He must begin to accept the doctrine that the most effective and exciting performance of a piece is the most authentic one histori- cally. Finally, the performer has the responsibility of continuing to educate himself by utilizing the literature on music which musicology produces. No longer should it be possible for the musicologist to make the accusation that "what many of the most influential performing musicians do not do is read, and what they particularly do not read is musicology."*

The choral performer has an additional responsibility which he has not always discharged as well as he might—that is, the performance of music of the quality which the musicologist would suggest to him. This is not the place to refight the battle about the repertoire of the average American chorus and what can be done to expand its horizons. Great strides in the broadening of repertoire have been made in the last generation, and there is reason for optimism that with the encouragement of musicology further progress can be expected. The hand of the musicologist can be seen, for instance, in the healthy trend to provide some unity in choral programming by the use of some system of association between pieces—be it musical, historical, textual, or whatever—in place of the indiscriminate scattering of many unrelated pieces on concert programs. Perhaps this influence may also stimulate more performances of major choral works as well as the shorter cyclic forms which add unity to our concert fare.

None of these responsibilities is so heavy as to be unbearable. Surely good will, knowledge, and cooperation between two groups that have so much to offer to each other and to the art of music are not too much to ask. Choral music has the most extensive repertoire of music of any kind, and the vast amount which still awaits hearing in its most beautiful possible performance makes any sacrifice worthwhile.

*Arthur Mendel, op. cit., p. 13.

FOUR

THE CHORAL CONDUCTOR AND TWENTIETH-CENTURY CHORAL MUSIC

Daniel Moe

> Everything is in flux.
> Heraclitus

> The ultimate goal of our strivings is indeed the unlimited and complete exploitation of all possible available tonal material.
> Bela Bartok

> All we have to do is to accept the proposition that, in musical terms, any sounds may occur in any combination and in any continuity.
> John Cage

The preceding statements say nothing about the specific characteristics of music in the twentieth century, but they do articulate unmistakably the tremendous scope of the contemporary sonorous revolution. The contrasting extremes of the revolution range from the latest experiments of Stockhausen or Xenakis to a simple folk song setting of Ralph Vaughan Williams. They include the unpredictable harmonization of an Ives psalm setting and the pointillistic texture of a Webern cantata. They encompass the charm of a Hindemith chanson and the dry, ascetic qualities of the Stravinsky *Canticum sacrum*. Since approximately 1910, composers throughout the world have, in fact, been experimenting with "the unlimited and complete exploitation of all possible available tonal material." It hardly needs to be pointed out that this situation has created numerous problems for the conductor as he attempts to come to terms with the musical expression of this new freedom. In the "Foreward" to Brock McElheran's excellent new book on conducting, Lukas Foss writes, "We are heading toward a new type of conductor, one who performs a difficult task indeed: the unraveling of new music, of new notations."*

Lest the conductor begin to feel too sorry for himself, it might be well to call attention to the fact that the composer is confronted by even greater difficulties as he approaches what Austin terms "the abyss of freedom."† He writes concerning Debussy that he "complained often of a paralysis of the imagination." In 1909 he (Debussy) wrote to Caplet, "No, it is not neurosis or hypochondria either, it is the sweet sickness of the notion of having to choose among all conceivable things".‡ The composer is perpetually searching for every new means of achieving variety while undergirding his expression with consistency and coherence. Recreating the composer's vision of "all conceivable things" is the challenge facing the modern conductor. One thing is sure, the conductor must begin with an open acknowledgement of the new "ground-rules." We have gone beyond the point where arguing about the validity of the new freedom will do us any good. It is a fact of twentieth-century artistic life.

In addressing oneself to the subject at hand, several other facts of life must be acknowledged. One of these is the realization that the members of the choral-conducting profession at about three quarters of the way through our century cannot share a common musical pedigree. The individual case history describing the process by which the conductor arrived at his present position and we would do well to jump into the arena with all the enthusiasm and vitality we can summon. This is not to say that we will respond to each new compositional effort with equal delight. Preferences there will be, and we have every right to them. What is required, however, is an attitude of fundamental openness and receptivity toward novel experience whenever and wherever we encounter it. We can begin acquiring this creative posture by worrying less about pinning labels on a particular chord or musical phenomenon and concern ourselves instead with the stream of melodic or harmonic events, even though certain moments of interpenetration may sound unruly or crude. We must also avoid linking the terms consonance and dissonance with any connotation of "beautiful" or "ugly." "No sound, considered by itself and detached from any context, can under any circumstances be other than neutral."§

*Brock McElheran, *Conducting Technique* (New York: Oxford University Press, 1966).
†William W. Austin, *Music in the Twentieth Century* (New York: W. W. Norton, 1966), p. 33.
‡*Ibid.*
§Ernst Toch, *The Shaping Forces in Music* (New York: Criterion Music, 1953), p. 15.

would be infinitely varied. Many are equipped with a laudable depth of background in all aspects of music. Others are not. The only thing that can be maintained with assurance is the fact of many levels of experience and proficiency. This applies as much to the twentieth century as to the sixteenth. In many cases, for example, the contemporary musical diet of the choral conductor is made up almost exclusively of three- to five-minute octavo pieces. Where this situation exists, the conductor must strive to become more aware of the larger musical events which form the background for these worthy but diminutive expressions. To put it another way, a deeper understanding of the literature must begin by seeing a work of William Latham, Alan Hovhannes, or Houston Bright in relation to the major achievements of Schoenberg, Bartok, Stravinsky, and Webern. By adding the names of Debussy, Prokofiev, Boulez, and Cage, we form a rather grand framework in which almost all other contemporary styles can be located. The serious conductor will immerse himself in the music of these composers and will certainly not restrict himself to their vocal compositions. With choral conductors representing such great diversity of background, a few comments of the major compositional currents in our century may be in order.*

TRENDS IN COMPOSITIONAL TECHNIQUES

Twentieth-century choral music does not lend itself to easy classification, and the assignment of one of the "neo" labels will contribute little, if anything, to greater understanding. Every work is, in fact, a law unto itself, and each composition must be approached with the expectation of discovering new revelations in medium and structure. From the choice of text to the final cadence, this new freedom in contemporary choral music can be observed. More specifically, it reveals itself in richly varied melodic contours, new pitch relationships, a "no-holds-barred" harmonic vocabulary, complex metric and rhythmic plans, and the free and imaginative use of unusual vocal declamation combined with instrumental ensembles which do not conform to the normal groupings of instruments. To complicate matters further, there is also a confusing variety of national, regional, local, and personal styles. In view of the fantastic quantity of material and the great divergence of forms and styles, is there no way of integrating the various musical components so that we can cut across the styles of individual composers, countries, and schools, creating some order out of the chaos? It would appear, at least to this writer, that there are several dominant trends in our music which tend to link the styles of certain composers without regard to their country of origin or their possible inclusion in one of the "neo" schools. The fundamental basis for the quasi-unity (hedging is mandatory here) of each group lies in a similar approach to melodic, contrapuntal, and harmonic

*The author acknowledges indebtedness to his former colleague, Professor Tom Turner of the University of Iowa, for initial insights into the classifications which follow.

usage.* The first classification would be those composers who, with some frequency, employ in their works a procedure which we shall label *chromatic dissonant counterpoint*. Aesthetically, this group is the lineal descendent of ultra-Romantic chromaticism of the late nineteenth and early twentieth centuries. Among its members are such composers as Mahler, Schoenberg, Berg, Webern, and Krenek. Perhaps its most revolutionary technical contribution to our century was the free use of all twelve notes of the chromatic scale organized according to certain tone-row or serial procedures. Fundamentally, however, all aspects of musical syntax were emancipated by these composers, not just dissonance. Representative choral works would include Schoenberg's early and nonserial *Friede auf Erde* and *De profundis* (Psalm 130); *Kantate I & II* of Anton Webern; and *Six Motets* (texts by Kafka) and the *Lamentations of Jeremiah* by Ernst Krenek. Ultimately, the influence of this group reaches far beyond its geographical point of origin in Vienna and extends itself into every major musical center of the world. Dallapiccola and Nono, Gaburo and Schuller, Valen and Wuorinen—all bear the marks of their encounter with chromatic dissonant expression.

It should be made quite clear, however, that the composers just mentioned, who with one or two exceptions came of age creatively after World War II, have evolved uniquely personal styles that have as little similarity to Schoenberg's style as Schoenberg's had with Bruckner's. At this moment in our century, at any rate, there is hardly a composer of note that does not owe some debt to this mode of musical thought.

The second major classification involves those composers who employ a procedure which we shall label *diatonic dissonant counterpoint*. This "school" represents a simple reaction to the extreme chromaticism of the late nineteenth and early twentieth centuries. Its principal exponents were active prior to World War II. It features a return to the diatonic scale as the basic source of its melodic material. Furthermore, it is based on the principle that *any* note of a given diatonic scale (or mode) can be successfully combined. Contrapuntally, the result is the free use of dissonance within a *diatonic* framework. In this music, chords of the second, fourth, fifth, seventh, ninth, and eleventh are commonly found. As a rule, there is a weakening of the sharp contrast between consonance and dissonance, and strong tonal progressions are frequently absent. Some authors use the term "pandiatonicism" in referring to this phenomenon. Humphrey Searle uses the term "expanded diatonicism" to good effect, especially in his discussion of the music of Stravinsky prior to *Agon*.† The choral conductor

---

*Making generalizations about the music of any century has its obvious limitations. The reader is therefore encouraged to consult some of the excellent books on twentieth-century music which are now available for treatment in depth. One excellent volume is Eric Salzman's *Twentieth-Century Music: An Introduction* (Englewood Cliffs, N. J.: Prentice-Hall, 1967).

†Humphrey Searle, *Twentieth Century Counterpoint* (London: Williams and Northgate, 1954), p. 22.

will have little difficulty in supplying names of composers for this category. Holst, Vaughan Williams, Kodály, Copland, Lukas Foss, Dello Joio, Stravinsky of the *Symphony of Psalms*, pre-*War Requiem* Britten, and a host of others come quickly to mind. Many of the most familiar works from the thirties and forties would fall under this classification, including those of Hugo Distler and his German contemporaries, and many recent American compositions. There still remains, of course, a great divergence of style among these composers. Further-more, while the conductor will discover many delightful moments of melodic color achieved by chromatic alteration in the music of Kodály or Dello Joio, these composers do have in common a fundamentally nonchromatic approach to melodic extension.

The reader has observed, no doubt, that we still have not assigned a convenient resting place for Hindemith or Bartok. Both these composers have written extensive passages that could be placed under either classification. While some sections of their works maintain a consistent diatonicism, others are highly chromatic. We might say with some degree of accuracy that both Bartok and Hindemith, along with a number of other composers, make free use of the twelve notes of the chromatic scale within a basically tonal framework. Searle comments about Bartok: "One can best sum this up by saying that his music invariably expresses tonality, but avoids normal diatonic elements."* Both composers can be recognized by their free use of dissonance, chromaticism, and resultant tonal fluidity. Neither employs consistently either diatonic or chro-matic dissonant counterpoint. Any appraisal of Bartok's style, however, must take into consideration his relationship with Hungarian folk music. He identified completely with his native culture and utilized folk material "as inspiration for free compositions wherein no actual folk tune may be cited, but into the texture of which Bartok has completely assimilated his knowledge of the scales and rhythms on which such tunes are based."† Bartok's free use of dissonance should always be seen within this context.

This brief discussion of Hindemith and Bartok, who obviously evade classification, leads to a third and even more relevant generalization regarding the music of the twentieth century. Since World War II, there has been a steadily increasing interaction among all styles of composition, resulting in a degree of consolidation. One can now observe an unmistakable synthesis of the principal lines of development. To a large extent, the two approaches cited have become fused. The lines are not as clearly drawn as they once were, and a kind of cross-fertilization has taken place. There is little question, however, that the greater influence rests with those composers of the chromatic dissonant persua-sion. Almost every young composer has been substantially influenced by serial procedure. Furthermore, a composer whose early works fell within a predomi-

---

Ibid., p. 46.
†Dika Newlin, "Four Revolutionaries," *Choral Music*, ed. Arthur Jacobs (Baltimore: Penguin Books, 1963), p. 319.

nantly diatonic framework, may, in fact, have undergone a radical restructuring of his musical intuition through repeated encounters with composers whose works are the stylistic offspring of Schoenberg and his followers. Igor Stravinsky, for example, was making extensive use of modified twelve-tone techniques toward the end of his life. To be sure, he remained unmistakably himself, but the influence is also unmistakable.

Another manifestation of the current trend is the composer who, while not actually employing serial methods, so naturally relates to that style that he intuits the harmonic relationships of twelve-note music without recourse to the method itself. One thinks of a diatonically predisposed composer like Paul Fetler, for example, who in the opening section of *Madman's Song* manifests a style which is harmonically indebted to serial texture but which does not actually employ twelve-note principles. There is a high degree of harmonic tension in this work, but it is realized by basically diatonic means. The motivation for the strong dissonance can be traced to the text itself, but Fetler arrives at his artistic result by the combined demands of linear inevitability and simple intuition. It is also significant that the pieces which precede *Madman's Song* in the set of choruses are not characterized by such extreme harmonic tension. The point of this rather detailed observation is, first, that choral composers today readily produce sections of works or even complete compositions by purely intuitive means which contain the kind of harmonic texture normally achieved by serial procedures. Second, choral composers do not hesitate to employ significant differences in harmonic and contrapuntal texture when the text or the dramatic situation requires it.

While the discussion thus far has concerned itself primarily with the melodic, harmonic, and contrapuntal dimensions of the new music, it must at least be mentioned that one of the most important aspects of the current revolution involves drastic innovations in the area of *rhythm*. Rhythm, of course, is the principle of organization that regulates the flow of melody, harmony, and counterpoint. As such, it is an essential ingredient in all music. In twentieth-century music, the varieties of rhythmic organization are so extensive that a systematic classification of any kind is impossible. Suffice it to say that our music is characterized by greater rhythmic freedom, less symmetrical patterns, a disdain for normal accentuation, metrical irregularity, and polyrhythms. There are numerous compositions that can best be described as rhythmically aggressive. In twentieth-century music, rhythm often becomes the primary motivating factor in generating the flow of harmonic movement. "The emancipation of rhythm" is certainly one of the primary causes for the vitality of contemporary music.

While the preceding comments characterize certain aspects of twentieth-century music, they are fragmentary at best and are merely intended as an introduction to contemporary style. They indicate nothing, except by implica-

Madman's Song is one of a set of five choruses published by Associated Music.

tion, of recent developments in the so-called *avant-garde*.* And at the very moment that our previous categories appear to have some relevance, our attention is drawn to the works of Messiaen, Berio, Partch, Brant, and Babbitt. The compositions of these men remind us again that "everything is in flux," that music is always in the process of "becoming"—becoming something other than it was. Commenting on this evolutionary process in music, Albert Roussell has written, "In art as in life there is no stable state, but rather a succession of continual transformations, and when a form of art seems to become fixed before us, its disintegration has already begun."† While these challenges to the established concepts of musical order are only mentioned, the dedicated conductor will make it his business to remain open to John Cage's proposition that "in musical terms, any sounds may occur in any combination and in any continuity."‡ In concluding this section, it should be emphasized that these recent experiments should not be viewed with alarm or in fear as a diabolical threat to the existence of other kinds of musical expression. John Cage, himself, with the wisdom and equanimity born of broad experience, puts the mind at ease by saying, "Each thing has its own place, never takes the place of something else, and the more things there are, as is said, the merrier."§

THE CONDUCTOR'S PREPARATION

Gunther Schuller, the eminent American composer who has also had considerable experience conducting twentieth-century music, comments on the problem which faces conductors today:

> The problems relating to the conducting of contemporary music are, as might be expected, as varied and unpredictable as contemporary music itself. An unprecedented plethora of compositional schools, techniques, conceptions, and philosophies dominate the current scene . . . . The art of conducting is presently being subjected to some rather fundamental re-evaluations, and in a few instances new compositional approaches have radically changed conducting techniques or eliminated them altogether.¶

This statement points up the complexity of the present situation. The conductor who lived and worked during the latter part of the nineteenth century

*For an excellent recent survey of twentieth-century developments, see the *Musical Quarterly*, January, 1965.

†Austin, *op. cit.*, p. 419.

‡John Cage, "Experimental Music," *The American Composer Speaks*, ed. Gilbert Chase (Baton Rouge, La.: Louisiana State University Press, 1966), p. 229.

§*Ibid.*, p. 232. See also the fascinating statements of new directions in experimental music by Harry Partch, Milton Babbit, William Flanagan, Earle Brown, and Charles Hamm which are included in this volume.

¶Gunther Schuller, "Conducting Revisited," *The Conductor's Art*, ed. Carl Bamburger (New York: McGraw-Hill, 1965), pp. 293-94.

had enough to worry about in preparing himself to conduct music as diverse in period and style as Josquin and Brahms. The modern choral conductor, in addition to pre-twentieth-century music, must now concern himself with the whole range of works from early Schoenberg to those of Luigi Nono. Within the latter category, he is confronted with the array of demands alluded to by Mr. Schuller: more composers than one man could possibly know well, each identifiable by characteristic stylistic traits; compositions by the hundreds containing a rich variety of moods and textures; new melodic and harmonic procedures; unusual metric and rhythmic configurations; new structural principles which involve understanding such terminology as serial, aleatory, and indeterminacy; new uses of both voices and instruments; an almost infinite variety of instrumental combinations *with* voices, with each orchestration implying unique problems resulting from the juxtaposition of different timbres, articulations, and sonorities. This list could, with little trouble, be expanded considerably. It is simply a highlighting of the major areas requiring special competence and understanding. The challenge is immense, and the choral conductor today must, indeed, know a great deal about many things.

Later in this volume, Julius Herford discusses some of the implications of an adequate knowledge of history and style on choral performance. Before proceeding further, it may be well to recapitulate briefly the relationship of one's knowledge of earlier periods to the performance of twentieth-century music. Some readers, with Gunther Schuller's statement still in mind, may reflect that this is the kind of reactionary posture they would expect from a "university choral man." This writer is convinced, however, that the conductor who attempts to wade into the mainstream of twentieth-century music without the requisite understanding of historical precedent will be severely crippled. In addition to the basic discipline which a systematic exposure to earlier music produces, the conductor with an adequate sense of history will, in most instances, perceive relationships between the old and the new which will significantly enhance his sensitivity to contemporary musical expression.

There are some rather specific ways in which the conductor's knowledge of musical tradition will influence what he does with today's music. First of all, it will actually affect, to some extent, the decisions he makes regarding the music he selects for study and performance. One is not likely to be intrigued by Krenek's contrapuntal manipulations in his *Lamentations of Jeremiah* or in Stravinsky's *Threni* without some understanding and appreciation for the imitative and polyphonic procedures of Ockeghem, Isaac, or Josquin. Second, a study of the past will sharpen the conductor's capacity to discriminate between those compositions which contain freshness, imagination, and solid craft, and those which do not. In short, he must be able to apprehend greatness in music when he encounters it. Certainly the ability to recognize greatness in both literature and performance is essential equipment for the serious conductor. The diligent and persistent investigation of the music of earlier periods cannot help extending the conductor's ability to recognize uniqueness in music, regardless of period.

There is another way in which the historical perspective of the conductor may influence his craft; it can have a profound effect upon how he realizes in sound much of the twentieth-century music which he conducts. When preparing a work which has an explicit stylistic affinity with compositions from an earlier period, an adequate sense of the style of that period will greatly simplify his task. To be specific, the successful realization of a motet of Hugo Distler will be greatly enhanced by an insight into the music of Heinrich Schütz. Whatever their differences, the music of Schütz and Distler has in common an emphatic declamation of the text set within the context of a contrapuntal texture. The stylistic kinship of these two composers is apparent to all who know their music. Similarly, a lack of empathy for Renaissance liturgical music will seriously handicap the conductor's capacity to reveal the inner substance of the mass settings of Igor Stravinsky or Vincent Persichetti.

The implications of what has just been said might be formulated into a principle that transcends historical epochs and styles: in choral music, the capacity to recreate a polyphonic texture satisfactorily applies just as much to the twentieth century as it does to the music of earlier periods. However, the secret of bringing off a polyphonic texture lies in the ability of each section to successfully fulfill the melodic requirements of its part. There is an "inherent urge of each voice toward linear self-preservation"* which must be satisfied. This leads us to consider an even more basic principle: there must be a primary concern for the individual line before a contrapuntal texture can be adequately realized. The choir whose sections lack the ability to shape a single phrase in isolation, that are unable to fulfill horizontal and linear potential, will be continually frustrated expressively. For the essence of music cannot be fully disclosed until each line is appropriately fashioned and molded.

Fortunately for the choral conductor, he has readily available a kind of music that can be of great assistance in heightening the melodic capabilities of his choir. That music is *plainsong*. It is the conviction of this writer that the choir that successfully masters the techniques required in singing chant well thereby possesses the ability to sing most phrases musically. The proper performance of plainsong might well be considered the foundation upon which we build our whole concept of choral performance in *all* periods. If, as has been stated, the successful realization of a polyphonic texture is dependent upon the ability to shape a single line, the mastery of the plainsong style could go a long way in helping us to obliterate squareness and inflexibility in all music. Erwin Stein comments that "the distinction between homophonic and polyphonic music is less important for the performer than for the historian. In a sense, *every texture is polyphonic*, and the features of each strand must be taken into account."† If we accept Stein's contention that "every texture is polyphonic," then the principle that plainsong is relevant to the performance of *all* music approaches universality.

In an excellent book entitled *Twentieth Century Counterpoint*, Humphrey

---

*Toch, *op. cit.*, p. 5.
†Erwin Stein, *Form and Performance* (New York: Alfred A. Knopf, 1962), p. 113.

Searle writes, "If Palestrina and Bach had not existed there would have been no Bartok or Schoenberg; every composer must learn all the lessons of the past before he can embark on new development himself. In fact, there is no break between modern music and that of the past."*

The preceding statement would be equally valid if "conductor" were substituted for "composer." The modern conductor's conception of music, his attitudes towards his craft, his musical preferences, and his sense of style are the result of the sum total of his musical experiences. While his current involvement in contemporary life and culture is an important shaping force in his general musical outlook, his relationship with his musical heritage also exerts a profound influence. With the possible exception of the Cage-Babbitt-Stockhausen experiments, performance adequacy in twentieth-century music cannot be divorced from proficiency in earlier epochs.

SELECTION CRITERIA

Before the conductor can begin his analysis and prerehearsal study of a contemporary composition, he must choose from among several hundred legitimate possibilities the particular work or works he wishes to program. This decision will be influenced by a variety of factors, including rehearsal time available, the degree of difficulty of the modern work, the scope and duration of the other parts of the program, peculiar ensemble strengths or weaknesses, instrumental resources required, available soloists, personal stylistic preferences, which composers were sung last year, and perhaps a few other considerations. With all these musical and extramusical influences, deciding which contemporary works to perform becomes a major problem by itself. The manner in which a conductor's knowledge of earlier music can influence his interest in particular contemporary scores, and how this knowledge can sharpen his power to discriminate has been discussed previously. Considering the sheer quantity of modern choral literature, the capacity to separate the worthy from the unworthy is a fairly basic tool.

One of the conductor's greatest challenges is the development of what Peter Yates calls "the awareness of fundamental individuality in music."† Any serious student of choral programming cannot help being both amused and perplexed by the literature selections of many conductors. One questions the rationale behind a decision to perform an inferior composition when a superior work, requiring no greater performance capability, might have been chosen. The only conclusion to be drawn from such action is that the conductor lacked the ability to recognize "fundamental individuality," or the absence of it, when he encountered it. The conductor must be utterly convinced about the worth of a work before he embarks on the long and arduous journey toward ultimate musical disclosure in performance. One does not bring this kind of commitment to a work that lacks uniqueness and "fundamental individuality." Perhaps if one

*Searle, op. cit., p. 1.
†Peter Yates, Twentieth Century Music (New York: Random House, 1967), p. 150.

is merely "reading" a new work this high standard of structural excellence can be relaxed. In most instances, however, the decision to perform a work without being "possessed" by it will produce a lack of conviction in both rehearsal and performance. What serious conductor has not experienced the initial hostility of his ensemble towards a contemporary composition transformed into full acceptance and commitment simply because he was utterly convinced of the worthiness of the work.

But what of the selection process itself? Are there any guidelines that will assist the conductor in making valid choices in the vast field of twentieth-century choral literature? By "valid" we mean, obviously, literature possessing the qualities of "fundamental individuality." This implies that the music will be well crafted, imaginative, and representative of *major* compositional tendencies. This also implies that it will worthily represent the text, contrast with other works programmed, and be within the performance capability of the chorus. As a result, the contemporary music selected for performance should contain enough musical substance to stand the strain of extensive repetition. Some recommendations for selection procedure are listed below:

1. The conductor's ability to recognize this literature will depend, in large measure, upon his prior knowledge of at least a small core of the generally accepted twentieth-century "classics."
2. *Begin* the search by examining the works of those composers who, by more or less common agreement, have made the most substantial contribution to the literature in terms of both quantity and quality. This has the salutary result of considerably narrowing the field.
3. When an examination of these works proves unproductive, move on to the next level of creative talent. (There is a certain nobility about being numbered among the ranks of composers at any level. Being a "minor" composer is not without virtue.)
4. While it is logical to begin with composers with whom the conductor is familiar, always be alert for the new and unrecognized compositional talent.
5. While vast quantities of literature are available from publishers, do not overlook the fact that, for a variety of reasons, many outstanding works remain in manuscript. This applies especially to composers in your own area for whom the conductor should feel a peculiar responsibility.
6. If the conductor's performance experience encompasses works which manifest primarily diatonic dissonant characteristics, stretch the mind and ear by attempting a small-scale twelve-tone work—for example, "The Dove Descending" by Stravinsky.
7. If Berger, Britten, Poulenc, and Thompson have been the principal musical diet, try Stevens, Pinkham, George, and Distler.
8. If the three-and-one-half minute contemporary octavo has been your limit, attempt something with greater scope and duration.

9. If you have never worked with instruments and voices, you have deprived yourself of the ultimate in sonorous pleasure.

10. If you can't find any literature from this century that really excites you, seriously consider changing professions.

The following is a representative listing of twentieth-century choral works which will satisfy the "core" requirement suggested in (1) above as well as provide the reader with the author's ideas about what constitutes "fundamental individuality" in the choral music of this period.

Representative Twentieth-Century Choral Works

Composer	Title	Publisher
Avshalamov, Jacob	Tom O'Bedlam	E.C. Schirmer
Barber, Samuel	Reincarnations	G. Schirmer
	Prayers of Kierkegaard	
Bartok, Bela	Cantata profana	T. Presser
*Bassett, Leslie	*Collect	World Library
Berger, Jean	Cantate Domino	Concordia
	Magnificat	J. Shepherd
	No Man Is an Island	T. Presser
Binkerd, Gordon	Ad te levavi	Associated
Bloch, Ernst	Sacred Service	Summy-Birchard
Britten, Benjamin	Hymn to St. Cecilia	Boosey & Hawkes
	Rejoice in the Lamb	
	War Requiem	
Chavez, Carlos	Tree of Sorrow	Mercury
Childs, Barney	Nine Choral Fragments	BMI (Canada)
Christiansen, Paul J.	This Is the Day	Augsburg
Copland, Aaron	In the Beginning	E.C. Schirmer
Dallapiccola, Luigi	Canti di prigionia	Associated
Dello Joio, Norman	To St. Cecilia	C. Fischer
Distler, Hugo	The Christmas Story	Concordia
	Singet dem Herrn	Bärenreiter
Effinger, Cecil	set of three	Elkan-Vogel
Felciano, Richard	*Pentecost Sunday—	World Library
	Double Alleluia	
Fetler, Paul	April	Lawson-Gould
	Jubilate Deo	Augsburg
Finney, Ross Lee	Pilgrim Psalms	C. Fischer
	*Still Are New Worlds	C.F. Peters
Finzi, Gerald	Magnificat	Oxford
Foss, Lukas	Behold, I Build an House	Mercury
	Psalms	C. Fischer
Gaburo, Kenneth	Ave Maria	World Library
	Psalm	
George, Earl	Cantate Domino	Summy-Birchard
	Songs of Innocence	
Ginastera, Alberto	Lamentations of Jeremiah	Mercury

Harris, Roy	Songs of Democracy	Mills
Harris, Russell	Tarye No Lenger	Summy-Birchard
Heiden, Bernard	Divine Poems	Associated
Hervig, Richard	Ubi sunt	(Unpublished)
Hindemith, Paul	Apparebit repentina dies	Associated
	Mass	
	Six chansons	
Honegger, Arthur	Joan of Arc	Durand
	King David	
Hovhannes, Alan	Magnificat	C.F. Peters
Ives, Charles	Three Harvest Home Chorales	Mercury
	67th Psalm	Associated
Karlen, Robert	*Dialogue	Art Masters
Kodály, Zoltán	Jesus and the Traders	Boosey & Hawkes
	Missa Brevis	
	Te Deum	
Kraehenbuehl, David	Ideo gloria in excelsis	Associated
Krenek, Ernst	Lamentations of Jeremiah	Bärenreiter
	The Seasons	Associated
Lenel, Ludwig	Magnificat	Summy-Birchard
	Three Pre-Reformation Chorale Motets	Concordia
Lidholm, Ingvar	Laudi	Mills
Ligeti, György	Lux Aeterna	C.F. Peters
Lockwood, Norman	Inscriptions from the Catacombs	Augsburg
LoPresti, Ronald	Alleluia	C. Fischer
McElheran, Brock	Patterns in Sound	Oxford
Micheelson, Hans F.	Es sungen drei Engel	Bärenreiter
Milhaud, Darius	Naissance de Vénus	Mercury
	Pacem in terris	
	Sacred Service	Ricordi
	The Two Cities	G. Schirmer
Nystedt, Knut	De profundis	Associated
Orff, Carl	Catulli Carmina	Schott
Penderecki, Krzysztof	St. Luke Passion	
Pepping, Ernst	St. Matthew Passion	Bärenreiter
	Te Deum	
Persichetti, Vincent	Mass	Elkan-Vogel
	Stabat Mater	
Petrassi, Goffredo	Magnificat	Ricordi
Pinkham, Daniel	Christmas Cantata	Robert King
	Requiem	C.F. Peters
	Stabat Mater	
Poulenc, Francis	Four Christmas Motets	Salabert
	Four Lenten Motets	
	Mass in G	
	Stabat Mater	

Rochberg, George	Three Psalms	T. Presser
Rorem, Ned	Four Madrigals	Mercury
Schoenberg, Arnold	De profundis	Leeds
	Friede auf Erden	Associated
Schuman, William	Carols of Death	G. Schirmer
	Prelude for Voices	
Stevens, Halsey	Magnificat	Mark Foster
Stravinsky, Igor	Anthem	Boosey & Hawkes
	Canticum sacrum	
	Mass	
	Symphony of Psalms	
Thompson, Randall	Frostiana	E.C. Schirmer.
	Requiem	
	The Peaceable Kingdom	
Thomson, Virgil	Missa pro defuncta	H.W. Gray
Tippett, Michael	A Child of Our Time	Schott
Vaughan Williams, Ralph	Dona nobis pacem	Oxford
	Lord, Thou Hast Been Our Refuge	G. Schirmer
	Mass in G minor	
Walton, William	Belshazzar's Feast	Oxford
Webern, Anton	Das Augenlicht	T. Presser
	Kantata I	
	Kantata II	
Wienhorst, Richard	Missa Brevis	Associated
	Magnificat	(Unpublished)

*These works are written for chorus and electronic tape.

While considering the possibility of performing a particular contemporary choral work, the conductor would do well to ask himself at least two other questions. First, is the composition recorded? If it is commercially released, the record jacket may contain valuable information that is not available elsewhere. Furthermore, any recording will give the conductor some insight into the work. Even a poor performance can produce positive results by clearly demonstrating what not to do. One word of caution about recordings needs to be expressed, however. With our sophisticated recording techniques and equipment, it is possible for recordings to lie, to be untruthful, to overemphasize one aspect of a performance at the expense of another. Clever microphone placement can produce a balance between sections, for example, that is rarely attainable in live performance. A good sound engineer can overcome other performance short-comings and can even minimize structural deficiencies in the music itself. Vocal ensembles with serious tonal problems can have these inadequacies covered up beautifully by the use of echo chambers in the recording studio. Just as we do not believe everything we read, we should not believe everything we hear. In any event, the wise conductor will rarely accept any performance, live or recorded, as definitive until after he has completed his own careful and exhaustive analysis. Records produced under the supervision of the composer can, of course, be especially valuable sources for the study of twentieth-century performance practices. A second question to be asked is whether or not the work to be performed is discussed in any current book, journal, or review. If so, such treatment may be a valuable source of information relating to previous performances, general background material, or the composer's compositional procedures. The necessity of being familiar with the basic bibliography in this area is obvious. Finally, if the composer lives within a reasonable distance, do not hesitate to request permission to discuss the score with him personally. A brief telephone conversation could also clarify questions concerning performance.

DEVELOPING A CONCEPT OF THE WORK

We shall now assume that the conductor has chosen the twentieth-century work which he plans to perform. With his ultimate performance objective of full musical disclosure in mind, what is required of him *before* he begins his rehearsals?

> The performer must have a crystal-clear conception of the music he is going to play, a conception which is necessarily in terms of sound. The better he understands the form, the clearer will be his conception. Form and sound must become identical in his mind. He ought to hear distinctly and vividly with his inner ear the exact shape of every passage, the extent of every crescendo, the accentuation of every phrase.*

This rather frightening statement ought to be repeated by conductors every night before retiring! Bela Bartok adds another dimension to the challenge: "the test of strength of true talent is shaping form."† Taken together, these two statements enunciate beautifully the most important objective of prerehearsal preparation: *developing a mental and aural concept of the complete work which embraces all its component parts, thereby enabling the conductor to assume a decisive role in the shaping of form.* "No man has the right to stand before an orchestra [or chorus]," writes Aaron Copland, "unless he has a complete conception in his mind of what he is about to transmit."‡ The formation of such a concept involves the complete assimilation of the music into the mind and ear of the conductor. This implies, incidentally, that the conductor possesses the capacity to project in silence a vivid sonorous image of his conception. He must, in fact, be able to hear the score in his mind. This

*Stein, *op. cit.*, p. 19.
†Austin, *op. cit.*, p. 229.
‡Aaron Copland, *Copland on Music* (New York: W. W. Norton, 1963), p. 137.

idealization of the total work becomes the yardstick by which he measures the actual sounds in rehearsal and performance.

There is nothing uniquely relevant to contemporary musical expression in the preceding discussion. The conductor's ability to develop a "crystal-clear conception" is a prerehearsal requirement for the music of every period. However, in twentieth-century music, the multiplicity of styles, structural procedures, and complex textures make the formation of an adequate conception problematic. Choral conductors need to remind themselves, especially with regard to contemporary music, that the possession of a clear image of the work prior to rehearsal is an absolute necessity. It is only with this kind of mastery that the conductor will be able to communicate to his ensemble, in word and gesture, the essence of what lies waiting but hidden in the music. While it must be admitted that a "complete conception" does not ensure successful execution, it is highly probable that if prerehearsal discipline is shoddy or superficial, the ultimate musical revelation will also be inadequate.

The participation of the ear in the process of creating the initial conception has already been suggested. It plays an even more strategic role, however, when it begins to function in the presence of actual sound. Gunther Schuller gives an emphatic reminder of the importance of the ear in controlling twentieth-century music when he writes: "One aspect of conducting has not changed: the role played by the ear. The ear is still the final arbiter, and in contemporary music, perhaps more than any other, no amount of baton dexterity can make up for deficiencies in either ear or mind."* In both the rehearsal and performance of a modern choral score, a continuously active, probing, examining ear is essential. The ear, however, must be prepared. It must be alerted and readied for its role of "arbiter" and diagnostician. This preparation is one of the principal functions of analysis. For the conductor, analysis is the process by which the mind and ear become ready. The task of the conductor, ultimately, is to shape form. In order to shape form, he must comprehend it. To comprehend means to analyze.

In analyzing twentieth-century choral music the conductor will encounter some elements which are common to the music of every period: melody, harmony, and rhythm. He will also discover such familiar compositional procedures as melodic extension, imitation, sequence, motivic transformation, variation, and recapitulation. Examination of the text will reveal various forms of declamation, including both syllabic and melismatic styles.

In utilizing these elements, however, the contemporary composer approaches them from his own moment in history and endows them with a distinctive quality which is consistent with his own modes of life and thought. While accepting certain aspects of his musical past, the composer has explored and exploited new areas of the sonorous realm. As a result, the conductor may discover, in addition to the characteristics mentioned above, such features as

*Schuller, *op. cit.*, p. 300.

parallelism, polyharmony, polyrhythm, metrical modulation, polyphony of both line and group, humming, *Sprechstimme*, both sung and spoken speech in simultaneous juxtaposition, and a few others. It is this great multiplicity of structural and textural detail that makes the analytical task of the conductor so formidable. There are other distractions.

In his discussion of twentieth-century harmonic practice,* Vincent Persichetti makes it clear that this music cannot be explained only in harmonic terms. The interdependence of melody, harmony, counterpoint, rhythm, and form must be clearly understood in all analytical procedures. This view stresses a concept of analysis which concerns itself with how the various musical elements interpenetrate, and no conductor will question the validity of this approach to contemporary music. To make it an operational principle, however, is another matter.

Adopting this analytical attitude as the guiding principle in developing one's "conception" is complicated by several factors. The first has already been mentioned: the sheer quantity of the musical elements requiring examination inhibits the understanding of their interdependence. Second, some twentieth-century compositions are unusually complex at one particular level. The special difficulty could reside in the harmonic, rhythmic, or contrapuntal organization. This means that detailed analysis of the individual feature becomes requisite to even a superficial knowledge of the score. The inordinate amount of time that may be required to fathom a work at just one of its levels may prevent an equally thorough analysis of the remainder of the work. The *Ave Maria* of Kenneth Gaburo is a case in point. The layout of the score and the infrequency of bar lines makes a separate rhythmic analysis of this work essential. Few conductors will sight-read this composition without stumbling once or twice. The same could be said for a host of other works from our century: *Belshazzar's Feast* of Walton, Britten's *Rejoice In The Lamb*, and the "Libera me" from the *War Requiem*, or the second movement of Ives's *Three Harvest Home Chorales* to mention just a few. In the harmonic area, special problems arise from the involved texture in *The Seasons* of Ernst Krenek, in the *Three Psalms* of George Rochberg, and in the *Requiescant* of Dallapiccola. The harmonic texture of these works will need to be isolated and examined in detail before thoughts of interrelationships can be considered. The need for similar treatment of complex contrapuntal passages in *Apparebit repentina dies* of Hindemith, in the *Te Deum* of Pepping, and in Stravinsky's *Threni* could also be cited. In a complex twentieth-century work, then, the conductor needs to guard against assuming that mastery and comprehension at one level of musical structure implies knowledge of the whole. An excessive amount of time spent mastering the rhythm, for example, may help to create a sense of total preparedness that is entirely unwarranted. Each separate musical component must, of course, be taken into consideration. The conscientious conductor will, however, strive for

---

*Vincent Persichetti, *Twentieth Century Harmony* (New York: W. W. Norton, 1961), p. 10.

an understanding of how all the levels of musical organization are integrated. The immediate purpose of his analysis will be to recognize, interpret, and synthesize all the stylistic features into a unified inner image: "the complete conception."

This emphasis upon discovering the essential character of the music presupposes a certain intellectual and spiritual posture on the part of the conductor. He is not one who imposes his own preconceived notions upon the music. Rather, he discovers the character and style in the structural features of the music itself. He is one who is content to serve the music. He is dedicated to the ultimate disclosure of what the music is. Every conductor would do well to take to heart the advice which is implicit in the following statement of G. Verdi: "I hardly think we need to have conductors and singers discover *new* effects: and for my part I vow that no one has ever, ever even succeeded in bringing out all the effects that I intended . . . . No one!"*

REPRESENTATIVE FEATURES
OF CONTEMPORARY CHORAL WORKS

The discussion which follows will concern itself with some of the structural features and integrating factors which may be encountered in the analysis of contemporary choral literature.

Text

In choral music, the text becomes a primary integrating factor. It is, in fact, the reason for the existence of the work. It plays a fundamental role in determining the type of composition (Mass, Te Deum, Oratorio), in motivating rhythm, melody, and structure and substantially influences the mood, texture, and duration of a given composition. Almost every composer of vocal music would agree that one of the most difficult aspects of the creative problem is the actual selection of the text itself. Just as the conductor strives for commitment to a composition before choosing it for performance, so does the composer strive for complete identification and involvement with the text before he proceeds with the compositional process.† There is too much at stake in terms of time and effort for the composer to be careless about his choice of text. The intensity of the relationship between the composer and the text is revealed in a letter which Gerald Finzi wrote to a friend: "I don't think everyone realizes the difference between choosing a text and being chosen by one."‡ Most composers covet the

---

*Bamberger, *op. cit.*, p. 312.

†See comments by Lukas Foss, Peter Racine Fricker, and Michael Tippett in *The Composer's Point of View*, ed. Robert S. Hines (Norman, Okla: University of Oklahoma Press, 1963).

‡Austin, *op. cit.*, p. 507.

feeling of "being chosen" by a text before the work begins. One senses this kind of rapport in Bartok's *Cantata profana*, Britten's *War Requiem*, in the *Dona nobis pacem* of R. Vaughan Williams, and in *A Survivor From Warsaw* by Arnold Schoenberg. The conductor would do well to accept the proposition that, with few exceptions, the composer is in dead earnest about the words he sets to music. Luigi Dallapicolla, for example, writes, "I have felt obliged to stick to very brief texts, just to achieve maximum comprehensibility through repetition."*

While the choice of text may reveal certain aspects of the mind of the composer, it reveals little about his specific attitude toward the whole process of using words in musical discourse.† Such concepts as word dominated, music dominated, subjective, objective, interpretive, and noninterpretive always contain a measure of ambiguity. They do convey the idea, however, that two composers may approach the same text in quite different ways. Compare, for example, the Mass settings of Stravinsky and Poulenc or the two settings of E. E. Cummings's *i thank You God* by Leland Sateren and Lloyd Pfautsch.

Let us now examine several ways in which the text influences, even creates form. If the composer decides upon a relatively short text of from eight to sixteen lines, it is quite possible that the broad, overall arch of the structure will become apparent to him almost immediately. The smaller details of the form may not yet have suggested themselves, but the dominant mood and spirit may have come into focus. As involvement with the text deepens, certain phrases may suggest a specific texture, a motif, or the possibility of utilizing repetition, variation, or refrain. An essentially lyric text may suggest accompanied melody as an ideal mode of expression. Words with a bold, affirmative ring may suggest the musical gesture of simultaneous declamation by all voices. Whatever else he may think, the conductor can be sure that the text has produced some vivid musical images in the mind of the composer and that his creative effort will be devoted to realizing their full dramatic potential.

The text chosen may have more specific implications in the motivation of structure. Take, for example, the text of the Mass. Most composers accept this challenge by agreeing from the outset to utilize the prescribed text of the ordinary. This means that the Kyrie, Gloria, Credo, Sanctus (with Benedictus), and the Agnus Dei will be set. A structure encompassing five large movements immediately presents itself. If the function of the setting is to be liturgical, the dimensions of each movement will be somewhat restricted, with the strong possibility that a considerable amount of syllabic treatment will be required. If the function of the setting is for concert use, nothing is to prevent the composer from dividing the various movements into substantial sections. With regard to the development of motifs, it is possible that the composer may decide on a

---

*Hines, *op. cit.*, p. 159.
†See the excellent article "Words and Music" by Howard Skinner in the May-June, 1967, issue of the *Choral Journal*.

cyclic treatment in which the Agnus Dei will recapitulate, in some way, themes or other musical elements which appeared in earlier movements. The *Mass* of Paul Hindemith features this kind of treatment in the last movement. The composer may decide, of course, not to utilize recapitulation and allow each movement structural autonomy, relying on the unity of contrast to give the overall setting some sense of design. Whatever the structure, the text of the Mass, by virtue of its familiarity, contributes an element of coherence.

A composition by Igor Stravinsky will serve to illustrate another example of the relationship of text to structure. *Anthem* (The Dove Descending Breaks The Air), based on a text by T. S. Eliot, provides an opportunity to savor a fairly recent work (1962) by one of our leading twentieth-century composers. It also serves to illustrate a composer whose early works fall into the diatonic dissonant category but who, in his later works, made free and frequent use of twelve-tone procedures. *Anthem* belongs in the latter category. Furthermore, while only forty-two measures in duration, it reveals compositional procedures which can be found in many larger compositions from this century. It also commends itself for study because it is inexpensive and can be readily performed by good high school and collegiate choirs.

The composer chose poetry with true nobility of expression (or was Stravinsky "chosen" by the text?). The theme is Pentecost with an implied emphasis on faith and an explicit stress on "fire." The poem is worthy of careful study.

> The dove descending breaks the air
> With flame of incandescent terror
> Of which the tongues declare
> The one discharge from sin and error.
> The only hope, or else despair
>   Lies in the choice of pyre or pyre—
>   To be redeemed from fire by fire.
>
> Who then devised the torment? Love.
> Love is the unfamiliar Name
> Behind the hands that wove
> The intolerable shirt of flame
> Which human power cannot remove.
>   We only live, only suspire
>   Consumed by either fire or fire.*

The overall structure is closely related to the text. The first four lines are set in two-part counterpoint by the women's voices emphasizing the words "terror" and "error"; the tenors and basses join the women for the last three lines of stanza one; in the first four lines of the second stanza, a two-part texture again is utilized but sung, this time, by the men. The momentum of this section moves forward to a harmonic and melodic emphasis of the word "flame"; the

*T. S. Eliot, *The Complete Poems and Plays* (New York: Harcourt, Brace & World, 1952), pp. 143-44.

women then join the men for the final three lines of stanza two. The music for the last three lines of stanza two is, incidentally, an almost exact quotation of the last three lines of stanza one. The structural symmetry of the work is revealed in Figure 4-1.

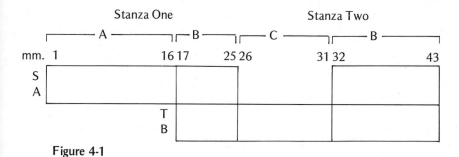

Figure 4-1

    The conductor's discovery that the text of a work is of the chorale or hymn type may also provide important clues relating to structure. The composer has several options in working with such a text. He may choose to ignore the traditional melody and set the text freely. He may decide to base the entire composition on the preexistent tune. If his decision is the latter, the conductor's analysis should begin with a precise identification of the tune and a thorough familiarization with its melodic and rhythmic design. Further study will reveal, in all probability, some type of variation or *cantus firmus* treatment. Knowledge of the basic melodic element will be crucial to an understanding of the total structure. A number of American, German, and Scandanavian composers have made significant contributions to this genre.

    Little has been said specifically about textual motivation of rhythm, melody, mood, and texture. It can only be stressed that an attempt to discern the manner in which the text motivates melodic and rhythmic elements, suggests structural relationships, and contributes to musical coherence will reward the conductor with special insights. The perceptive conductor will have no trouble finding contemporary choral literature in which the interaction of text and music is abundantly evident. The examination of this dimension of the modern choral score should be one of the first steps in the analytical process.

Music

When the conductor has thoroughly familiarized himself with the text, he can focus his attention on specifically musical elements and their interrelationships. Contained in the following list are some of the principal ways in which musical materials are organized and integrated in twentieth-century choral literature. The list is by no means comprehensive; it is hoped, however, that these categories will provide flexible guidelines for some of the structural principles that will be encountered in the music. Musical structure, furthermore, is the larger arena in which the interdependence of various elements can be observed. The categories are described as follows:

1. Works in which *tripartition* is in evidence. This is a favorite term of Ernst Toch and has analytical relevance to all music. It is also known as *A B A* form or, more fundamentally, as exposition, development, and recapitulation. Regardless of how the phenomenon is titled, the principle is the same. It implies that "the affinity and correlation of the flanking parts will always be felt against the middle part."*

In dealing with structures of this type, the conductor must isolate the motif or musical idea contained in the opening section, determine the nature of the contrast or tension in the middle section, and be alert for a recapitulation that is *not* an exact repetition of the opening. This concluding section will need special attention. The twentieth-century composer is particularly fond of camouflaging his recapitulation by means of significant modification or variation of his original material. He may drastically alter his motifs, regroup them, or even substitute new ideas for ones used earlier in the composition. This latter treatment may, in fact, function as a recapitulation without any literal reference to earlier material.

2. Works in which *variation technique* is extensively utilized. Several types of variation technique can be found in contemporary choral literature. First, in such works as *A Boy Was Born* by Britten and *The Christmas Story* by Hugo Distler, variations are based upon a given theme (original or someone else's), and the structural substance of these works is the systematic working out of a set of variations on the theme. The individual variations utilize the melodic, harmonic, and rhythmic qualities of the theme as the basis for motivic modification and transformation.† David Kraehenbuehl's *Ideo gloria in excelsis Deo* is a shorter work demonstrating this technique.

Second, there are works in which *free variation* is evident. Essentially, this category includes all the ways in which a composer handles and manipulates his musical motifs. More specifically, however, free variation involves the manner in which a musical motif is developed. Development in this sense implies thematic metamorphosis. Inasmuch as every composer transforms his musical material in a personal way, this dimension of the structure provides an important clue to the work's individuality and fundamental character. *This Is the Day* of Paul J. Christiansen and *Music When Soft Voices Die* of Lloyd Pfautsch are excellent short examples of free-variation technique.

Third, works which employ a chorale *cantus firmus* reveal another aspect of variation technique. There are a number of contemporary cantatas and motets based on chorale tunes which demonstrate how variation can be utilized in these

---

*Toch, *op. cit.*, p. 163.
†The author's *Easter Canticle* and *Fall Softly, Snow* are less extensive examples of this treatment.

forms. Works by Lenel, Micheelsen, Bender, Pepping, Distler, and Wienhorst are illustrative.* Furthermore, a large number of hymn-anthems would also come under this classification. The passacaglia involves another type of variation treatment. The third movement of the Hindemith *Apparebit repentina dies* is a beautiful example of this type. The conclusion of the Honnegger *Christmas Cantata* is in reality a huge quodlibet combining several familiar carols, another aspect of variation treatment. Finally, there are those works such as the Cantatas of Anton Webern, which could best be described as continuous variation involving all aspects of the musical structure but which are not based on a given theme or *cantus firmus*. It should be noted that in all types of variation, the transformation of musical motifs involves the utilization of well-known contrapuntal devices including canon, free imitation, augmentation, diminution, inversion, and *stretto*.

3. Works that contain sections or complete movements in *fugue*. Obviously, linear and rhythmic features are influenced by twentieth-century practice. Furthermore, subject-answer relationships in twentieth-century fugue writing reveal significant differences when compared with fugues of Bach, Haydn, Beethoven, or Bruckner. However, works like the *Symphony of Psalms*, the *Te Deum* settings of Kodály and Pepping, and the Christmas cantatas of Menin and Effinger contain individual movements which can best be explained as fugues.

4. Works in which overall coherence is achieved by *utilization of additive forms*. This type has much in common with the principal features of the Renaissance motet or a seventeenth-century verse anthem. Each successive phrase of text is set forth with a new musical motif. In most instances, there is no ascertainable thematic relationship between the successive musical ideas. Each new statement may be an extension of the texture of the preceding material or it may be a stark contrast. The treatment can be either chordal or imitative. The structure can best be described as the sum total of the various parts added together. The middle section of the *Magnificat* of Halsey Stevens is an excellent example of this type of writing. In addition to the unifying effect of the text, the composer with a sensitized intuition can create a fundamental unity without recourse to motivic development as such. He does this at one level by sensing when to make the new material an extention of the texture of the preceding motifs and when to make it contrasting. If each new section manifests an organic relationship between text and music, the unity of that section is assured. The coherence of the total structure results, then, from the cumulative effect of a sequence of individual unities.

5. Works in which *refrain* or *rondo-like* sections contribute significantly to structural integration. One of the best illustrations of this type is *In the Beginning* of Aaron Copland. Cast in the form of a large rondo, the story of creation covering the seven days unfolds as an antiphonal dialogue between

---

Christ Jesus Lay in Death's Strong Bonds and *The Seven Words of Jesus Christ from the Cross* by Richard Weinhorst utilize this type of variation technique.

soprano solo and chorus. Each section is introduced by the soloist, extended by the chorus, and concluded with a refrain. It should be noted that this particular work also makes liberal use of variation technique with the material from the choral parts frequently being derived from the motif set forth by the soprano soloist.

6. Works employing *ostinato* patterns. This device has also been used by composers for centuries. Its usefulness as a means of bringing coherence to musical form has not been lost to twentieth-century composers. In the choral music of our century, *ostinato* can be found in the shape of rhythmic, melodic, or harmonic reiteration. Stravinsky, for example, makes frequent use of *ostinato* patterns in his music. The Raffman *Triptych* begins with an *ostinato* structure involving both harmony and rhythm. "The Unknown Region," the second of William Schuman's *Carols of Death*, is an exciting study of rhythmic *ostinato* undergirding motivic development. Many other examples could be cited.

7. Works in which *accompanied melody* is the basic unifying element. There are numerous examples of modern choral works in which a beautifully contoured melody imposes its unity upon the total structure. The composer may choose, of course, to complement the tune with supporting voices which contain their own autonomous unity, and he often does. However, the well-constructed melody may need little more than a secure harmonic base to succeed in its expressive purpose. Many of the works of Francis Poulenc can best be explained when approached as accompanied melodies. Poulenc frequently uses the additive method as a means of melodic extension. While his choral structures always convey a sense of the "long line," closer examination may reveal a carefully connected string of essentially short melodic motifs. The familiar *O magnum mysterium* demonstrates this procedure.

8. Works in which antiphony endows the music with a measure of coherence. There is a subtle unity which results from the mere deployment of two contrasting bodies of sound, even when the response of the opposing group is not motivically related to the other. Antiphonal treatment in and of itself becomes a powerful unifying element. To be sure, many contemporary composers do relate the musical material of the two groups, but the conductor should be open to instances of responsorial procedure in which dissimilar elements are juxtaposed. A number of compositions for two or more choirs can illustrate this category. *The Peaceable Kingdom* and the *Mass of the Holy Spirit* by Randall Thompson employ opposing groups, using basically related musical material. In the *Coronation Te Deum* of William Walton and the *St. Matthew Passion* of Ernst Pepping, the opposing choirs often respond with dissimilar musical material.*

These, then, are some of the manifestations of structure and form in

---

*In the author's unpublished cantata *One People—One God*, for double chorus and symphonic winds, the opposing groups are further differentiated by having different texts throughout.

twentieth-century choral music. It should be remembered, however, that these structural features can be found in the works of composers with quite dissimilar harmonic, rhythmic, and melodic characteristics. A composition that is harmonically integrated by serial methods, for example, can make extensive use of tripartition, variation techniques, or fugue as structural features. A composer who achieves harmonic coherence by using diatonic dissonant means can also write fugues and construct *A B A* forms. Tripartition, for example, exists in the music of both Berg and Hindemith. Variation techniques are the common property of both Schoenberg and Distler. Imitative and fugal textures can be found in both Webern and Kodály. It is well to keep in mind that in most of the great musical masterpieces, whether they be by Bach or Bartok, a high level of integration and coherence exists at all levels.

While the conductor must concern himself with the structural features outlined above, his analysis must also inform him of the means by which melodic, harmonic, contrapuntal, and rhythmic coherence is achieved. There are a number of excellent books and articles which are devoted to this aspect of twentieth-century music. As a result, a systematic presentation here will not be attempted. Before moving on to a discussion of actual performance problems, however, one brief digression may be in order. In the music of many contemporary composers, one of the prevalent means of realizing harmonic integration is through their use of twelve-tone or serial techniques. When these procedures and their resultant sonorities are encountered in music, too many conductors become apprehensive and fearful. In order to attempt to overcome some of the insecurity which results from these encounters, one work which coheres harmonically in this manner will be examined.

The *Anthem* by Stravinsky has already been referred to within the context of the discussion which related text to form. It has been shown that the structure of this work (*A B C B*) is intimately related to the structure of the text. The repetition of the *B* section contributes significantly to formal coherence. Our special concern here, however, is the means by which Stravinsky achieves harmonic and contrapuntal coherence. While it may not be immediately apparent, closer examination of the score reveals that integration at these levels is realized by the composer's use of twelve-tone procedures. The various forms of the row which are utilized are set forth in Figure 4-2.

While it would be tempting at this point to launch into a note-by-note analysis, the discovery of how Stravinsky uses the row in *Anthem* will be left to the individual reader. Without ready access to the full score, such row-chasing here would be tedious, at best. Those who do proceed with a detailed analysis, however, should be aware of the fact that Stravinsky does not slavishly adhere to textbook rules regarding twelve-tone writing. He does not hesitate, for example, to repeat notes, and he does this even before the first statement of the row is completed [measure 3 in both soprano and alto parts.] One should also be alerted to the frequent use of enharmonic notation, such as F being the equivalent of E-sharp. For those conductors whose analytical and performance

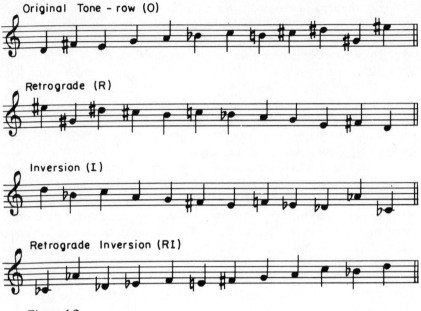

Figure 4-2

experience with serial music is lacking, a careful study of Stravinsky's compositional procedures in this work is strongly recommended.

The principal purpose of this discussion is to demonstrate that the *A B C B* structure of this composition is undergirded by a highly integrated harmonic and contrapuntal scheme. The coherence at these levels is realized by the inspired use of twelve-tone procedures which, incidentally, fall within the framework of the chromatic dissonant style. In his discussion of Stravinsky, William Austin writes that *Anthem* is one of the composer's "most thoroughly graspable works, a piece worthy to stand beside a Bach chorale or an anthem of Gibbons."* The validity of this judgment has been corroborated in numerous performances of this composition by the present writer.

When the subject of music which utilizes some form of row technique is raised, the question is often asked: is the capability to respond to and appreciate a composition that employs serial procedures dependent upon an actual knowledge of the "row" itself? Emphatically, no! In the first place, the speed with which the notes of any twelve-tone composition are projected into the ear makes the intellectual comprehension of the row and its permutations an acoustical impossibility. The complexity of the contrapuntal texture and its accompanying rhythmic design create additional aural demands. Second, the overwhelming

*Austin, *op. cit.*, p. 531.

impact which works like the *Violin Concerto* and *Wozzeck* of Berg or *Moses and Aaron* of Schoenberg have upon audiences has nothing to do with their comprehension of the row as such. The row is an integrating element at only one level of the musical composition. It is the sense of coherence, coupled with imaginative fantasy, at every level of these works that accounts for their expressive power and eloquence. In response to a letter from Kolisch who asks specifically about this question, Schoenberg replies, "Do you really think that it (row analysis) is useful to know this? I cannot really imagine it . . . ."* On the other hand, inasmuch as this technique is used as extensively as it is in twentieth-century music, every conductor ought to have some experience in depth with music which is integrated in this fashion. One can be fairly safe in assuming that during the next few decades, composers will be using this means of achieving musical coherence more rather than less.

SPECIAL PERFORMANCE PROBLEMS FOR THE CONDUCTOR

While an extensive treatment of twentieth-century performance practices is beyond the scope of this presentation, several major areas of concern will be touched upon in the space that remains.

Accuracy

In the performance of twentieth-century choral music, the conductor must strive for absolute fidelity to the composer's intentions as indicated in the score. While all aspects of the music are included in this statement, special emphasis is here being placed on *pitch* and *rhythm*. To mention these at all may seem unnecessary, but there are enough instances of inaccuracy and lack of precision in the performance of contemporary choral music to justify calling attention to the need for continual vigilance in these areas. Here again, analysis is the key to success. If the conductor's ear has been properly prepared, he will recognize instantly any inaccuracies of pitch or rhythm and will proceed immediately with remedial action. It may be worth noting that a conductor who is quite capable of approaching a Mozart, Beethoven, or Brahms score without reference to the keyboard may not be able to do so with a modern score. The conductor must be absolutely secure in his understanding of the various pitch relationships before he enters the rehearsal. This will often necessitate some special keyboard work during the analytical process. Modest vocal resources may justify some sympathy and understanding for the ensemble with improper balance, inadequate diction, or occasional difficulties with intonation, but there can be little sympathy when wrong notes or rhythms are in evidence.

*Ibid., p. 305.

Tempo The conductor who attempts to remain faithful to the intention of the composer is inevitably led to questions relating to tempo and tempo determination. Erwin Stein writes:

> In our time, metronome figures have become a generally accepted method of fixing the tempo. Stravinsky gives sometimes no other than metronomical tempo indications, while Bartok indicates every section of a movement in minutes and seconds. But paradoxically the exact observation of the figures does not guarantee the right tempo: too strict an obedience dulls the music. Schoenberg says in his scores: "Metronomical figures are not to be taken verbally, but only as a guide" (Andeutung). A famous conductor once confessed that he never looked at the figures; yet his tempi are convincing because he realizes the musical structure.*

Tempo is, in fact, "a function of the structure. It must allow the music to sound characteristic . . . . If the tempo is wrong, everything is distorted."† If the conductor's concept of the structure and style of a composition is adequate, the problem of the tempo will, in most instances, have taken care of itself. In twentieth-century music, then, the metronomic markings should be considered as one piece of external evidence contributing to the determination of the proper tempo. The more substantial evidence will, in all likelihood, be found *within* the music itself. Most contemporary composers would agree that metronome indications should always be considered approximate. The frequency with which "circa" is used provides ample proof. Out of respect for the composers, however, it is always a wise policy to *begin* with his indication. If, after thoughtful study and rehearsal, the suggested tempo does not satisfy the demands of the music, modifications may be in order.‡ Conductors who have had experience doing premiere performances would verify the fact that metronomic markings are often changed after the composer has actually heard the music for the first time. This is one reason why a composer is always grateful for a performance of a work prior to publication or to the preparation of a final manuscript edition.

Intonation Every conductor has had the experience of arriving home after a particularly trying rehearsal, wondering how it was possible that his ensemble could perform so badly out of tune. After one such experience, the author drafted the following memorandum to his choir for study and consideration at the next rehearsal:

> Perfect intonation in the ensemble is unattainable without a perfect unison in each section. Among the enemies of a good unison are: Inadequate breath

*Stein, *op. cit.*, p. 53.
†*Ibid.*, p. 48, 54.
‡Houston Bright, "The Composer Looks at the Choral Conductor," *The Choral Journal* (January-February, 1967), 24-25.

support, bad posture, poorly produced tone, closed ears, un-unified vowels, sloppy intervals and excessive vibrato.

Every top-notch choral group habitually makes minor pitch adjustments while singing as a matter of course. Learn to think certain intervals "high." Learn to think certain intervals "low." Be especially cautious about half steps and differentiate clearly between minor and major thirds. No interval, however, can be sung carelessly. The musical context will determine the precise 'treatment' required.

Expend maximum listening effort at phrase endings and cadential points. Beware of out of tune singing on loud passages. On a long, loud note, anchor the pitch firmly. Relate the pitch of your section, mentally, to all other notes of any given chord. Couple your intellect with your ear. Anticipate problematic passages and intervals.*

Comments similar to these have undoubtedly been made to most choral groups at some time or other. They touch upon the generally accepted causes of poor intonation and apply, of course, to the music of every historical epoch. Twentieth-century choral music, however, does contain some special intonation problems, and while they can only be alluded to here, it would seem unwise to ignore them completely. Most recent books and articles on conducting at least acknowledge that the harmonic and intervallic aspects of contemporary music place new demands upon the ear of the performer. The actual discussions of the inherent problems, however, are generally inadequate. Even McElheran's excellent book on conducting passes over this large if nebulous area of ensemble technique with the single statement that intonation (and tone) "would require a special book."† To be sure, a separate volume on this important subject would be most welcome. As far as is known, however, no such work can be anticipated by choral conductors, at least in the immediate future. In the meantime, there are major sevenths to get in turn, tone clusters to balance, vocal glissandos to realize and, to use Auden's marvelous phrase, "the time being to redeem from insignificance" (tomorrow's rehearsal!).

Before proceeding to specific problems, one point needs to be made clear: the conductor must assume that, with the exception of those composers espousing chance or indeterminate methods, the majority of contemporary composers have not made their harmonic, melodic, and contrapuntal decisions capriciously. They do, in fact, care about a faithful and precise reproduction of the pitches they have notated. "With Stravinsky," writes Aaron Copland, "one senses that the place of each note in each melody and chord has been found for it only after a process of meticulous elimination."‡ Stravinsky himself corroborates this assessment by saying, "Pitch and interval relationships are for me the primary

---

*Daniel Moe, *Responsibilities of the Choir Member* (Minneapolis, Minn.: Augsburg, 1965), p. 2.
†McElheran, *op. cit.*, p. 104.
‡Copland, *op. cit.*, p. 94.

dimension."* On the basis of this statement, the conductor who performs Stravinsky will not be able to rationalize lack of precision in pitch and interval relationships by assuming that the composer was interested in only an approximation of the notational symbols in his score. Every conductor who has performed Stravinsky knows the extent to which full musical disclosure is dependent upon the accurate projection of each interval and chord into the ear of the listener. Daniel Pinkham, another composer who is also an active conductor, states that in Stravinsky "good intonation is imperative if one is to grasp the resulting vertical structure and sonorities."† The finely chiseled features of his music require that the singers have a particular dedication to achieving clarity of intervallic detail. It can be assumed, furthermore, that Stravinsky's concern with pitch and interval relationships is shared by most composers. The conductor who takes this concern of the composer seriously will, therefore, do all in his power to make good intonation a characteristic of his performances of twentieth-century music.

In dealing with the special problems of singing in tune, it should be reemphasized that no single aspect of choral technique can ever be neatly isolated. Tone, diction, vowel formation, rhythmic consistency, style, and intonation are all interdependent. As a result, artistic choral singing can be achieved only when all elements of technique are successfully synthesized. With this axiom clearly in mind, the discussion of intonation can continue.

1. *Quality and size of tone in relation to intonation.* While contemporary composers usually give explicit directions regarding tempo, and occasionally dynamics, very few suggestions are ever made about other aspects of performance. Considering the frequency with which footnotes are utilized in books and journals today, it seems strange that there are so few explanatory comments in musical scores. One notable exception is Kenneth Gaburo's preface to his short motet *Ave Maria*, which contains some very definite performance directives. The fact that he is also the conductor of an unusual university vocal ensemble which devotes itself almost exclusively to the performance of new music gives additional substance to the comments. The following statement gives a clear indication of the composer's overall intent: "In no case should there be a perceptible break in sound. In effect, the work should sound as continuous, legato, sustained, still as possible . . . . Textural punctuations do not constitute breaks in linear continuity."‡ (The dynamic range, incidentally, is limited to *piano or pianissimo* throughout.) Gaburo then gives this interesting and explicit direction concerning the kind of tone quality he desires for *Ave Maria*: "The normal [in this composition] singing voice is *senza vibrato*." In performing this

---

*Igor Stravinsky and Robert Craft, *Themes and Episodes* (New York: Alfred A. Knopf, 1966), p. 24.

†Daniel Pinkham, "Intonation, Dissonance and Sonority," *Bulletin* of the American Choral Foundation, Inc., III, No. 3 (March, 1961), 6-7.

‡Kenneth Gaburo, *Ave Maria* (Cincinnati, Ohio: World Library of Sacred Music, 1965).

work, the quiet intensity which results from the continuous *senza vibrato* and *legato* style is remarkable. It is a beautiful demonstration of the expressive power of musical understatement, especially when programmed between other contemporary compositions with a more aggressive style. The particular relevance to this discussion, however, is the composer's request for a *senza vibrato* and the effect which this type of tone quality has upon intonation in this composition.

Gaburo's harmonic and contrapuntal technique, like Stravinsky's, reveals a meticulous concern for pitch and interval relationships. Major and minor seconds, major and minor sevenths, along with augmented fourths, are used frequently as a part of the contrapuntal interplay. Performance experience with this and with other twentieth-century compositions in which these intervals predominate convinces one that the musical texture is more clearly delineated when the *senza vibrato* style is utilized. This statement must *not*, however, be construed as an advocation of this vocal style for all contemporary choral music. There are many other stylistic factors which can affect tonal amplitude. Major portions of the *Te Deum* of Kodály, the *Stabat Mater* of Poulenc, or Honegger's *King David*, for example, are unthinkable in a *senza vibrato* style. What is being suggested here is simply that the more stringent the dissonance in a harmonic or contrapuntal texture, the greater the need for a degree of tonal restraint. Tonal restraint in this usage implies a modification of the tone quality in the direction of *senza vibrato*.

Daniel Pinkham observes in this regard that

> another curious phenomenon of sonority in dissonant music, or at least in music in which there are difficult intervals in the vocal lines, is that the vocal production may change .... [Some] singers seem to turn off or to narrow somewhat their omnipresent vibrato and attempt to sing with a much straighter tone, with the aim of hitting the note squarely in the middle. This thinner sound probably does help in pitch definition, and in fact may make for a cleaner execution of a chromatic polyphonic texture.*

The application of this principle can be noted in the recordings of Webern's choral music. Also of interest is the fact that many high school choirs are more successful at disclosing the harmonic dimensions of strongly dissonant contemporary choral music than some college and university choirs with their greater maturity of tone. A fairly dissonant, multivoiced harmonic texture often becomes blurred and imprecise when the weight of tone is too heavy or when the pitch of an individual section of the chorus lacks sufficient focus. The choral conductor should remember in this connection that the bass section must take special care to produce a perfect unison so that the overtones arising out of the bass part are unambiguous. It is imperative, of course, that every section strive for perfect unison.

*Pinkham, *op. cit.*, p. 7.

To summarize, what is ultimately required of our ensembles in the performance of all music is enough vocal flexibility to be able to make quick modifications of the weight and focus of tone in response to an expressively strategic harmonic event. This implies, of course, that the expressive function of some chords may require greater emphasis upon the vertical dimension than others. Or to put it yet another way, while our primary concern as conductors will be with the flow of the musical line, certain harmonic events may become important enough to justify a momentary preoccupation with the underlying chord itself. In these instances, the quick modification of tone referred to above should be utilized by the ensemble. There will always be, of course, works like the Gaburo *Ave Maria* which call for this type of tonal restraint throughout.

2. *Balance in relation to intonation.* That lack of balance in a given chord can adversely affect intonation is common knowledge. At times, such imbalance actually produces poor intonation. In other instances lack of balance creates the illusion of being out of tune when, in fact, the notes in the chord are actually correct. Whether the intonation problem of a given chord is illusory or real, the composer's harmonic intent is still being misrepresented. Remedial work in rehearsal is required in either case. Figure 4-3 gives examples of potentially problematic chordal combinations in contemporary music.

Figure 4-3

If the harmonic implications of these chords are to be successfully realized, each note must have approximately the same dynamic weight. In each case, except (d), the definition of the major second is crucial. If these chords were scored for three trumpets or three woodwinds the problems would be greatly minimized. When scored for women's voices, however, at least one section must sing *divisi* and herein lies the difficulty. If the composer happens to call for *divisi* altos and the alto section is weaker than the soprano section, poor balance is assured, and the composer's harmonic language is only partially realized. In all probability, the preponderance of soprano tone will ultimately produce intonation problems, especially if the passage using such chord construction is extended. It should be obvious that in such cases, the notation of the composer should not be obeyed literally. A few second sopranos should drop to the first alto part and several first altos should sing with the second altos. Very few composers, if any, would object to such a decision on the part of the conductor. At least one composer expressly requests such redistribution of voices. In *No Man Is an Island*, Jean Berger states in an infrequent footnote: "If not enough altos with good low range are available, two or three tenors may sing in unison with the alto part, measures 1-9."*

Another potentially problematic situation involving balance arises when voice parts cross. When the tenors are required to go above the alto part, for example, or the basses above the tenors, balance and/or intonation can momentarily be jeopardized. The *Ad te levavi* of Gordon Binkerd has such a passage. The alto line drops below the tenors for about one measure. As is often the case in such instances, this places the alto section in its least effective range dynamically, while the tenor line remains fairly high. It is imperative here that both the tenor and alto sections be aware of what is taking place in the vocal orchestration. Both sections will need to consciously compensate for this arrangement of the voice parts. The alto line must be projected with extra effort and the tenors will need to avoid ruining the balance by holding back slightly.

One additional problem requiring special treatment is the strongly dissonant chord in which the composer inadvertently (carelessly might be a more appropriate word) assigns a note which is crucial to defining the dissonance to a voice in the weak part of its range. If the tenors are assigned an F on the top line of their staff against an alto F-sharp on the first line of their staff, the resultant minor second dissonance is bound to lack definition unless the alto section comes close to matching the dynamic level of the tenors. With the usual tonal brilliance of tenors on that pitch, coupled with the probable lack of brilliance in the alto part, balance cannot be taken for granted. In cases like this, the composer is helpless without an alert and imaginative conductor. Badly voiced chords will always require some adjustment of dynamics on the part of the ensemble if the vertical dimension of the sonority is to be fully realized, and most conductors have encountered such moments in contemporary scores. A careful prerehearsal analysis will disclose the existence of these balance problems, however, and the musical context will often suggest the nature and extent of the adjustment required. In conclusion, it may be well to warn the conductor that some composers who possess a solid foundation in instrumental orchestration lack a similar foundation in vocal "orchestration." A composer may be acutely aware of the changes of timbre which occur as an oboe moves from its middle range to a high E. He may not be as aware of the similar changes which take place in the voice as it moves from middle to upper range. Composers are not infallible beings, and when such lack of awareness is encountered, the conductor must bring his imagination to bear on the problem.

3. *Articulation and its effect upon intonation.* A recent experience with the Oklahoma All-State Chorus pointed up the degree to which articulation or declamation affect intonation. In rehearsing the Halsey Stevens *Magnificat*, a three-measure sequence of moderately dissonant homophony was giving trouble. In order to get the vertical and melodic relationships stabilized, the familiar practice of taking one chord at a time was attempted. This chorus, an alert and

*Jean Berger, *No Man Is an Island* (Bryn Mawr, Pa.: Theodore Presser, 1953), p. 2.

talented one, quickly got the individual chords "lined up." The phrase was then attempted in tempo, and there was no problem getting to the end of the phrase without a breakdown. However, the intonation itself was hardly better than it had been before the intensive dissection of each chord. It was obvious that there was still much insecurity in the chorus, rhythmically as well as intervallically. Inasmuch as the section in question was far from being under control by the chorus, another route had to be explored. It was noticed that beginning consonants were being lazily articulated, the shape of the phrase was generally static with little stress on the breath undergirding either primary or secondary accents, and the tone quality itself was lacking in focus. As the chorus began to exaggerate the declamation, and achieve more precision in intervallic movement, the intonation improved substantially.

Similar experiences could be described by every conductor. What happened in Oklahoma, however, did serve to reinforce the notion that adequate projection of text, articulation, and precise rhythmic delineation must be coordinated with an emphasis upon listening, proper tone quality, vowel unification, and clean intervals if good intonation is to be achieved.

Meter and Proportion

As has been stated earlier, there is a considerable body of contemporary choral literature which involves various conducting techniques not frequently utilized in pre-twentieth-century music. Much of this music requires, especially, that the conductor refine and perfect his capacity to control more intricate and complex rhythmic organization. The extent to which irregular meters, polyrhythms, and complex proportional systems have become commonplace makes it essential that a conductor be able to handle these difficulties with precision and with authority. Certainly one of the principal reasons that choruses have difficulty with twentieth-century rhythms is that too many conductors are themselves rhythmically insecure. The conductor who steadfastly refuses to acquire the techniques necessary to control contemporary rhythms will invariably shy away from works which contain special rhythmic challenges. As a result, he deprives himself and his chorus of the delights which irregular meter and asymmetrical phrase structure can provide.

While irregular metric schemes are potentially problematic, an understanding of a few basic principles will enable the conductor to cope with most of the music of our century. In order to facilitate our discussion, the specific comments will be related to the musical example in Figure 4-4. The *Mini-Gloria** was written for conducting classes at the University of Iowa and contains problems which are characteristic of many contemporary works.

*Reprinted from *Problems in Conducting* by Daniel Moe, 1968. By permission of Augsburg Publishing House, Minneapolis, Minn., copyright owner. This short conducting exercise, along with some of the analytical comments which follow, are reprinted here with the kind permission of the publishers.

Figure 4-4 Mini-Gloria

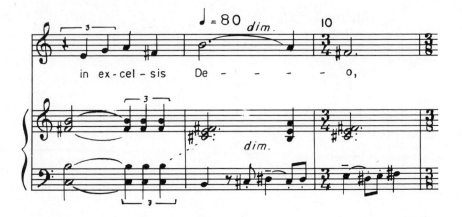

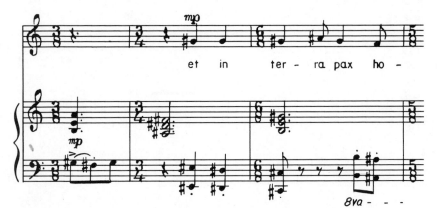

Figure 4-4 (cont.)

Figure 4-4 (cont.)

Figure 4-4 (cont.)

1. The first problem is found in mm. 3, 4, and 5, and involves controlling the 3/4-3/8-2/4 sequence. The rule that applies here is the following: the basic unit of pulse, which in this case is the quarter note, remains constant until a change of tempo is specifically indicated by the composer. This means, of course, that the value of the eighth note, a subdivision of the quarter, also remains constant. The successful control of metric irregularity depends upon the consistent subdivision of the basic unit of pulse in the mind of the performer. Therefore, when moving through the 3/4, 3/8, and 2/4 bars in this example, the conductor and the ensemble must be thinking the eighth note subdivision in the 3/4 measure. What is being emphasized here is thinking subdivision rather than conducting subdivision. Conducting subdivided beats should be done with great discretion and will, in fact, be an infrequent practice. Thinking subdivision,

however, must become an almost constant practice, especially when performing contemporary music.

2. Measure 4, the first 3/8 bar, must not be performed as a triplet. In twentieth-century music, notes should be performed as triplets only when a ⌐——3——⌐, or the number 3, appears above the notes.

3. Concerning triplet figures in general, it is well to bear in mind that triplets can and should be performed accurately. While many other rhythmic problems could be cited, triplet groupings are so common in our music that the inability to project them successfully will seriously jeopardize effective performance. A vague approximation of triplet patterns in contemporary music will not suffice. The relationships between the triplets in Figure 4-5 should be thoroughly understood by choirs and conductors.

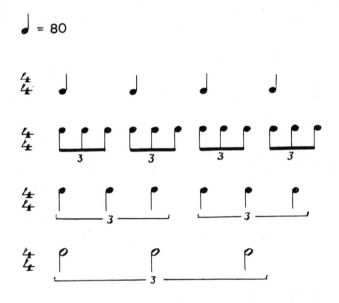

Figure 4-5

Notice that the quarter-note triplets can be defined precisely when seen and felt in relation to the eighth-note triplets. Similarly, the half-note triplets can be defined precisely when seen and felt in relation to the quarter-note triplets. Note the two different kinds of triplets in m. 29. It should not be necessary to beat triplets for the voices in this measure.

4. While changes of meter require special care and understanding on the part of the conductor, an even greater problem involves sudden changes of tempo. This problem, incidentally, is as acute in earlier music as it is in our own.

In m. 6, there is a drastic change of tempo from ♩ = 120 to ♩ = 60 . This situation can be managed easily if m. 5 is carefully subdivided in the conductor's mind. The half note in m. 5 becomes the quarter note in m. 6. Or, the quarter note in m. 5 becomes the eighth note in m. 6. Returning to Tempo I in m. 7 should be no problem.

    5. A more sophisticated problem is found in m. 9. In moving from ♩ = 120 to ♩ = 80 the conductor must think eighth-note subdivision on the last two beats of m. 8. The quarter-note triplets must not be allowed to distract. The eighth notes in m. 8 become triplet eighth notes in m. 9. The notational equivalent is as shown in Figure 4-6.

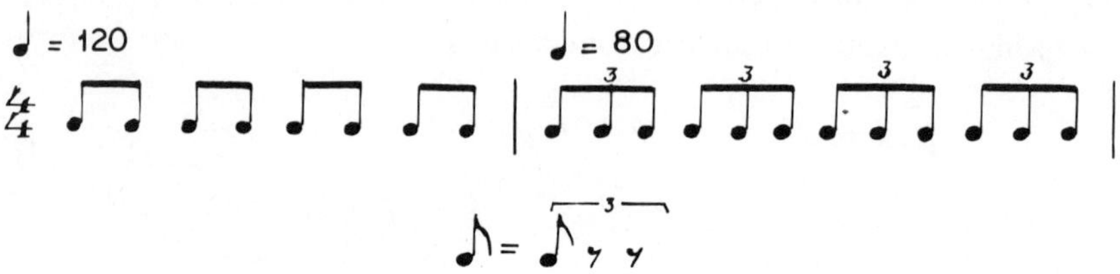

Figure 4-6

    Dramatic changes of tempo such as these are certainly not new to music. Renaissance composers, for example, were particularly fond of achieving contrast in their music by means of such proportional relationships. The concluding section of *Jubilate Deo* by Giovanni Gabrieli illustrates one of the most common proportional situations in late-sixteenth-century music. The relationship is as follows:

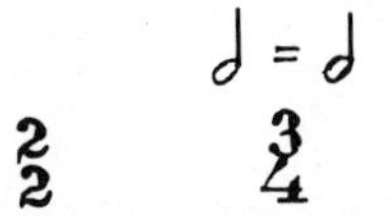

    The Victoria *O magnum mysterium* and the *Haec dies* of Gallus are two more of the many works which could be cited to demonstrate the frequent use of such procedures. The author's *Prelude and Hodie** contains a contemporary application of this Renaissance practice:

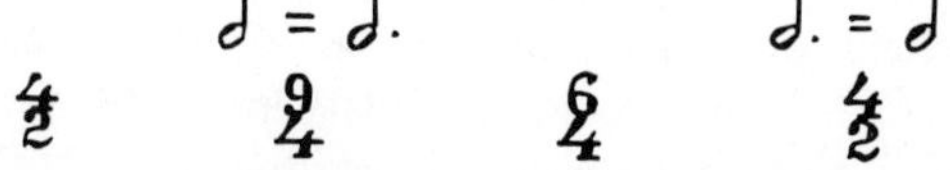

    By thinking quarter-note triplets against the half notes in the 4/2 bar, the transition to the 9/4 bar will be accomplished with no difficulty. Numerous

*Daniel Moe, Prelude and Hodie (Bryn Mawr, Pa.: Theodore Presser, 1959).

additional examples of twentieth-century works containing similar problems could be given. The interested conductor is encouraged to examine a full orchestral score of the Britten *War Requiem*. This composition contains a fascinating array of proportional relationships which typify this aspect of contemporary music.

6. Returning again to the *Mini-Gloria*, the clue as to how to conduct the 7/4 bar, m. 25, is found in the accompaniment. The solution: ♩ + ♩ + ♩.

7. In the passage from m. 10 through m. 16, think eighth notes constantly. In m. 16, the vocal line indicates a grouping of ♩. + ♩. + ♩ . The conductor who can successfully control this phrase possesses the skill and poise to handle most of the rhythmic problems in twentieth-century music at least prior to Cage and Stockhausen.

8. While this treatment of meter and proportion is only an introduction to the subject, a discussion of these problems should not be concluded without some mention of what is, undoubtedly, the most frequently misread metric arrangement in twentieth-century choral music: 4/4 to 3/2 to 4/4. There appears to be more confusion about this relationship than most others. The confusion arises over the question of the relationship of the quarter note in a 4/4 or 3/4 or 5/4 bar, to the quarter note in the 3/2 bar. Stated very simply, the rule is as follows: When moving from 4/4 to 3/2, unless the composer specifically indicates a change of tempo, the duration of the quarter note in both measures remains constant. The quarter note in the 4/4 bar *equals* the quarter note in the 3/2 bar. The quarter note in the 4/4 bar does *not* equal the half note in 3/2. Some scores will indicate this relationship above the staff: m. 22 in the *Mini-Gloria* is a case in point. However, most scores do not indicate the relationship in this way, and, while such an indication might be advisable, it is certainly not necessary. In either case, the rule stated above applies: the quarter note remains the same unless the composer indicates otherwise.

Another conducting technique which must be thoroughly understood and mastered before the rhythmic control of contemporary music (or any other music) can be assured is the preparatory beat. In discussing the implications of communicating via gesture, Leonard Bernstein comments that "the chief element in the conductor's technique of communication is the preparation. Everything must be shown . . . before it happens."* In a similar vein, Furtwängler has written that "it is not the moment of the down-beat itself, nor the accuracy and sharpness with which this down-beat is given, which determines the precision achieved by the orchestra, but the *preparation* which the conductor gives to this down-beat . . . ."† In a subsequent statement in the same article, he challenges the mind with an idea that may have peculiar relevance to the contemporary

---

*Leonard Bernstein, "The Art of Conducting," *The Conductor's Art*, ed. Carl Bamberger (New York: McGraw-Hill, 1965), p. 272.

†Wilhelm Furtwängler, "About the Handicraft of the Conductor," *The Conductor's Art*, ed. Carl Bamberger (New York: McGraw-Hill, 1965), p. 211.

situation: "If the preparation is that which most strongly influences the sound of the instrument, could not one imagine a style of conducting which would renounce the final points of every beat . . . and make use only of the preparation as such?"*

The experienced conductor, it is suspected, will have no difficulty understanding the implications of this statement. He realizes that, in an oversimplified sense, conducting is nothing more than a chain or sequence of preparations. He knows that he cannot, with impunity, "renounce" the final points of every beat. However, he also knows that the point of the beat has a greater influence upon what happens *after* the beat than it has upon what happens at the instant the beat is delivered. Clarification of this concept is extremely difficult without access to physical illustration. It is the conviction of the author, however, that this whole area is a greatly neglected one in too many conducting courses. It would make a fascinating topic for a graduate seminar. Suffice it to say here, that in attempting to extend his capacity to control twentieth-century music, the conductor would do well to seriously rethink his attitudes relating to the function and use of preparation. If an adequate gesture of preparation precedes every musical event, precision and control are assured.

VOICES WITH INSTRUMENTS

If these pages had been written in the 1950s, a section on the special problems of voices and instruments in twentieth-century choral music might have received scant attention. This would not have been because such literature did not exist, but because in many high school, college, and church situations this literature was not being frequently performed. Today, however, a review of representative programs reveals considerable interest in vocal literature involving various combinations of instruments. Even in the Midwest where the prevailing preoccupation has been with *a cappella* literature, more and more choirs are programming works which call for piano, brasses, woodwinds, and strings. This growing fascination with more variety of texture in choral music is due to several factors. First is the new understanding of Renaissance performance practice on the part of conductors, coupled with the availability of good performance editions of this literature. Second, this "demythologizing" of the so-called *a cappella* period has had a subtle effect upon composers who are now, in increasing numbers, contributing to a significant new literature for voices and instruments. There is little question that the musicologist has had a profound impact not only upon the methods of performing earlier music but also upon the creation of new music. The sonorous excitement of well-performed Gabrieli, Monteverdi, and Schütz has been a powerful motivating factor for composers as they have sought to expand their choral color palette. The extensive bibliography of literature in

* *Ibid.,* p. 213.

this genre, especially works utilizing chorus with brasses, has made some new demands upon both conductors and choruses.

1. In the preparation of instrumentally accompanied twentieth-century choral music, the choral conductor cannot content himself with means of communication which apply only to singers. In the first place, the gesture language of the conductor must speak with equal authority to both instrumentalists and vocalists. Every indication of nuance, phrasing, and dynamic gradation must take place within the context of a beat pattern that will be legible to all performers. There is no justification for conducting words in the presence of instrumentalists. Second, the rehearsal language and vocabulary must be extensive enough to communicate effectively with brasses, woodwinds, and strings as well as with the chorus. Attendance at rehearsal of orchestras and bands should become a requirement for all undergraduate choral conductors. With the virtuoso writing for percussion in much twentieth-century music, special attention should be given to this area as well. It should also be obvious that special familiarity with keyboard problems of both piano and organ are a normal part of the conductor's basic equipment. The modern choral conductor should be secure enough of himself in the instrumental field to make quick, incisive, and pertinent comments relating to articulation, bowing, phrasing, tone quality, balance, and intonation. It goes without saying that similar requirements are incumbent upon the instrumental conductor who works with voices.

2. The choral conductor who was weaned on short three-minute madrigals, anthems, and motets must expand and develop his capacity to conceptualize the larger more extended works for voices and instruments. Such compositions are likely to involve greater density of texture by virtue of the presence of the instrumental sonority, more than two changes of tempi, more complicated transition sections, special problems of balance and ensemble, extended maintenance of rhythmic pulse, and greater exaggeration of choral declamation than what is required in the short unaccompanied work. Each of the preceding aspects of the larger modern work could well receive extensive coverage. They are simply listed here to provide some guidelines for further study and analysis. How can the conductor develop his capacity to deal successfully with these problems?

If a conductor has rarely or never worked with instruments and voices, he would be ill-advised to begin with the *Symphony of Psalms*, or the *Apparebit repentina dies* of Hindemith, or the Pinkham *Christmas Cantata*. He might begin, however, by programming a modestly extended work for brasses and chorus such as Robert Washburn's "A Child This Day Is Born." This well-conceived composition, while only about six minutes in duration, will challenge the conductor in all the areas listed above. Furthermore, if for any reason the brasses cannot realize their parts or the second trumpet player does not show up for the performance, the piano could always be utilized in an emergency. There are a number of similar contemporary works that could function well as the means by which the conductor grows in his ability to conceptualize larger works.

3. With the infinite variety of instrumental and vocal combinations possible, no conductor can take the orchestration of a twentieth-century work for granted. One should assume nothing. If the full instrumental complement is not clearly stated in the vocal score, the full score must be consulted and the sooner the better. The unexpected discovery of a part for alto sax, flugelhorn, or harp three weeks before a performance can add unnecessary trauma to the conductor whose anxiety quota has already been overextended. Obviously, the best time to take the orchestration into consideration is during the selection process itself. The work which contains a virtuoso first trumpet part, for example, cannot be programmed unless such a player is available. This leads to another important point.

4. The conductor must be able to determine from the score whether or not the difficulties inherent in the instrumental parts can be successfully mastered by the available performers. There is a slight tendency on the part of choral conductors to underestimate the ability of their choirs and overestimate the abilities of the instrumentalists.

5. The conductor must realize that in twentieth-century choral works calling for small instrumental ensembles, he will be requiring instrumentalists whose major performance experience is in large bands and orchestras to become *chamber musicians*. There is a vast difference between being alone on the first trumpet part of Dello Joio's "St. Cecilia," and being a part of the whole trumpet section on Owen Reed's "La Fiesta Mexicana."

6. In choral works utilizing brasses such as the Dello Joio or the *Christmas Cantata* of Daniel Pinkham, the brass ensemble should be extensively rehearsed prior to the first rehearsal with the chorus. While another conductor may assist in these rehearsals, it is imperative that the conductor who will ultimately take the performance have at least one rehearsal with the brasses alone. The first rehearsal of the combined forces is psychologically very important. If properly prepared for, it should culminate with a feeling of genuine enthusiasm for the work on the part of all participants. In most cases, the chorus arrives at this rehearsal with a fairly mature concept of the music. It is grossly unfair to the chorus, then, to move through this rehearsal with a brass group that has seen the music only once if at all. The choral conductor would be well-advised not to accept the assurance of the band director who maintains that there are no real difficulties in the brass parts and that his players will have no trouble sight-reading the score. Some of this writer's most distressing performance experiences at festivals have been with high school instrumentalists whose leaders quietly assured me as the curtain went up that "there were no real problems in the brass parts." This may have been true, but even superior technical competence does not ensure adequate balance, acceptable intonation, or a sense of the appropriate style and subtleties of nuance and phrasing that mark the adequately prepared performance. As was stated earlier, this is instrumental chamber music. As such, it requires even more intensive preparation than with a larger group if the music is to speak with its full potential.

7. In twentieth-century choral music which utilizes instruments, dynamic levels and balance will require the conductor's special attention. If the instruments are brasses, the problems are even greater. A small group of four brass instruments will maintain its identity with no trouble at all even when opposed by a chorus of 400 voices. If the chorus is diminished to 100 voices and the brass choir increased to eight, the voices can, with little exertion on the part of the brasses, be inundated. When this occurs, there may be an overall sense of excitement in the performance, and the applause may be substantial, but in all probability the music has been desecrated. Brasses have as much difficulty playing softly well as voices do singing softly well. Much discipline will be required to achieve adequate results and some restraint will be mandatory for the brasses. The conductor is usually safe in marking the dynamic levels of the brass parts down one degree before he ever begins rehearsing. Brass fortissimos should be reserved for moments when the voices are not singing or for the final cadence. Some composers understand this problem completely and their scores are wonderfully transparent, allowing the vocal declamation to cut through without excessive exaggeration. Other composers do not understand the problem at all, and the conductor must exercise great care in such works. While much more could be said, these remarks will at least alert the conductor to a source of potential trouble in choral works accompanied by brasses.

8. In instrumentally accompanied choral music, the simultaneous juxtaposition of contrasting modes of articulation requires special attention. For example, in the "Kyrie" of the Stravinsky *Mass* (m. 16) the composer sets forth a sustained, imitative choral texture on "Christe" that is essentially lyric, against a short, dry, *staccato* articulation in the woodwind *ostinato* figure. In order that the contrasting character of the opposing timbres can be clearly audible, it may be advisable to exaggerate both the instrumental *staccato* and the intensity of the choral *sostenuto*. The brevity of the section requires, furthermore, that the two opposing types of articulation become operative from the very first note in this passage. In fact, the style must be conceptualized in the minds of each performer in the preparatory instant *before* the phrase begins. This is just one of many instances in this work in which simultaneous contrasts of articulation occur. Contemporary choral literature is full of such occasions, and the conductor must be especially alert at these moments. The tendency will be for the distinction between timbres to become blurred. The opposing groups must be encouraged to maintain their autonomy in the sphere of articulation and phrasing. When this happens, the counterrelation of the opposing elements is thrown into bold relief, and the total effect of the composer's intent is realized.

POSTSCRIPT

Since this chapter was completed in the Fall of 1967, dramatic changes have taken place in the area of choral performance. Penderecki was a name known only to a few, and his music to even fewer. Now recordings of his music are readily available and his *St. Luke Passion* has been successfully performed in the United States with several of our collegiate choral groups involved. In 1967, Knut Nystedt's *De Profundis*, a work which contains numerous tone clusters and vocal *glissandi*, had been performed by only a handful of college choirs. Since then, this work has appeared on numerous college and university programs and has even been done successfully by some of the better high school choirs. In 1967, choral music utilizing electronic tape was, with a few notable exceptions, restricted to avant-garde experimental ensembles. Now choirs from colleges such as Oberlin, St. Olaf, and Augsburg include compositions for tape recorder and choir on their tour programs. The modes of musical composition have undergone radical changes in a very short time, and composers such as Berio, Ligeti, Davidovsky, Feldman, and Childs are being heard more frequently on choral programs.

It would be difficult if not impossible to bring this discussion of twentieth-century choral music completely up-to-date in this concluding Postscript. Furthermore, it would be grossly unfair to treat the music of the composers mentioned above superficially or in haste. A detailed discussion of recent avant-garde composers must, therefore, be left for another time—and possibly to someone else. Suffice it to say that, while the performance problems of the new music are great, they are by no means insurmountable. The new notation *is* decipherable when approached with an open mind, a creative imagination, and a solid analytical capability. Conductors who have exposed themselves and their choirs to this music speak glowingly of the rewards that can be anticipated from such endeavors. Indeterminate and aleatoric expressions, furthermore, appear to have special relevance to many of our young people. We owe it to them and to ourselves to become better acquainted with this music.

This chapter has called attention to some of the special challenges and problems which present themselves in twentieth-century choral music. Hopefully, this discussion will lead to more freedom, less fear, and a more open attitude on the part of choral conductors towards the choral expression of the last fifty years. This music, to be sure, "sings differently, it rears itself more suddenly and plunges more precipitously. It even stops differently. But it shares with older music the expression of basic human emotions . . . whatever else it may be, it is the voice of our own age and in that sense it needs no apology."*

*Copland, *op. cit.*, p. 255.

FiVe

THE CHORAL CONDUCTOR'S PREPARATION OF THE MUSICAL SCORE

Julius Herford

SCORE READING

The skill of score reading is one of the musician's most basic achievements. Music notation is not an easily accessible medium to convey musical thought. Even the correct spelling of graphic symbols and the correct rendition of musical detail is a demanding task; in the case of early music handed to us in an archaic form of notation it often presents insurmountable problems. The musician, of course, needs to develop his reading ability far beyond the stage of the correct spelling of details; he must be able to read musical context and musical thought. A performer fails badly presenting no more than a multiplicity of musical details instead of a concept of the work as a whole. The skillful composer has given to each of his compositions its unique proportions, timings, and spacings as he conveys the "order" of his work by means of musical notation. The authentic written or printed score provides the most direct access to the thought processes of the composer. Listening to a performance one hears the work as conceived by another musician; reading the score one is alone with the work and is given a chance to arrive at his own personal concept. Such an aim implies a quality of

177

reading which conceives thought and, ultimately, conceives the work as a whole. It demands a long, even ceaseless process of learning.

In order to understand in depth a single work of a composer, one must be familiar with many of his works. The single work must be viewed within the context of his entire creative output and even this must be understood within the wider perspective of the musical style of the historical period in which it was conceived. Therefore, a study of a musical work in depth is interdependent upon its study in breadth as well.

An approach to score studies as outlined above is not unfamiliar to musicians who know of the philosophies and theories of Heinrich Schenker and Ernst Kurth. The more specific procedures of musical analysis which follow must be understood within the frame of such attitudes and general thoughts.

The limited space of one chapter necessitates a condensed, even limited choice of materials. Since this discussion is directed to the choral musician and deals specifically with his preparation and study procedures, musical examples are chosen from major choral works of the standard performance repertory. The analytical studies in depth are limited to a single, similar movement from several cyclic choral-orchestral works. These are selected from composers of different, although not far removed, style periods so that individual and historical characteristics may easily be compared. The reader should be forewarned that a superficial reading will not bear fruit. On the contrary, a concentrated study, with score in hand, is essential for complete musical understanding. A prerequisite for the intense score study as suggested in the following is a reasonable mastery of the mechanics of score reading. The student's focal point and aim is the perception of the musical logic with which the work unfolds from beginning to end.

THE MOZART *REQUIEM*, K. 626 (1791): INTROIT

The Overall Form

We take as our first example the Introit "Requiem aeternam" of Mozart's *Requiem* (K. 626).* Intensive studies begin with *silent* score studies. It should be one's first endeavor to gain a comprehensive point of view by the determination of the overall form of the piece. Graph 5-1 gives a picture of the overall form of the Introit. The graph is self-explanatory, although the following remarks may be helpful:

Bar numbers: In 7, 8, the tie indicates that the musical phrase overlaps into bar 8. The same is true for 14, 15, 18, 19, etc.

---

*Recommended scores: *Orchestral Miniature Score, Eulenburg No. 954,* 1932, edited by Friedrich Blume; or *Neue Mozartausgabe* (New Mozart Edition), Bärenreither, 1965 (Serie I, Werkgruppe I, Teilband I, p. 37), edited by Leopold Nowak.

Text:	Only the beginning and ending words of the textual phrase are given.
Keys:	Small letters stand for minor keys; capital letters stand for major keys.
$\underline{V}$: d	Dominant of d minor (14^3 = third beat of m. 14).
$\underline{VII°/I}$: F	Diminished seventh degree of F, leading to tonic of F major (14^4 = fourth beat of m. 14; 15^1 = first beat of m. 15).

The Introit is in a quasi-sonata form, starting with an orchestral introduction. The sonata exposition consists of five fugal entrances of the first theme. The second theme falls on the second textual phrase ("et lux perpetua . . ."). As is customary in a sonata whose main key is in the minor (here: d minor) the second theme is in the relative major key (here: F major). The second theme reappears in the recapitulation (m. 43) in B-flat major, a fifth lower from the key of its first appearance. In accordance with a century-old tradition, the musical divisions coincide with the divisions of the textual phrases.

GRAPH 5-1

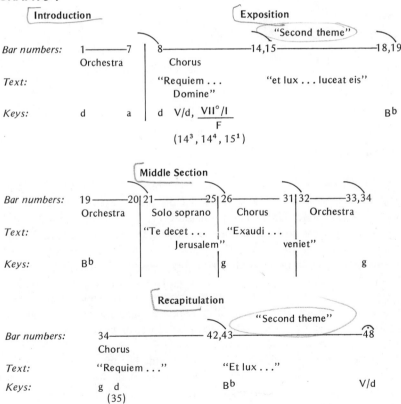

Essential Details within the Overall Form

Taking a second look at the score, we will read more detail but keep the overall form well in mind. It goes without saying that the reader must perceptively follow the observations in the score.

Introduction (mm. 1-8¹)

Mm. 1-8¹: The woodwinds enter with the *Requiem* theme consisting of five tones (Figure 5-1).

Figure 5-1

The order of entrances is as follows:

Instrument	Bar and Beat	Pitch
First bassoon	m. 1²	d (subject)
Second basset horn	m. 2²	a (answer)
First basset horn	m. 3⁴	d (subject)
Second bassoon	m. 4²	a (answer)

The four fugal entrances follow each other in irregular time distances of four, six, and two beats. After the presentation of the theme, each wind instrument continues with an independent line to measure 7¹. The polyphonic texture of the winds is accompanied by a rhythmic harmonic pulse of the strings. All the string parts, however, are of some melodic interest; some double melodic lines of the winds (the second violins double the first bassoon at mm. 1-4, the first violins double the second bassoon at mm. 2-3). This harmonic-rhythmic accompaniment pulses underneath the polyphonic texture of the woodwinds, loosening it and moving it on. One might call it an orchestrated and notated continuo realization. The organ part is marked *tasto solo*, which means that the string sonority is not to be mixed with the sonority of organ chords. Such an accompaniment is a homophonic device which underlies the polyphony of the winds. Polyphonic-homophonic mixture is significant in Mozart's late style (from 1781-82 on). Here, in the *Requiem* Introit, it is an integral element of the composition, sounding, indeed, very "Mozartean"; however, the same technique used by him in his "new instrumentation" of Handel's *Messiah* (K. 572, 1789) falsifies the semi-improvisational character of the Baroque continuo realization.

After a rather decisive cadence in a minor, ending at m. 7^1, the main key of d minor is quickly reestablished (mm. 7^2-8^1). The dynamic marking *piano* lasts from m. 1 to m. 7^1. A sudden *forte* is marked from m. 7^2 on, and the texture changes from m. 7^2 to m. 8^1 to the simple chord progression above the cadential steps of the bass: A G F E D. Mozart notates here three *colla parte*
$$(7^1) \qquad (8^1)$$
trombones (alto, tenor, bass trombones) in his manuscript fragment (see *Neue Mozartausgabe*, Ser. I, Workgroup I, Pt. I, p. 3).*

The trumpet-tympani punctuation is another Baroque device. It is used in this Introit at mm. 7^4-8^1, 13-14^3, and, at the end, mm. 43-46^1 and m.48—in all cases at sectional or subsectional endings. At mm. 7^4-8^1 it punctuates the d minor cadence as the ending of the introduction and simultaneously announces the first choral entry which is the beginning of the exposition.†

Exposition (mm. 8-19^1)

Mm. 8-15^1: The choral voices enter with the *Requiem* theme in the rising order of bass, tenor, alto, soprano, alternating as subject and answer, and in *stretto* imitation, following each other in the regular time distance of two beats. A climactic fifth entrance in the soprano occurs at m. 12^2. The melodic tessitura from voice to voice spans from the low d in the bass (m. 8) to the high f in the soprano (m. 13^3) as *one* huge melodic arch.

The winds and low strings (violas, celli) double the voices. The high strings (first and second violins) add this time a more intensive syncopated pulse to the otherwise polyphonic texture. The fugal exposition ends with a semicadence in d minor at m. 14^3.

To continue our observations, the two musical examples given in Figures 5-2 and 5-3 serve as the structural skeletons of mm. 1-7^1 and mm. 8-14^3.

*Friedrich Blume omitted these trombones in the Eulenburg score edited by him. He admitted this omission to be erroneous (*Musical Quarterly*, April, 1961, p. 162, ftn. 31).

†The baroque device of trumpet-tympani is still used in the pedal-point fugue of the Brahms *Requiem*.

Figure 5-2 Mm. 1-7[1]

Figure 5-3 Mm. 8-14[3]

A superficial comparison of the two examples shows the relative lucidity of the texture in the example shown in Figure 5-2 versus the higher degree of density in the example of Figure 5-3—the *piano* versus the *forte*, the greater rhythmic-harmonic motion, and the entrances of the theme following each other more closely in the second example. In Figure 5-2 the reader must supplement in his mind the sonority of soft low woodwinds (basset horns and bassoons) and the still, almost solemn string pulse underneath the polyphonic wind texture; in Figure 5-3, the *forte* choral voices doubled by instruments and, above this, the dramatic, syncopated pulse of the high strings. The music does not come to a stop at the semicadence in d minor (m. 14³), where, theoretically speaking, the fugal exposition ends.* It moves on to m. 15¹ with a modulation to F major, which is accomplished with two chords: VII and I in F major (mm. 14⁴-15¹).

Mm. 15-19¹: The second theme of the sonata form appears in the relative major key on the words "et lux perpetua luceat eis." This is, as mentioned before, a traditional procedure, and it is also customary to cast the words "et lux perpetua" in a brighter key. The musical texture changes from m. 15 on, to syllabic choral declamation, which is echoed by the woodwinds in an antiphonal manner. The harmonic rhythm widens expressively. Throughout mm. 15-17¹ an F chord is held. Starting as a tonic of F major at m. 15, it is intensified by adding the pitches E-flat (m. 16) and G (m. 17) and hereby converting it into the dominant seventh and dominant ninth of B-flat major.

Middle Section (mm. 19-34¹)

Mm. 19-34¹: The middle section is "framed" by two orchestral bars. They are alike as to musical material and structural function. They start the section (mm. 19-21¹), reaffirming the cadence of B-flat major twice, in which key the middle section begins. They also end the section (mm. 32-34¹), reaffirming the key of g minor, the concluding key of the section. The solo soprano sings the first verse of Psalm 64: "Te decet hymnus..." (mm. 21-26¹), and the chorus sings the second verse: "Exaudi orationem meam..." (mm. 26-32¹). The melody sung by the solo soprano and, in the second verse, by the choral sopranos is based on the ninth psalm tone, the so-called *tonus peregrinus*.† The accented syllables of the words "decet," "hymnus," "Deus," "Sion," "tibi," "reddetur," "exaudi," "meam," and "te" fall on weak beats of the bars. This is probably done to preserve the nonmetrical character of the Gregorian psalm tone. The Gregorian melody floats on a polyphonic string accompaniment (mm. 21-26¹) which is formed out of a motif appearing for the first time in the first violins and the first bassoon at m. 20 (Figure 5-4). This motif sounds new when it is heard for the first time, but it is actually the diminution inversion of the main theme.

how? ↑

(a)

*The "fugal exposition" (mm. 8-14³) is the first subsection of the "sonata exposition" (mm. 8-34¹).

†Bach uses the *tonus peregrinus* in the "Suscepit Israel" of his *Magnificat* as *cantus firmus* in long notes. The *cantus* is played by a trumpet in the early version in E-flat major (BWV 243a), by an oboe in the later version in D major (BWV 243). Michael Haydn uses the first psalm tone in his *Requiem* in C minor (1771) at the "te decet hymnus" (see L. Nowak's Introductory Notes, *Neue Mozartausgabe*, Ser. I, Workgroup I, Pt. I, p. xv). Mozart used the *tonus peregrinus* in 1771 in the final chorus of *Betulia liberata*.

(b)

Figure 5-4 (a) M. 20, first violins and first bassoon; (b) m. 1, first bassoon

The string accompaniment uses also the diminution in the original direction (Figure 5-5).

(a)

(b)

Figure 5-5 (a) M. 21, second violins; (b) m. 22, first violins

The second verse of the psalm is accompanied with a dotted rhythm which must be played in the baroque manner of the French overture dot:

Recapitulation (mm. 34-48)

The recapitulation is an intensified repeat of the exposition: mm. 34-43[1] correspond structurally to mm. 8-15[1]; mm. 43-48 correspond structurally to mm. 15-19[1].

Mm. 34-43[1]: The fugal exposition is now bithematic. The second fugal theme is formed out of the diminution inversion and the diminution *recte* (original direction) of the main theme. The double entrances follow in this order ("I" refers to the first fugal theme, "II" to the second):

Double Entrance	Voices	Pitches	Measures
1	bass (I)	d	34
	alto (II)	a	
2	tenor (I)	a	35^4-36
	soprano (II)	e	
3	alto (I)	g	37^4-38
	tenor (II)	d	
4	soprano (I)	f	39^4-40
	bass (II)	c	

The four double entrances are arranged in such a way that each of the choral voice sections enters twice, singing once the first fugal theme and then the second, or vice versa. The interval relation between the first and second themes is at the higher fifth or the lower fourth; the time distance between the two themes is one and one half beats. The four double entrances follow each other at the distance of six, eight, and eight beats (mm. 34^2; 35^4; 37^4; 39^4). The modulatory process is more intense than in the corresponding section of the sonata exposition. It is as follows:

Keys: g   d   a   g   F   (d)   Bb

Bars: 34   35   37   39   41   42   43

It is expanded to nine bars (mm. $34-43^1$; Figure 5-6) compared to the seven bars before (mm. $8-14^3$; compare Figure 5-3).

35

Figure 5-6 Mm. 34-43[1]

Figure 5-6 indicates the sixteenth-note motion of the second fugal theme only here and there. In other words it is reduced here to its basic step progressions: it is the skeleton structure of the fugal double exposition as it appears in the recapitulation (mm. 34-43[1]). Comparing it to the fugal entrances of the sonata exposition (Figure 5-3), the reader will easily notice a further intensification.

Mm. 43-48: The second sonata theme is now in B-flat major. It, too, is intensified compared to its first appearance at mm. 15-19[1]. It moves upon the strongly forward-leaning bass progression: Bb-A-G#-A (mm. 43, 44, 45, 46). Pausing emphatically for an eighth rest after the semicadence in d minor (m. 46[2]), the words "et lux perpetua luceat eis" are repeated softly and solemnly (mm. 46[2]-48). The Introit ends on the repeated half-close in d minor, with a composed *ritard* implied by the tympani rhythm:

Form: A Process in Motion

With the maturing ability to read musical context, mind and ear function more and more closely together. Graph 5-1 gives the impression of a well-organized overall form with its sectional and subsectional divisions overlapping each other (mm. 7, 8, etc.) but the picture of the graph, as the eye sees it, is much more static than the music heard by the ear.

Comparing the musical examples given in Figures 5-2, 5-3, and 5-6, eye and ear relate the three fugal expositions of the instrumental introduction, the sonata exposition, and the recapitulation to each other and detect a measurable process of intensification. Considering the place of the three fugal expositions within the overall form, the degrees of intensification are most logically related. The composer is in complete control of the stream of energy as it flows throughout the entire form, and he guides it securely toward climaxes and away from them. This stream of energy flows even through cadential interpunctuations. It does not stop fully at any place except at the very end when it has fulfilled itself. This phenomenon of consistent and controlled motion to the end may be called "form in motion" or "form as a process in motion." It is the living breath of the music. A further glance into the score (Graph 5-2) elaborates upon it.

GRAPH 5-2

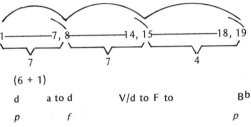

Measure numbers:	1————7, 8————14, 15————18, 19				
Measure groupings:	7		7		4
Subdivisions:	(6 + 1)				
Keys:	d	a to d	V/d to F to		B♭
Dynamics:	p	f			p

Pivot Points The downbeats of mm. 8, 15, and 19 are *pivot beats*; they have double functions. The introduction ends at the downbeat of m. 8 (the d minor cadence resolves here), and it is also here where the exposition begins. The double function is indicated in Graph 5-2 by one long tie ending here and another starting from here, both meeting at this one point. The new impulse generates from the three upbeats in the strings (m. 7^2-7^4) and receives a new impetus from the trumpet-tympani punctuation (mm. 7^4-8^1), as indicated in the graph by the short tie: 7, 8. The energy accumulated at the downbeat of m. 8 "motivates" the forceful, syncopated pulse in the violins. It streams through the a minor cadence at m. 7^1 and then presses forward to m. 8^1. That is especially noticeable in the bass progression, shown in Figure 5-7. A similar situation is found at m. 15^1. The energy streams through the half-cadence at m. 14^3 and moves on to m. 15^1 (Figure 5-8). The enforcing impulse at m. 14^4 is indicated by the small tie: 14, 15.

(a)   (d)

Figure 5-7 Mm. 6^4-8^1

Figure 5-8 Mm 13³-15 (begins on m. 15, ends on downbeat of m. 19)

The new subsection (the second theme on "et lux perpetua") begins, and the first part of the sonata exposition ends on the downbeat of m. 15.

The third pivot point (m. 19¹) will be discussed below. The ear hears these pivot points actually twice, as an ending and a beginning, as shown in Graph 5-3.

GRAPH 5-3

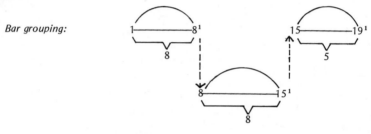

We refrained from this *musical* notation of bar groupings (8-8-5) in Graph 5-2 for the practical reason of making the number of bars within the bar groups identical to the number of bars counted in the score.

Subdivisions of Bar Groups The subdivision of the seven-bar group (mm. 1-8¹) into 6 + 1 bars directs the attention to the a minor cadence at m. 7¹ as a momentary stopping point, which is, of course, neutralized through the imme-diate continuation. Similar subdivisions within larger bar groups occur at two other places in the Introit:

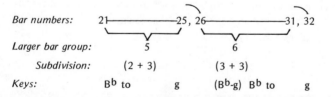

The first of these subdivisions is heard through the repeated B-flat major cadence at m. 23¹ (at the end of the textual phrase). The music modulates in the following three bars (mm. 23-26¹) to g minor. The downbeat of m. 23 is a pivot point. The 3 + 3 subdivision of the 6-bar group is heard as follows:

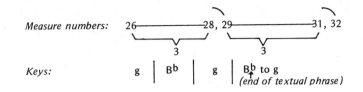

Measure numbers:

Keys:

Inflectionary Dynamics

The dynamics are marked *piano* from mm. 1-7[1]. But this marking cannot be taken too literally since the ear clearly hears increase and decrease of intensity in these bars. The melodic top pitches rise:

Pitch	Instrument	Bar and Beat
d^1	first bassoon	1^2
a^1	second basset horn	2^2
d^2	first basset horn	3^4
f^2	first basset horn	5^1

Together with this melodic intensification occurs a harmonic increase of intensity. Both melody and harmony reach their peak of intensity at exactly the same point: m. 5^1. The harmony brightens through a passing modulation to C major (m. 5: II^7-V-I of C major) and, then, the energy dissipates, coming to a momentary resting point on the tonic of a minor (m. 7^1). This increase and decrease of melodic and harmonic intensity, this brightening and darkening of color does not permit a statically held *piano*. Though the basic quality of *piano* must be preserved throughout these bars (precisely to m. 7^1), the *piano* must be modified in an inflectionary sense along with the melody and harmony.

Dovetailing Procedures

The discussion of the pivot point at m. 19^1 has been postponed so that the subtlety of the transition from the middle section to the recapitulation may be treated here with ample thoroughness. After the word "luceat" has been sung *forte* (at m. 17), it is repeated *piano* (at m. 18) and the accentuation is on the second syllable: "luceat." A slight minorish shadow falls on the second beat of m. 18 (diminished chord: E-G-Bb-Db).

The second bassoon cadences melodically in a decisive way (Figure 5-9), and the sopranos join in the last two beats (Figure 5-10). The first violins do not

Figure 5-9 Mm. 18-19[1]   **Figure 5-10** Mm. 18-19[1]

contribute to this finite effect of the cadence. Instead, they proceed hesitantly (Figure 5-11). The repeated three sixteenth-note figure is a composed slight

Figure 5-11 Mm. 18-19[1]

ritard, and the violins conclude at m. 19 with an imperfect and feminine melodic cadence. The B-flat major cadence ·is then repeated twice. The second basset horn cadences again firmly (Figure 5-12). However, here the first basset horn

Figure 5-12 Mm. 19-20[1]

converts the finality of the repeated cadence into another imperfect and feminine ending (Figure 5-13).

Figure 5-13 Mm. 19-20[1]

The first violins approach a complete cadence but leap high at the downbeat of m. 20 (Figure 5-14). The continuo basses, violas, second violins, and second

Figure 5-14 Mm. 19-20

bassoon repeat the B-flat cadence for a third time at mm. 20-21[1], but the first violins, doubled by the first bassoon, initiate at m. 20[1] a flowing sixteenth-note pulse by presenting the diminution inversion of the main theme for the first time (Figure 5-15). The top melody pitches ascend in mm. 19-20[1] from d to f (Figure 5-16).

Figure 5-15 Mm. 20-21[1]

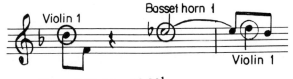

Figure 5-16 Mm. 19-20[1]

The sixteenth-note pulse springs forth and moves on in the accompaniment of the first verse of the psalm tone; therefore, if any finality was felt in the B-flat major cadence at m. 19[1], it was weakened by the first violins. The first basset horn repeated the imperfect feminine ending of the violins at mm. 19-20[1] and led on to the first violins, which, supported by the first bassoon, initiated at m. 20 a new sixteenth-note motion. This and the implied ascent of the top pitches from d^2 to f^2 (mm. 19-20) cause the ear to hear the B-flat major cadence on the downbeat of m. 21 as a logical continuation rather than an ending point.

A rather typical dovetailing procedure links the middle section with the recapitulation. The recapitulation begins, as far as musical materials are concerned, at m. 34. On the downbeat of m. 34 falls a recurrence of the g minor cadence, the key in which the middle section ends. The recapitulation should, of course, begin in d minor, the main key of the Introit, but at the first thematic bar of the recapitulation, a modulation to d minor does take place, which concludes on the tonic d minor at the downbeat of m. 35. In other words, the harmonic beginning of the recapitulation has been shifted to its second thematic bar.*

Brief Summary

We have passed through three stages of silent score studies:

1. The determination of the overall form (Graph 5-1).
2. The observation of the structurally essential details as they occur within the overall form (pp. 181-186).

*A similar dovetailing procedure is found in the first *Kyrie* of the *B minor Mass* by Bach. A new thematic section begins with the entrance of the theme in the second soprano on f-sharp (m. 48); the cadence in f-sharp minor is resolved at m. 49, where also the first soprano and the bass end their phrases. Because of these strong melodic endings and the harmonic ending at m. 49[1], the entrance of the second soprano at m. 48 seems anticipated rather than the harmonic beginning being postponed.

3. The form in motion or form as a process in motion. This motion flows through the cadential points. The composer controls the increases and decreases of tension, leading the incessant motion logically toward climaxes and again away from them. All elements of composition, melody, harmony, rhythm, dynamics, as well as the tightness or looseness of texture, are conditioned by this stream of energy.

Exercises

Mental Exercise   The following mental exercise done in order will enhance the mastery of the overall form:

GRAPH 5-4 Memorization Chart

```
⊢————————7, 8————————⊣4, 15————————⊣8, 19

19————— 20, 21⊢—————————25, 26————————31, 32————————33, 34

34—————————42, 43—————————48
```

Stage 1: Graph 5-4 gives the measure numbers of Graph 5-1. Fill in the information given in Graph 5-1 and omitted here. This should be done by heart. You may pencil the information in thinly once to check whether it is correct but then erase it. Do this as often as necessary until you are securely oriented in the overall form.

Then reading the graph, find in the score the information given in the graph at any point, and vice versa,—that is, be sure that when reading the score, you always know where you are in the graph (i.e., in the overall form).

Stage 2: Review the more detailed observations (given on pp. 183-191) and, looking at Graph 5-4, fill them in mentally on the graph (not writing them in!). This may be done for awhile, section by section, until you are fully aware of the main musical events and where they occur in the overall form. Your knowledge must be precise. Of fugal entrances, for instance, you must know bar, beat, pitch, subject, answer, instrument and/or voice, as well as time distances from entrance to entrance.

Stage 3: The most important achievement is the awareness of the *form in motion*. It does not suffice to be aware of chord progressions, modulations, and cadences as isolated events, but one must hear them as processes within the larger musical context. One relates these events to those which precede and follow them. "Pivot points" (discussed above) take on different meanings, whether related to that which precedes them (i.e., pivot points conceived ·as ending points) or that which follows them (points of beginning). The same is true for single chords. The a minor chord at m. 3^3 is the second degree of g minor if related forward to the g minor chord at m. 4^1 but if related backward to m. 2^4 it is the tonic of a minor. If accurately related backward to the d minor beginning (m. 1) and forward to m. 8^1, the a minor chords are V of d minor, and the g minor chord is IV of d minor. The chord progression from m. 5^1 to m. 5^3 is heard by itself as II-V-I of C major. The a minor chord at m. 7^1 is, as pointed out before, on the way to d minor. The ear must conceive the harmony *in motion* from one strategic structural point (here, m. 1) to the other strategic structural point (here, m. 8^1) until the ear hears the harmony in motion from the beginning to the end of the piece.

Audible Exercises We now leave the stage of *silent* score studies and continue with *sounding* exercises, which, in another way, will help toward an intelligent understanding of the score.

1. Sing the first bassoon part, mm. 1-7, and play on the keyboard the continuo bass or the entire string accompaniment.
2. Sing the alto part mm. 34-37 and play the bass part.
3. Make similar exercises with any combination of voices and/or instruments. These exercises are carried out in one conceived tempo (for technical reasons, it may be slower than the "right" tempo) and in a *listening* (not *performing*) state of mind. The sounds of the voice and of the keyboard should balance each other in a quality not addressed to an audience.
4. The musical examples in Figures 5-2, 5-3, and 5-6 were notations of the fugal expositions at mm. $1\text{-}7^1$, $8\text{-}14^3$, and $34\text{-}43^1$, reduced to their structural skeletons. They were notated above so that the reader might relate them to each other in terms of degrees of tension as reflected in the looseness or tightness of their textures. It was also to complement in his mind the omitted "notes" and the orchestration. We now come back to these structural skeleton reductions in order to animate the reader to produce such reductions himself in later studies. Figure 5-17 shows the continuo bass line of mm. $13^3\text{-}19^1$, reduced to its basic progressions. Reading the skeleton notation of Figures 5-18 and 5-19, the increase of intensity of the second "et lux perpetua" section (Figure 5-19) is again most obvious in comparison with the one shown in Figure 5-18.

Figure 5-17 Mm. $13^3\text{-}19^1$

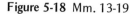

Figure 5-18 Mm. 13-19

Figure 5-19 Mm. 43-48.

THE BERLIOZ *REQUIEM*, OPUS 5 (1837): INTROIT AND KYRIE

Less than half a century lies between the time of composition of Mozart's *Requiem* fragment and Berlioz's *Grande Messe des Morts*. This brief historical span of time witnessed the rise and fall of Napoleon and produced Beethoven's gigantic musical work, both of which events left their mark on the political and musical scenes of Europe. The *Requiem* compositions of Mozart and Berlioz are telling examples of the change in musical style which took place during the time between the late eighteenth and early nineteenth centuries.

Mozart was commissioned to write his *Requiem* for the exclusive and intimate memorial service held at the court chapel of Count von Walsegg. Berlioz wrote his *Requiem* for a pompous government-sponsored memorial service to be held at L'Eglise des Invalides in Paris. Though external circumstances, general or personal, never fully explain characteristics or changes of style, they did condition, to an extent, the chamber proportions and liturgical quality of Mozart's *Requiem* and the grandiose dimensions and gigantic apparatus of the Berlioz *Requiem*. One must also take into consideration the personal state of the gravely ill Mozart, who was writing his own *Requiem*, his mind directed toward the eternal. In contrast, Berlioz, at approximately the same age as Mozart, was only at the beginning of his creative life. Ambitious, full of new ideas, he was searching for a creative outlet. We read in his *Memoirs* (German edition, p. 223):

> I had a long-standing desire to compose the text of the *Requiem* and, once commissioned, I threw myself into the work with a kind of wrath. My head seemed to burst from ideas. Scarcely had I sketched the plan for one piece when already the idea for another came to mind. It was impossible to keep pace in writing with the flow of ideas, and I invented a kind of stenography (short-hand) which served me well, especially in the 'Lacrymosa.' The work was completed very quickly and a few changes were made at a much later time. They are found in the second edition published by Ricordi, Milano.*

Comparative Examination of Composition Techniques

A thorough examination of composition techniques gives us a more substantial insight into characteristics and changes of style than do the external circumstances. Music is of a material which leaves imprints finer than wax. For those who can truly read what the composer has written, the musical text speaks an unmistakable language. The comparison of two compositions written by different composers at different historical periods must place in relief the uniqueness of each of the two works. Each has ultimately to be understood and evaluated in its own right.

One does not expect to find Mozart's elemental, impersonal thematic materials and his Classical restraint in a work of Berlioz, the first French Romanticist. It is, nevertheless, amazing how the difference in attitude reveals itself in all facets of composition. Consider for instance, the purpose or function of Berlioz's introduction to the Introit and Kyrie in the first movement of his *Requiem*, and compare it to the opening of Mozart's *Requiem*. Mozart begins, so to speak, *in medias res* and immediately presents the main theme and an imitative exposition based on it. Berlioz sets the scene for that which is to come in the foreboding ascending steps which gather momentum in the three phrases of the first 25 bars. Mozart needs no "setting of the stage" (although we may technically call the first eight bars an introduction), while Berlioz wishes to

*The Broude Brothers edition is a reprint of the Ricordi score.

prepare the listener for things to come, to create in him the proper state of mind.

The Shape of the First Theme

The shape of the first theme reveals unmistakably the attitude of utter self-involvement. The first basses present the main theme immediately after the introduction (Figure 5-20).

Re - qui - em ae - ter - - - nam

Figure 5-20 Mm. 26-31

The theme is sung *mezza voce, piano* by thirty-five first basses. Starting in a high register (d^1), the melody falls in three descending thirds. The e-flat is held for three long bars ($\downarrow$ =69) and then resolves by sinking one half step to the "d," the octave below the starting pitch. The melody is syllabic except for the two-tone ligature on the last syllable of the word "requi*em*." The sixteenth rest on the second beat is taken off the b-flat; it is actually a notated breath mark which enables the singers to prepare for the emphatic recitation of the word "aeternam" and then to sing through to the end of the phrase. If Berlioz had felt this line horizontally, the e-flat would be heard as the tone of greatest harmonic tension—a minor seventh, or three descending thirds below the starting tone (d^1-b^b-g-e^b). On the contrary, he harmonizes mm. 26 and 27 with the tonic of g minor and mm. 28-30 with the c minor sixth chord (IV^6 of g minor), which takes the linear tension out. The composer substitutes for it the agogic marking *poco f* $>$, a brief attack fading away quickly and diminishing to the end. The long-held note on the second syllable of the word "aeternam" traditionally expresses "eternity." The theme is indeed a highly expressive rhetorical pronunciation of the words "requiem aeternam," a plea for eternal rest uttered even more urgently through the hovering vocal sound (*mezza voce*) and the *piano*.*

Overall Form

Berlioz, like Mozart, organizes his first movement in sonata form. This had been a standard procedure for large-scale choral compositions since Haydn and remained so for a long time after Berlioz. Another standard procedure, especially for sacred choral music, found in both Berlioz and Mozart, is the alternation of polyphonic and homophonic textures.† The difference between the Classicist

---

*A comparison with the idiomatic, neutral *Requiem* theme of Mozart makes the personal, expressive quality of Berlioz's theme still more obvious.

†The specific fugal structure and the simultaneity of contrapuntal and homophonic texture in Mozart's Introit are, as mentioned before, typical for his late style.

Mozart and the Romanticist Berlioz lies in the timing, spacing, and the proportioning of the form.

Berlioz's overall organization of his Introit and Kyrie in the broadest sense is as shown in Graph 5-5.

GRAPH 5-5*

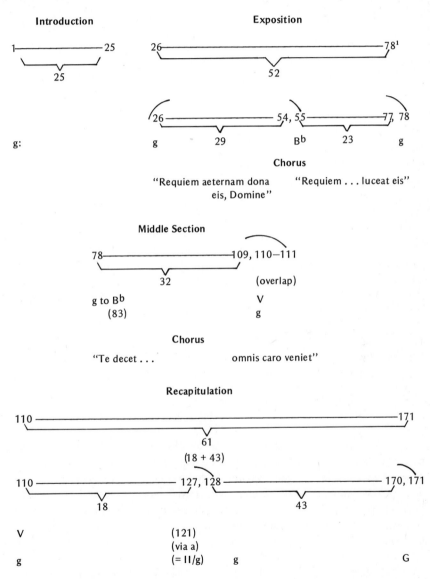

*Compare Graph 5-1. The notation used in Graph 5-5 is the same as that used in Graph 5-1. In 26, the tie indicates the beginning of the string accompaniment at 25^2.

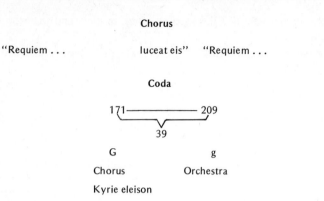

Berlioz integrates the text "Kyrie eleison, Christe eleison" into the organizational fabric of the first movement. He builds a lofty coda on these words, while Mozart treats them in an independent double fugue which is thematically related to the Introit.

More Detailed Analysis

Following a procedure similar to that used before, we will now take a more detailed look at the structure of each section in the opening movement of Berlioz's *Requiem*.* A charting of the introduction is given in Graph 5-6.

GRAPH 5-6 Mm. 1-25

Andante un poco Lento (♩ = 69)

Introduction

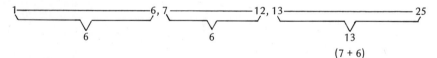

Mm. 1-25: The three phrases are separated by rests of almost two bars (grand pauses). They all ascend from the low register of the violins and violas. The first phrase begins *piano* (played by twenty-five second violins and twenty violas!) and ascends from g-d^1 (*poco crescendo*). It ends in the rhythm given in Figure 5-21 on the highest tone (d^1). This may be interpreted as an instrumental recitation of the word rhythm: "requiem." The second violins and violas are here (mm. 3-6) doubled by two oboes, two English horns, and six French horns

---

*The first measure is counted as a full measure despite the quarter rest on its first beat. The rest is felt as an impulse to the melodic ascent in the same way as in measures 7 and 13.

Figure 5-21 Mm. 3-6; second violins and violas

which enter *piano* and are otherwise marked dynamically like the strings. The second phrase (mm. 7-12) ascends a minor sixth (g-e^b), a half step higher than the first phrase. The second violins and violas, starting the ascent as they did in the first phrase, are now marked *meno piano* and are doubled by eight bassoons. The "requiem rhythm" on the highest tone (e^b) is orchestrated as before but the number of French horns is doubled (twelve French horns). The third phrase rises a minor tenth (g-b^{b1}, mm. 13-19). Second violins and violas begin the ascent with the string basses entering imitatively seven beats later. This is followed by the first violins, entering here for the first time, which imitate the string basses two beats later. The orchestration and the dynamics (*mf, crescendo molto, sf*) are proportionally intensified. The "requiem rhythm" is on the dominant chord of g minor and the orchestra *tutti*.

The massive number of voices and instruments and the instrumental doublings are carefully calculated coloristic effects. The transitional dynamics are graded exactly. Orchestration and dynamics which were integral structural elements in the Classical period become independent elements of primary importance in the Romantic period.

Exposition

The First Large Subsection of the Exposition

The exposition is divided into two large subsections: 26-54, 55-78^1 (see Graph 5-5). The first of these two large subsections is subdivided as follows:

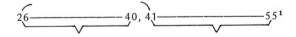

Mm. 26-41^1: The first 15 measures (26-40) contain three entrances of the first theme. It is a quasi-fugal exposition with the second and third entrances being "modulatory." We will call this and similar textures *imitative expositions*.

The first imitative exposition is bithematic. The second theme starts with a chromatic descent (Figure 5-22).

The descent of this theme, later called *contrapuntal theme*, seems to be a free inversion of the introductory ascent (Figure 5-23). The accented syllables of the first three words fall on weak beats of the bar.

Figure 5-22 Mm. 28-33; first tenors

Figure 5-23 Mm. 13-17; second violins

A third important element of this first imitative exposition is the polymetrical accompaniment of the strings. The musical excerpt shown in Figure 5-24 makes this complex texture clear (the first basses and first tenors are here

Figure 5-24 Mm. 25^2-29^1: (a) first theme; (b) contrapuntal theme

notated an octave higher). The rhythm of the strings is a displaced 3/4 meter, starting each time on the second beat and ending on the first of the bar following.

We shall now look at the first imitative exposition (mm. 26-41), analyzed in Graph 5-7.

GRAPH 5-7 First imitative exposition: mm. 26-41^1:

mm. 26—41^1	(a), first theme;	(b), contrapuntal theme

15

First sopranos:		(a)		(b)
First tenors:	(b)		(a)	
First basses:	(a)	(b)		(a) false entry

Bars:	$\lceil$(a)	26	30	34	38
	$\lfloor$(b)	28^2	32^2	36^2	

Pitches:	$\lceil$(a)	d	g	f	e^b
	$\lfloor$(b)	c	g	e^b	

Doubling instruments:	bassoons *pp*	bassoons *pp*	flutes oboes English horn	celli basses
Keys:	g	to	B^b	V/B^b (40)

The three complete entrances of the first theme follow at four-bar intervals, and since the theme is six measures long the entrances follow each other in *stretto* imitations. The basses enter on d^1 (dominant of g minor); the sopranos on g^2 are given a tonal answer (the first interval is shortened to a descending second: g^2-f^2: this answer modulates to B-flat major). The tenors enter on f^1 (dominant of B-flat major) and are a subject in B-flat major. The three entrances are *piano*, *mezza voce* and not doubled by instruments.

Graph 5-8 indicates clearly the relation of the entrances of the contrapuntal theme (b) to those of the first theme (a) in terms of distances (two bars and one beat) and intervals.

GRAPH 5-8 Mm. 26-39

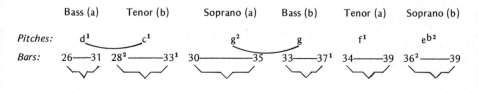

	Bass (a)	Tenor (b)	Soprano (a)	Bass (b)	Tenor (a)	Soprano (b)
Pitches:	d^1	c^1	g^2	g	f^1	e^{b2}
Bars:	26——31	28^2————33^1	30————35	33——37^1	34————39	36^2————39

As shown, the entrances of the (a) and (b) themes overlap each other. The chromatic descent of (b) is doubled by instruments which phrase *pp-legato* (quarter notes) while the voices phrase in eighth notes followed by eighth rests (Figure 5-25). A false entrance of the (a) theme (mm. 38-41[1], basses I/II, beginning *poco forte diminuendo* at m. 40) uses only the third fall of the first six notes of the theme which line out the dominant-seventh chord of B-flat major (e^b-c-A-F).

Figure 5-25 Mm. 28-31[1]

The contrapuntal style of this ingenious, adventurous, and superbly skillful Romanticist is indeed harmonically saturated.

Mm. 41-55[1]: The musical texture changes in the next fourteen bars. A gentle plea—"dona, dona eis, Domine"—is repeated twice, the second time somewhat more urgently. The tenors have the melody, the simplest possible melody, harmonized in parallel thirds and sung warmly, *espressivo*. English horns and bassoons and, at the first repeat, the French horns double the tenors. Here the sopranos, doubled by the flutes, oboes, and clarinets, weave garlands of broken chords around the tenor melody. Such purely coloristic treatment of voices may well have meant to Berlioz's more conservative contemporaries a shocking departure from rule and regulation. The vocal and string basses continue throughout the displaced 3/4 meter on an F-pedal, which is raised to F-sharp at the more urgent second repeat (note the harmonies!), and then sinks back to F-natural and resolves to B-flat when the sopranos and tenors (both *divisi*) sing *pianissimo* "requiem aeternam." A tender plea, an early impressionistic pastel landscape: will a prayer of such secular beauty be heard above?

The Second Large Subsection of the Exposition

Mm. 55-70: The scene changes back to a second imitative exposition, which is pictured in Graph 5-9.

GRAPH 5-9 Second imitative exposition: mm. 55-70

First and second
   sopranos   (a)

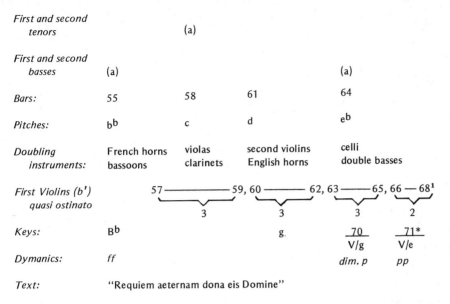

First and second tenors		(a)		
First and second basses	(a)			(a)
Bars:	55	58	61	64
Pitches:	b^b	c	d	e^b
Doubling instruments:	French horns bassoons	violas clarinets	second violins English horns	celli double basses
First Violins (b') quasi ostinato	57 ———— 59, 60 ——— 62, 63 ——— 65, 66 — 68^1
	3	3	3	2
Keys:	B^b		g.	70 / V/g, 71* / V/e
Dymanics:	ff			dim. p, pp
Text:	"Requiem aeternam dona eis Domine"

* Enharmonic change.

The four entrances of the main theme follow in distances of three bars and at the interval of ascending steps: B^b-C-D-E^b. The dynamics are *fortissimo* and each entrance is instrumentally supported. This is in utter contrast to the first imitative exposition (Graph 5-7), where the four entrances of the main theme followed each other in four-bar distances, the last three at the interval of descending steps: G-F-E^b. The dynamics were *piano, mezzo voce*, and the entrances were not supported by instruments.*

The first violins repeat a somewhat altered version of the contrapuntal theme (b') four times. These repeats follow at the distance of three bars (at mm. 57, 60, 63, and 66). They set a three-bar grouping of their own against that of the entrances of the main theme. This is a polymetrical procedure similar to the displaced 3/4 meter of the preceding subsection at mm. 25^2-52. The celli support the ascending steps of the vocal bass with the rhythm ♪♫♫♩ from mm. 57-62^1. This invigorating rhythm takes over in other parts. The climax (*fortissimo*) is reached at the start of the *tutti* (m. 66). After the *diminuendo* (mm. 67-69), an enharmonic change (e^b equals d#) spreads a tender light

*Bach contrasts fugal expositions in choral works by setting the first exposition for concertists only, with light orchestral accompaniment, and the voices are not doubled by instruments. The second exposition is sung by the full chorus and the voices are doubled by the instruments. See, for example, the "Et in terra pax" fugue of the B minor Mass: first exposition mm. 21-37^3, second exposition mm. 43^3-60^1.

upon the words "et lux perpetua." This is followed by a cadence in g minor on the words "luceat eis" (Figure 5-26).

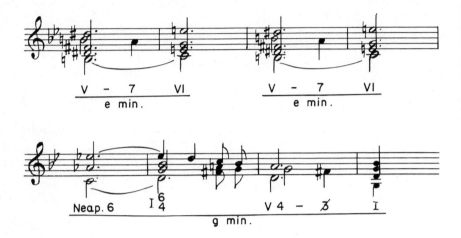

Figure 5-26 Mm. 71-78[1]

This momentary brightening of the harmonies is a coloristic effect, a harmonic pictorialism of sensuous beauty. How basically different is this Romanticism from Mozart's Classical simplicity of brightening the tonality from d minor to F major, the closest structural or functional relationship, at the corresponding textual point of his *Requiem* Introit!

Middle Section (mm. 78-111[1])

Mm. 78-98[1]: The first tenors and then the first basses sing the first verse and the first line of the second verse of Psalm 64, a variant of the simple tune which the tenors had sung before when pleading gently "Dona, dona eis" (Figures 5-27 and 5-28). The texture is now still airier. The celli begin the middle

Figure 5-27 Mm. 41-44

senza accel. e largo

Te de - cet hym-nus De - us in__ Si - on __

Figure 5-28 Mm. 83-88

section alone, modulating from g minor to B-flat major (Figure 5-29). The 4/8 figure within the 3/4 bars suggests a 2/4 within the 3/4. The bassoons have a b$^\flat$ pedal (mm. 82-98[1]). The flutes and oboes draw a thin line in long notes high above (Figure 5-30), which is then repeated (mm. 90-98[1]). The horns double the second half of the tenor melody (Figure 5-31) (mm. 85-89, again in m. 93, etc.). When the first basses answer the tenor (Figure 5-32) (and again mm.

non stringendo

mf

Figure 5-29 Mm. 78-82

Figure 5-30 Mm. 81-90

Figure 5-31 Mm. 85-89

Figure 5-32 Mm. 87-88

95-98), clarinets and English horns (both *divisi*) fill in with harmonizing chords. This is, indeed, an orderly procedure. None other than a Frenchman could ever express a scriptural prayer with such sophisticated simplicity (compare this with the simple purity of the *tonus peregrinus* at the corresponding place in Mozart). The markings *non stringendo* and *senza accelerando e largo* remind us not to rush but to keep the tempo moving slowly and in a dignified manner.

Mm. 99-111: The texture becomes fuller from m. 98 on, but notice that the voices and the strings (except for the celli) are now marked *piano*. The canon between first sopranos, doubled by flutes and oboes, and the second sopranos, doubled by English horns and clarinets, is marked *pianissimo*.

The second line of Psalm 64, second verse ("ad te omnis caro veniet"), is given a new melody. It is sung first by the tenors (m. 101³), then by the basses (m. 102³) a fifth lower. The tenors start an ascending scale progression at m. 105², doubled by violas, second violins, bassoons, and from m. 107² on, also clarinets. Starting *mezzo forte* the dynamics rise (*crescendo molto*) to *forte*, linking with an overlapping into the recapitulation (mm. 110-111¹). This stepwise ascent is a melodically augmented return of the ascent in the introduction (mm. 13-20), now rising from g¹-a².

Recapitulation (mm. 110-171¹)

The recapitulation has two large subsections corresponding structurally to those of the exposition (see also Graph 5-5):

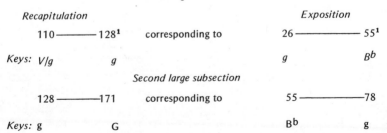

The two large subsections of the exposition modulate from g to B-flat and then return from B-flat to g. The two large subsections of the recapitulation begin in g minor, with the first subsection ending in g minor and the second ending in G major. The main part of the middle section is in B-flat major, the coda in G major/g minor. This is a logical procedure for the sonata-like *A-B-A'-C* organization.

We shall now look at an analysis of the third imitative exposition (Graph 5-10).

GRAPH 5-10 Third imitative exposition: mm. 110–115

First and second sopranos		(a)		
First and second tenors	(a)		(a)	
First and second basses	(a)			
Bars:	110	112	114	115
Pitches:	d	g	e^b	
Doubling instruments:	celli double basses French horns (C)	first violins flutes, oboes French horns (C)	second violins bassoons French horns (E^b)	
Keys:	g	to		B^b
Dynamics:	ff	ff	ff	
Text:	"Requiem aeternam dona . . ."			

Mm. 110-115: The pitches at which the three entrances of the first theme start are the same as those of the bass, soprano entrances, and the incomplete entrance of the first and second basses of the first imitative exposition (compare Graph 5-7) at m. 26 (bass: d^1), m. 30 (soprano: g^2), m. 38 (first and second basses: e^b). It is noticeable that the entrances of the first theme occur in the first imitative exposition at the distance of four bars, in the second exposition (Graph 5-9) at the distance of three bars, and now at the distance of two bars, a gradual metrical condensation and intensification. The sonorities (*fortissimo* and instrumental doublings) resemble those of the second imitative exposition but are here further intensified by the basses and sopranos in octave doublings.

Mm. 116-128: A sudden dynamic softening (voices, *pianissimo*; woodwinds, *piano*) occurs at m. 116. The liturgical text at this point is changed from "eis" to "defunctis," and at mm. 118-119 the *diminuendo* on "et lux perpetua luceat"* is now lengthened considerably (mm 117-128). A new orchestration effect is the long mordent written out in flutes and clarinets (mm. 120-125).

Graph 5-11 shows an analysis of the fourth imitative exposition.

GRAPH 5-11   Fourth imitative exposition: mm. 128-146

First and second sopranos	(a)		(b')		(b')	

First and second
sopranos   (a)   (b')   (b')

First and second
tenors   (a)

First and second
basses   (b)   (a)

Measures: 129   131² 132 134² 135   137   138

Pitches:
(a)   d   c   b♭   e♭
(b)   g   f   (incomplete)

Doubling   second   second
instruments: violin | cello viola | violin   cello   cello

First violin;
woodwinds: 128—130| 131—133| 134—136| 137—139| 140—141| 142—143| 144   146¹
                    ⌣   ⌣   ı   ⌣   ⌣   ⌣   ⌣
English   3 | 3 | 3 | 3 | 2 | 2 | vi⁶/g
horn (b')
  quasi ostinato   con soprani   dim.   p.

Keys: g

                           (a) entrances = ff
Dynamics: (b) entrances = mf   sf > > sf >
                           (b') entrances = f >

Text: "Requiem aeternam, dona eis Domine"

Mm. 128-146: The fourth imitative exposition corresponds structurally to the second one (Graph 5-9). The four entrances of the first theme follow each other at the distance of three measures (129, 132, 135, and 138). The three complete entrances of the first theme follow at the interval with descending steps (unlike the second imitative exposition in which the four entrances of the first theme follow in ascending steps b♭-c-d-e♭). Thematically, this is the richest imitative exposition inasmuch as the first theme and the contrapuntal theme

---

*Note the change of the Latin syntax at mm. 127-128 to "eis luceat," as seen before at measures 102-104, where the tenors have "caro omnis" instead of "omnis caro."

(both supported instrumentally) and the b' (*quasi ostinato*) appear simultaneously. The entrances of the first theme and the contrapuntal theme follow in
descending fifths (d-g-c-f-b♭-e♭). In the sonata exposition the words "et lux
perpetua . . . luceat eis" were stated only once in a brief but effective expression
(mm. 72-78). They are stressed a great deal more in the recapitulation (mm.
118-128), while the third imitative exposition (mm. 110-115) is strongly abbre-
viated. Now, after the fourth and most intensive imitative exposition, the "et lux
perpetua" is treated most spaciously. The first violins and flutes repeat over and
over the second bar of the b' theme (mm. 146-157) (Figure 5-33).

Figure 5-33 Mm. 146-158[1]

Mm. 146-171[1]: Under this the basses sing the words "et lux perpetua" on
a monotone (mm. 148-149), and thus supported, the whole choir recites the
whole phrase twice *(pianissimo)*. The voices and string basses start a stepwise
descent from measure 143 on:

C	B♭	A♭	G		G	F	E	E♭		D	D
143	144	145	146		151	152	153 154 155	156 157	158 159 160		161
"Dona eis Domine"			"et lux perpetua"		"et lux perpetua"	"luceat eis"		"et lux perpetua"	"luceat eis"		"luceat eis"
ff dim. p					*pp*				*p < ff > p* *V/g*		

The French horns in C double the descending bass progression at mm. 150-156
with long notes (g-f-e-e♭), and from mm. 156-159 the French horns in E-flat
sustain the e-flat. The dynamics rise in the voices to *forte* (dominant chord of g)
at m. 160, *decrescendo* immediately to *ppp* (m. 162), rising once more to *forte*
(m. 165), which is followed by *un poco riten., pp* (flutes and clarinets marked
dolce, assai ascend in eights and descend again, mm. 169-171[1]). The prayer for
light eternal is dimmed and shines on the far horizon until it fades into the
prayer for mercy.

In Graph 5-12 we analyze the Kyrie Eleison-Christe Eleison.

GRAPH 5-12 Coda: Kyrie Eleison—Christe Eleison; mm. 171—209

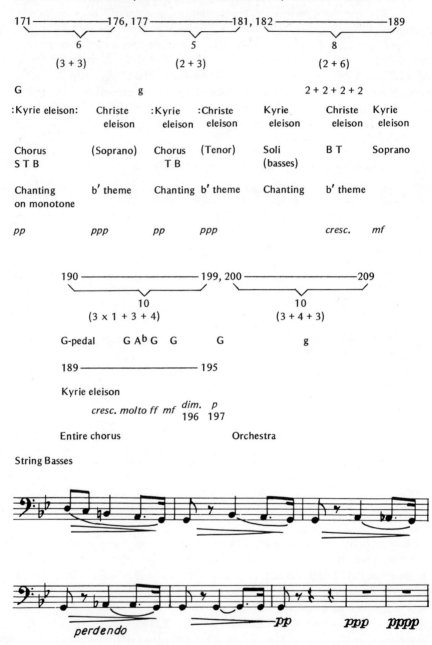

(Mm. 202—209)

Conclusion and Exercise

Mozart and Berlioz chose extraordinary orchestrations for their *Requiem* compositions. Mozart's *Requiem* is written in a quasi-Baroque style which was considered "archaic" in his time, while Berlioz employs unusually large choral and orchestral forces. Mozart felt compelled to use his particular orchestration to emphasize the liturgical quality of the text [he had already composed previously in the first movement of his mass fragment in c minor (K. 427) in this then outmoded, contrapuntal style]. Berlioz was intrigued by the Latin text of the *Requiem* because it lent itself to the new sonority effects for which he was seeking an outlet.

Here are some of the different stylistic trends observed in the Introit movements of the two *Requiem* compositions:

Mozart	Berlioz
Terraced dynamics *piano-forte*	Transitional dynamics *poco cresc.* to *cresc. molto;* agogic *sforzati*
Restrained range of dynamics	Extreme dynamic range
For his time, archaic (Baroque) tendencies: basso continuo, trumpet-tympani punctuations, *colla parte* trombones	For his time, bold progressive tendencies: Basso continuo abandoned, romantic coloristic orchestration of special skill and originality
Linear polyphony simultaneous with harmonic accompaniment of homophonic nature	Polyphony penetrated by vertical (harmonic) element

Both have in common the alternation of polyphonic and homophonic sections.

Chamber proportions of form and orchestration (18-20 strings, 4 low woodwinds, 2 trumpets and timpani, basso continuo)	Huge numbers of singers and instruments (Introit: 20 woodwinds, 12 French horns, 108 strings—25:25:20:18; 210 singers—80SS, 60TT, 70BB)
Concise structure	Expansive structure

Structural Memorization Graph

1. The memorization chart (Graph 5-13) is identical to Graph 5-5 but indicates nothing more than the mere bar numbers of the overall form.
2. The student of the score should mentally supply the information of Graph 5-5 concerning the overall form.

GRAPH 5-13 Structural Memorization graph

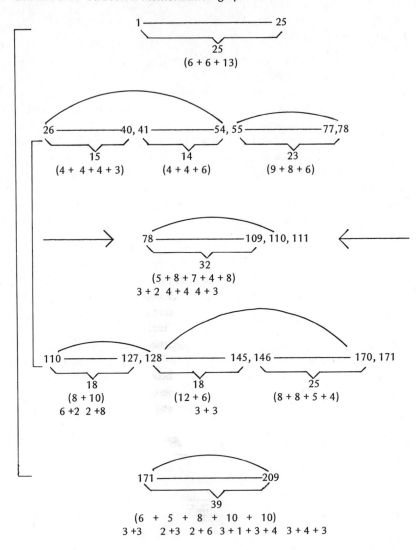

3. He should then fill in the more detailed information section by section:
    a. Introduction (described on pp.198-199).
    b. Comparative detailed study of the four imitative expositions: mm. 26-41[1] equal mm. 110-128[1] and mm. 55-78[1] equal mm. 128-171[1]. This study should encompass the following: time distances and pitches of the entrances of the first theme; time distances and pitches of the entrances of the contrapuntal theme; relationships

of time distances and pitches of both themes to each other; the *quasi ostinato* theme (b'); and other items such as displaced meter (polymeter), keys, cadences, dynamics, instrumental doublings, and text.

c. The homophonic sections: transitions from polyphonic to homophonic sections or separations; texture (choral, orchestral); dynamics; text (word and phrase repetitions).
d. Introduction and coda or the outer sections (beginning and end).
e. The middle section (center).
f. The relative proportions of these sections and their relationships to each other (contrast and similarity).

The "form in motion," the musical logic by which the form unfolds or generates from beginning to end, is of ultimate importance. To sense the function or purpose of each section, subsection, each element, and each detail within the form as a whole is the highest aim of our studies. It must be understood that the introduction prepares (the plot has not yet started), that the highly polyphonic sections are climactic moments of action, the homophonic lyrical sections are moments of relaxed action, the middle section is the axis, and the coda is the exit (Figure 5-34).

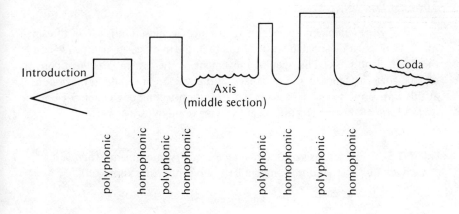

Figure 5-34 The architectural blueprint

The tempo is even throughout but changes quality: there is the time of no action, the time of great action, and the time of relaxed action; there is the slowly flowing center section and the two corresponding large subsections to the left and right of the center (sonata exposition and sonata recapitulation). There is finally the fading of energy into silence, the coda.

BRAHMS: *EIN DEUTSCHES REQUIEM,* OPUS 45 (1868): FIRST MOVEMENT

At the time of composing their *Requiems,* Mozart was thirty-five years old (1791), Berlioz thirty-four (1837), and Brahms thirty-five (1868). Mozart at the age of thirty-five had reached an almost ageless maturity, Berlioz at thirty-four was a youthful and, indeed, a highly gifted eccentric. Brahms at thirty-five was an ardently searching soul, with his final aim as a composer not yet in sight; a devout disciple of Beethoven, he had in his own judgment not yet reached the stage of maturity to fill the large form (symphony and string quartet) with meaning. His first string quartets (Op. 51, 1-2) were not completed until 1873, his first symphony (Op. 68) not before 1876. The *German Requiem* was his first and remained his only choral-orchestral composition of oratorio size. It received its final form of seven movements after approximately ten years of sporadic concentration on its composition. In the year 1866, the year of Brahms's greatest concentration on the composition of the *Requiem,* six movements were completed and performed as an entity. The present fifth movement was added for a subsequent performance in 1868.

The First *Lied* Idea

As with Schumann and Chopin, Brahms's genius flourished in the small form. Their most personal ideas came to life in the microcosm of the *Lied* and in the short piano piece. The opening movement of the Brahms *Requiem* consists of *Lied* ideas juxtaposed and organized in the fashion of sonata form. Brahms is at this time a master of expansion and transition techniques. Graph 5-14 of the overall form of the opening movement will make this clear.

GRAPH 5-14 An Analysis of Brahms *Requiem*: first movement* (*ziemlich langsam und mit Ausdruck*—moderately slow and with expression)

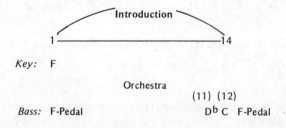

Key: F

Orchestra

(11) (12)

Bass: F-Pedal   D♭ C   F-Pedal

*Refer to Edition Eulenburg, *Ein deutsches Requiem*-Johannes Brahms, Opus 45. The English text by R. H. Benson, copyright C. F. Peters Corp., New York, London.

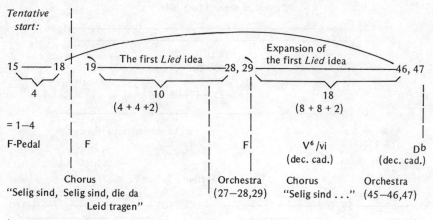

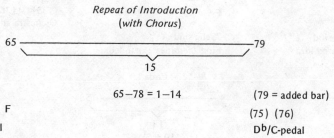

Tentative
start:

15 ———— 18 | 19 — The first *Lied* idea — 28, 29 — Expansion of the first *Lied* idea — 46, 47

4 | 10 (4 + 4 +2) | 18 (8 + 8 + 2)

= 1–4

F-Pedal | F | F | V^6/vi (dec. cad.) | D^b (dec. cad.)

Chorus | Orchestra (27–28,29) | Chorus "Selig sind ..." | Orchestra (45–46,47)
"Selig sind, Selig sind, die da Leid tragen"

(New Testament: Matt. 5:4)

The second *Lied* idea

47 ———————— 64, 65

18 (8 + 8 + 2)

D^b | D^b to F

"Die mit Tränen säen, werden mit Freuden ernten" | Orchestra

(Old Testament: Psalm 126:5)

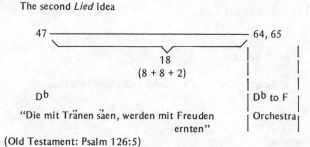

Repeat of Introduction
(*with Chorus*)

65 ——————————— 79

15

65–78 = 1–14 | (79 = added bar)

F | (75) (76)

Bass: F-pedal | D^b/C-pedal

"Sie gehen hin und weinen"
(First line of Ps. 126:6)

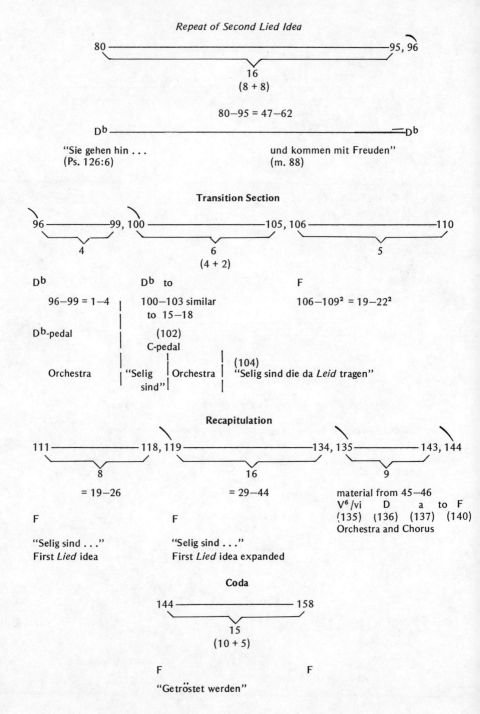

Repeat of Second Lied Idea

80 ———————————————————————— 95, 96

16
(8 + 8)

80–95 = 47–62

D♭ ———————————————————————— D♭

"Sie gehen hin . . .   und kommen mit Freuden"
(Ps. 126:6)   (m. 88)

Transition Section

96 ——— 99, 100 ——————— 105, 106 ——————— 110

4   6   5
(4 + 2)

D♭   D♭ to   F

96–99 = 1–4   100–103 similar $106-109^2 = 19-22^2$
               to 15–18

D♭-pedal   (102)
                 C-pedal

Orchestra   "Selig Orchestra   (104)
               sind"   "Selig sind die da *Leid* tragen"

Recapitulation

111 ——————— 118, 119 ——————————— 134, 135 ——————— 143, 144

8   16   9

= 19–26   = 29–44   material from 45–46
                               V^6/vi   D   a to F
F   F   (135) (136) (137) (140)
                                Orchestra and Chorus

"Selig sind . . ."   "Selig sind . . ."
First *Lied* idea   First *Lied* idea expanded

Coda

144 ——————— 158

15
(10 + 5)

F   F
"Getröstet werden"

Structural Skeleton of Introduction
(Figure 5-35)

Figure 5-35 Mm. 1-15[1]

The introduction announces, indeed, a dark, very "Brahmsian" F major quality in timbre (orchestration), and in harmonic content cello II, cello I, viola II, and viola I enter with chromatically descending lines at the intervals of the fifth and fourth (mm. 2, 3, 5, and 7) (Figure 5-36). The harmony flattens in mm. 1-11 gradually to a G-flat six-four chord (Figure 5-36) anticipating the harmonic timbre of the secondary key of D-flat major which appears at m. 47

Figure 5-36

("second theme"). The G-flat six-four chord is heard in the context of these introductory bars as a Neapolitan six-four chord followed at m. 12 by an F major six-four chord. The strings then descend further and resolve at m. 15 with the F major tonic.

Exposition

Mm. 15-29[1]: The chorus enters at m. 15, intoning the first words of Matthew 5:4 ("selig sind"). The bars 15-18 repeat mm. 1-4, but above the harmonic progression of mm. 15-17[1] (alias 1-3[1]) the sopranos sing the first three tones of the first *Lied* melody. This tentative entrance of the chorus spreads a consoling light upon the darkness which has prevailed so far. The measures 15-16 (alias 1-2) are sung *a cappella* by the chorus, while at mm. 17-18 (a literal instrumental repeat of mm. 3-4) violas are added. The entire first *Lied* idea (mm. 19-29[1]) is sung by the chorus *a cappella* except for the first horn which sounds tenderly into the beginning of the *a cappella* sonority (at mm. 19-20) (Figure 5-37).

Figure 5-37 First two notes of the *Lied*

The first half-period of the *Lied* ends in the sopranos at m. 22 but the three lower voices continue and end the half-period with an a-minor chord (mediant of F major) at m. 23[2] (Figure 5-38). The sopranos start the second half-period on the second beat of m. 23, singing into the ending a minor chord of the three lower voices. The chord progression at mm. 21[3]-23[2] has a modal (Aeolian) flavor (Figure 5-39). The whole period ends at m. 27[1]. The instruments repeat the whole close in F major, the two violas in *Stimmtausch* (interchange of voices) and partial augmentation. (Mm. 27-29[1]: Vla. I = Alto; Vla. II = Soprano; Vc I = Tenor; Vc. II, III and Cb. = Bass.)

Figure 5-38

Figure 5-39

Mm. 29-47[1]: An expanded version of the *Lied* melody follows. The eight bars of the original version (19-27[1]) are expanded to sixteen bars (29-45[1]). The first half-period is now eight bars long (29-37[1]). The sopranos start the melody with a descending minor sixth,

a pitch inversion of the rising major third

with which the sopranos began the original version (m. 19). Following this, the orchestra answers the chorus antiphonally (mm. 30 and 32), flutes, horns, and trombones join the chorus (m. 34), and the latter instruments sound here for the first time (on the word *"Leid"*). Chorus and orchestra conclude the first half-period together, ending (m. 37^1) on a deceptive cadence (V^6 of d minor). The second half-period is also expanded to eight bars ($37-45^1$). The oboes begin the melody; violas and celli I and II accompany with an animated eighth-note pulse. The chorus repeats the oboe melody, and at the height (mm. $41-42^1$) the pulse intensifies to eighth-note triplets. The expanded *Lied* version concludes like the original version with an F major cadence (the voices at mm. 43-44 resemble the instrumental repeat at mm. 27-28), and the instruments repeat the last two bars (mm. 45-46), concluding with a deceptive cadence (on D-flat major, the Dorian sixth of F major). The key of D-flat major was prepared at m. 11, and the deceptive cadence at m. 37 has prepared the ear for the stronger deceptive cadence at m. 47, but the secondary key of the movement still sounds fresh and unexpected.

The Second *Lied* Idea

Mm. $47-63^2$: The second *Lied,* based on an Old Testament text (Psalm 126:5) is sufficiently contrasted to the first *Lied* by key relation (major third down) and through a new orchestration (at least two harps enter m. 48) and choral texture. The melody wanders from voice to voice (Figure 5-40).

Figure 5-40 Mm. 47-55.

Brahms, an ardent Bach student, uses here the Bachian "sigh-motive" (Figure 5-41) to pictorialize *Tränen.* The string basses have an inversion (Figure 5-42).

Figure 5-41

Figure 5-42 Mm. 48 and 50

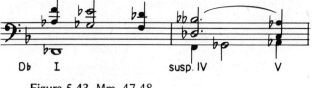

Figure 5-43 Mm. 47-48

The chord progression at mm. 47-48 is shown in Figure 5-43. The bar grouping is as symmetrical as in the first *Lied*:

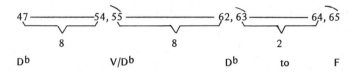

Measure 55 is a pivot bar where the half-close (ending the first half-period) falls together with the strong downbeat at the beginning of the second half-period in the tenors (Figure 5-44).

wer— den mit Freu -

Figure 5-44

Sopranos, basses, and altos imitate at half-bar distances. These downbeat impulses initiate the joyful passage. The English translation* changes these strongly entering impulses to upbeats (Figure 5-45). This is a regrettable distortion of the composer's intention.

Ten.: shall   reap, shall_ reap_

Figure 5-45 Tenors

Repeat of Introduction

Mm. 65-79 (mm. 65-78 = 1-14): The introduction (mm. 1-14) is repeated. The voices sing into the originally instrumental introduction the first line of Psalm 126, verse 6: "Sie gehen hin und weinen." The introduction repeated

---

A German Requiem (New York: G. Schirmer, n.d.). Piano-vocal score.

takes on the meaning of a procession of mourners. Measure 79 is added, sounding like a fermata on C preparing the deceptive cadence of D-flat major (Figure 5-46).

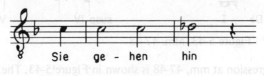

Sie   ge - hen   hin

Figure 5-46 Mm. 78^4-80^2

Repeat of Second *Lied* Idea

Mm. 80-95, 96 (= 47-62, 63): There follows a repeat of the second *Lied* idea. The first half-period (to m. 88^2) is now based on the first two lines of Psalm 126:6. The second half-period (mm. 88-95) is on the third and fourth lines of verse 6.* The student of the score must pay particular attention to the subtle changes in repeated sections by comparing them with their first appearances—for instance, bars 73-76 (alias 9-12) with the soprano *melisma* on "weinen" doubled by flutes and oboes. The variants in mm. $80-96^2$ (especially 80-87) compared to $47-64^2$ (respectively 47-54) are particularly interesting.

Transition Section

Mm. 96-100: The piece begins for the third time, bars 96-99 equal mm. 1-4 of the introduction, bars 100-103 are analogous to mm. 15-18, and bars 104-105 are inserted. The secondary key of D-flat major is preserved to m. 100, the modulation to F major starts at m. 101. Bars 106-109 are a quotation of the first phrase of the first *Lied* (mm. 19-22) but in the new sonority; flutes—with the theme in the first flute and the altos supported by the first horn providing the "bass," leave no doubt that this is still a tentative preparation for the recapitulation which follows at m. 111. The tenors at mm. $109-111^1$ are extending the preparation.

Recapitulation (mm. 111-144)

Mm. $111-135^1$: Bars $111-119^1$ recapitulate mm. $19-27^1$ (note the orchestral support at mm. 115-118). Bars 27-28 are here omitted. The expanded *Lied* version is repeated in mm. $119-127^2$ (= $29-37^2$) with some alterations as the exchange of roles of chorus and orchestra (mm. 119-123). The second half-period is recapitulated literally in mm. 127-134 (= 37-44). The instrumental repeat of the last two bars in mm. 45-46 of the exposition is again omitted. On

*The text here is: "und kommen mit Freuden und bringen ihre Garben." It should be noted that Brahms eliminates the "und" at the tenor entrance (downbeat of m. 88) to preserve the downbeat impulse.

the downbeat of m. 135 reoccurs the deceptive cadence V⁶ of VI. The composer does not recapitulate the "second theme" (which he had already repeated in mm. 80-95).

Mm. 135-144¹: An ingenious orchestral transition to the Coda follows. The V⁶ to VI chord is now leading to D major (m. 136), which, in the light of the a minor chord (m. 137), is heard as a major subdominant to a minor (IV-1/a). The motivic material is taken from mm. 27-28. The woodwinds sound it first (Figure 5-47). The strings repeat it *minore* (Figure 5-48). Notice the A-pedal in the horns (mm. 135-138³). At m. 138² starts a *stretto* imitation of this motive (Figure 5-49).

Figure 5-47 Mm. 136-137

Figure 5-48 Mm. 137-138

Figure 5-49 Mm. 138-142

Coda (mm. 144-158)

A relatively new thematic phrase appears first in the tenors in contrary motion to the ascending opening tones of the first *Lied** (Figure 5-50).

*The last movement begins with this phrase (soprano: mm. 2-4¹).

Figure 5-50   Mm. 144-150

The energy flares up once more to *forte* and then fades away. The sound disappears like a cloud on the horizon. The woodwind choir, the *pizzicato* strings, and the harps remain, the latter increasing the speed to triplets like a dying heartbeat.

THE FAURÉ *REQUIEM*, OPUS 48 (1886): INTROIT AND KYRIE

We conclude our chapter on structural score studies with a study of the opening movement of the Fauré *Requiem*. A direct line leads from the Fauré *Requiem* to Stravinsky's *Symphony of Psalms* (1930). The lucid craft and noble emotional uninvolvement of Fauré's music is more than superficially akin to the crystalline coolness and masterful skill of Stravinsky's. It is also the refreshing newness of Fauré's musical syntax (not yet of musical vocabulary) which in a way prepares Stravinsky's coining of a new, twentieth-century musical language.

No greater distance can be imagined than that between Fauré's daylight openness of texture, timbre, and form and Brahms's autumn mixtures behind which stands the struggle from desperation to hope and faith which draws the listener warmly and very personally into it. There is no "issue" behind Fauré's music; its only issue is music itself, *l'art pour l'art*, one might say, and, most assuredly, *Ars Gallica* versus *Ars Germanica*. There is also a great difference in kind between Berlioz's ambitious pomposity and Fauré's unassuming simplicity and newness.

Fauré had received his early musical education in the École Niedermeyer in Paris, which he attended from his tenth to his twentieth year of age (from 1855 to 1865). Here he learned Gregorian chant and twentieth-century polyphony. Of course, it was accompanied chant and *a cappella* vocal polyphony as the nineteenth-century understood or misunderstood it. Nevertheless, Fauré absorbed the spirit of chant and of modality, and it became an integral part of his own musical language. His *Requiem* is a noticeable example of it.

The composition of the *Requiem* falls at the threshhold of Fauré's second creative period, the time of his second piano quartet, op. 45, and the songs, op. 43. He lived and composed to 1924 (his last composition is his only string quartet in E minor, Op. 121). At this time Bartok had written his second string quartet (1917), his *Improvisations on Hungarian Folksongs* (Op. 20, 1920), and his *Dance Suite* for orchestra (1923). Schoenberg had fully established his twelve-tone method. It remains, of course, an open question whether, or to what extent, at the time of his last years the old master (in his late seventies) realized the new development in music. Since 1910 he had been rather handicapped through deafness; in his last years he was unable to hear music.

Graph 5-15 is an analysis of Fauré's *Requiem*.

GRAPH 5-15   An Analysis of the Fauré *Requiem**

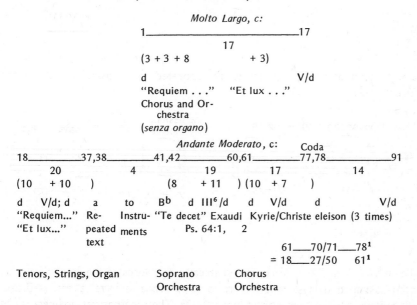

*This analysis is based on *Partitions d'orchestre de poche*, J. Hamelle, Editeur, Paris (J. 4650), USA © 1900; and on the vocal score, J. Hammelle, Editeur, Paris, H. T. Fitz-Simons, Chicago © 1944. There are numerous discrepancies between the two scores; the authenticity of either score is doubtful.

The *Molto Largo* (1-17) is a slow introduction (♩=40). The *Andante Moderato*, the main section of the movement, is almost twice as fast (♩=72). The music of the "Requiem aeternam" (18-27) is repeated on "Kyrie eleison" (61-70); the music of the "Exaudi orationem meam" (50-61') is repeated on "Christe eleison" (71-78').

Molto Largo

Mm. 1-17: The first seventeen bars are based on descending steps in the strings which move with extreme slowness (Figure 5-51).

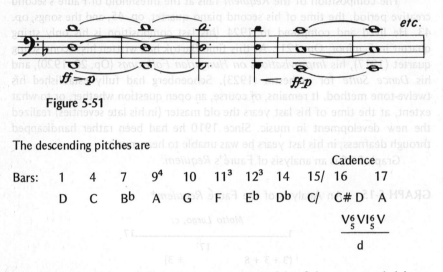

Figure 5-51

The descending pitches are

Bars:	1	4	7	9⁴	10	11³	12³	14	15/	16	17
	D	C	B♭	A	G	F	E♭	D♭	C/	C#D	A

Cadence

$$\text{V}^6_5 \text{ VI}^6_5 \text{ V}$$
d

The *ff* punctuations of the strings are supported by 2 bassoons and 4 horns (Figure 5-52).

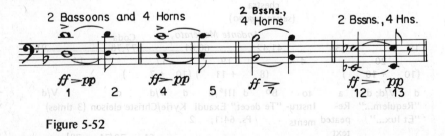

Figure 5-52

The chorus (S A T T B B) chants syllabically the words of the Introit over the softly sustained strings: (mm. 2-6 are to be *pp* rising to *forte* at mm. 7-10, and diminishing to *p, pp,* and *ppp* at mm. 11-17). The supernatural slowness is not unlike Stravinsky's *Symphony of Psalms* (Finale, rehearsal numbers 22 and 26.)

In the first six bars a touch of modality is felt (Figure 5-53).

Requiem   aeternam   dona eis   Domine
　2　　　　　3　　　　　4　　5　　　6

Figure 5-53

The tonal center throughout the movement is unmistakably "D," but the chords from m. 11 on scarcely fit into any kind of a d minor key or Dorian mode. The harmonic style is in its own way as fresh and new as that of Debussy's *La Damoiselle Elue* (1887-88). There is an angularity of harmony but also an ease with which chord progressions are far removed from the D tonality of the piece. The suspension B-flat in the strings speaks for the angularity or harshness, while the voices move on to the thirdless F chord (first two beats of m. 8). There is also the passing tone "A" in the strings underneath the empty E-flat chords (m. 9⁴), and the "G" sustained in the strings while the voices move to "C" in soprano and tenor and "A" in alto and bass (first and second beats of m. 11). The easy voice leading and singability gives a lightness and naturalness to the chords far removed from the D tonality (Figure 5-54).

Figure 5-54

Andante Moderato (mm. 18-91)

18 —————————————— 27, 28 ———————————————— 37, 38

10   10

18 —————— 23, 24 —————— 27, 28 ————31, 32 ———— 37, 38[1]

3 times 2   4   2 times 2   6   a
(= mm. 18-21)

d   d   to

"Requiem . . .   "Et lux   "Requiem . . . Domine"   "Et lux . . .
Domine"   luceat eis"   luceat eis"
                                                                (m. 35)

Instruments   Tenors   Instruments   Tenors
only   (m. 20)   only   (m. 30)

Strings and organ

Mm. 18-38[1]: The organ enters here (fonds de 8 p.); it mainly doubles the strings with a kind of written-out continuo realization. The strings have a two-part texture: viola I, II and cello I are in unison, cello II and contrabass are in octaves. The texture changes somewhat in m. 27 and mm. 28 and 29, the beginning of the "consequent" where the viola I plays the first two notes of the melody which were played by the top voice of the organ at mm. 18-19. At mm. 32-38[1] the first violas double the melody of the tenors. The orchestration is flexible and subtle. The choice of specific instrumental timbres and the exclusion of others (in the first movement there are no violins I, II, flutes, clarinets, brass, and tympani) anticipates in its own way Stravinsky's and Webern's varied instrumental palette. The separation and specific function of each sonority group is obvious from the very beginning of the movement where two bassoons and four horns support the dynamic punctuations of the descending line of the strings, and the chorus sings into the softly sustained sound of the strings.

Mm. 38[2]-41: If there is any doubt of Fauré's sensitivity for timbre, the instrumental transition shown in Figure 5-55 completely dispels such doubt. The sound of the trumpets is heard here for the first time: the first trumpet and the second horn carry the top melody in m. 38, and the trumpet alone takes it in m. 39 (Figure 5-55).

Figure 5-55

Mm. 40 and *41* prepare the timbre of the following section, and Vc. I, II are introduced in m. 41 to prepare the (*piano dolce espressando*) counter melody of the celli in the following bars.

Mm. 42-49:

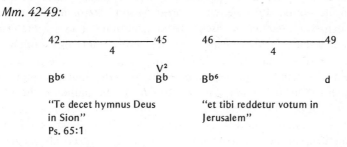

42————————45   46————————49
        4   4

                V²
Bb⁶   Bb   Bb⁶   d

"Te decet hymnus Deus   "et tibi reddetur votum in
in Sion"   Jerusalem"
Ps. 65:1

Mozart, Berlioz, Verdi, and other composers of the nineteenth century who cast the *Requiem* Introit into a quasi-sonata form base the middle section upon this psalm text and give to it contrasting musical materials. A slight change of texture, timbre, and expression may be felt at this point in Fauré's setting (the sopranos sing a new melody and the celli play the counter melody), but basically the pastoral tranquillity of the beginning of the *Andante Moderato* is continued. Even the trio setting is similar here and there (here: soprano melody, celli countermelody, both doubled by the organ, which adds as the third line a bass melody). A contrast occurs with the setting of the second psalm verse:

Mm. 50-61:

50 ——————53   54 ——————57   58——————60, 61
        4   4   3

III⁶   III⁶   d
d   D

"Exaudi orationem meam"   "ad te omnis caro veniet"   "omnis caro veniet"
Ps. 65:2

The dynamics are highly stylized:

Bars: 50   /   51   /   52   /   53
         "Exaudi,   exaudi,   orationem   meam"
         ff   >   p   <   ff   >   p

Bars: 54————————————————57   58————————————61¹
         "ad te omnis caro veniet"   "omnis caro veniet"
         ff   dim. p

The organ (*anches et fonds* from m. 49) doubles the chords sung by the chorus, the strings play a broken chord melody in large intervals—not unlike that of m. 18 and following—the bassoons double the celli, and the four horns fill in harmonically at mm. 51 and 53 (= piano bars), and at mm. 57-58.

The harmony is boldly widening the harmonic vocabulary of d minor; the tonic of d minor stands unmistakably at m. 49 and again at m. 61.

Mm. 61-78[1] : Mozart in his *Requiem* writes a mighty, independent double fugue on the words "Kyrie eleison" "Christe eleison"; Verdi devotes to this text a large expressive section by itself; Berlioz integrates it as a coda into the opening movement of his *Grande Messe des Morts*; Fauré does nothing of the sort. He repeats on the "Kyrie eleison" the music used before on the words "Requiem aeternam" at the beginning of the *Andante Moderato* (mm. 18-27), and on the "Christe eleison" he repeats freely the music of the "Exaudi orationem meam," the second psalm verse (mm. 50-61). These unusual procedures of recapitulating prevent any hint of sonata form. Fauré is not architecturally minded, but he is most capable of producing a masterfully proportioned form. With sonata form of the late nineteenth century one associates dramatic contrasts. Fauré's *Requiem* setting is epic and lyrical by nature. Just as the *fortissimi* are not dramatic outcries, so the form is not accumulative and contrasting but a kind of meaningful narration, and foremost, it is music well proportioned dynamically and structurally.

Coda (mm. 78-91)

$$78\underline{}85 \quad 86\underline{}91$$
$$8 \qquad\qquad\qquad 6$$

(2 times 4)

The Coda is like the music of the entire movement, linear and most singable. It is specifically of a linear chromaticism not heard before in this piece. The first celli and second violas begin a chromatically ascending line at measure 78 and the first violas follow a bar later. The prominent sound of this concluding section is that of the strings and the organ beneath the strings. Notice that the organ is marked *p al fine* in the last six bars, while the strings are marked *pp sempre al fine*. This marking may have something to do with the acoustics and the placement of the organ at the Église Madeleine, where the first performance of the *Requiem* took place, but it is also an indication that the organ sound should be softly present.

The chorus sings "eleison" three times in unison and *pp* into the string sound, doubling the notes of the first violas (mm. 81-82), then of the first celli (m. 85), and then holds the d for the last six bars. The horn (mm. 84-86) doubles the top voice of the organ, which in turn doubles the first celli and then sustains, together with the chorus, the d but is tacet for the last two and a half bars. Doublings like these which occur throughout the piece are indicative of the subtlety of orchestration, and they are, indeed, most effective at the close of this movement.

BOOKS AND OTHER MATERIALS
FOR THE CHORAL MUSICIAN:
A SELECTED LIST

James G. Smith

Although this bibliography includes a number of entries which are directly related to the foregoing essays, it is not intended simply as a list of supplementary reading materials. It is far more general than that, covering a wide range of literature concerned with the choral music repertoire and its performance. Some of the entries are basic and are, or should be, familiar to every choral musician; others are less well known but nonetheless valuable sources of information. The likelihood that members of the choral profession will find them useful, interesting, and stimulating has been the primary consideration governing their selection for inclusion in this list.

Some of the more specific criteria by which selections have been made are the following:

1. General historical studies have been included only if they are in large part devoted to choral music. Thus, for example, Reese's contributions to the

Norton series, because they deal with historical periods in which choral music was of primary importance, are included; Einstein's comparable study of the nineteenth century, which contains relatively little about choral music, is omitted.

2. Biographical works have been cited only if they provide substantial coverage of their subjects' choral music.

3. In general, recently published works have been preferred; invariably, however, this consideration has been subordinated to the more important one of quality.

4. Certain dated but important works on choral music (e.g., Coward's *Choral Technique and Interpretation*) have been included precisely because they are dated and important and, therefore, of historical interest.

5. Sixteenth-, seventeenth-, and eighteenth-century sources have not been included; they are treated in Donington's *Interpretation of Early Music* and can be located with reference to the bibliography found there.

6. Certain items have been included because their subject matter is of widespread current interest. Thus, for example, the Cowells' book on Ives, though it does not meet the stated requirement for biographical studies, is included.

7. Some journal articles and dissertations appear in this list simply because they are representative of the present state and trends of such endeavors; others of equal merit could have been cited, but there has not been sufficient space for all of them.

8. Potential usefulness, rather than specific orientation, has determined the selection of technical manuals (on conducting, singing, pronunciation, etc.). In some cases (Marshall's *Manual of English Diction* is an example), this has resulted in the inclusion of publications which are not specifically concerned with choral music.

9. Although works in English have been favored, those in other languages which are unique sources of valuable information have not been excluded.

One other factor has played a major role in determining the composition of this bibliography. Whenever possible, works have been cited which are themselves substantial sources of bibliographic information. In accordance with this consideration, the final section below is devoted entirely to reference· materials: dictionaries, catalogues, lists, bibliographies, and indices. Selection of the periodicals which are cited has also been influenced by the reviews and lists of choral music and of books about choral music which they frequently contain. Books and articles, too, have been chosen for inclusion with a view to their potential bibliographic usefulness as well as to their intrinsic merit as basic sources of information.

This bibliography is, therefore, a two-directional instrument. It lists important works drawn from the literature concerned with choral music; it is also, by virtue of the bibliographic information contained in the cited works, a reference key to that extensive body of literature from which it has been drawn.

The bibliography is divided into five sections: (1) books, (2) periodicals, (3) periodical articles, (4) miscellanea—that is, articles in yearbooks and *Festschriften*, pamphlets, dissertations, and so on, and (5) reference materials.

BOOKS

Abraham, Gerald, ed. *Handel: A Symposium*. London: Oxford University Press, 1954.

Abraham, Gerald, ed. *The New Oxford History of Music*, Vol. IV: *The Age of Humanism, 1540-1630*. London: Oxford University Press, 1968.

Ades, Hawley. *Choral Arranging*. Delaware Water Gap, Pa.: Shawnee Press, 1966.

Adler, Kurt. *Phonetics and Diction in Singing: Italian, French, Spanish, German*. Minneapolis, Minn.: University of Minnesota Press, 1967.

Apel, Willi. *Gregorian Chant*. Bloomington, Ind.: Indiana University Press, 1958.

Apel, Willi. *The Notation of Polyphonic Music, 900-1600*. Fifth edition, revised and with commentary. Cambridge, Mass.: Mediaeval Academy of America, 1953.

Arnold, Denis, and Fortune, Nigel, eds. *The Monteverdi Companion*. New York: W. W. Norton, 1972.

Arnold, Franck Thomas. *The Art of Accompaniment from a Thorough-Bass*. 2 volumes. New York: Dover Publications, 1965.

Austin, William W. *Music in the Twentieth Century from Debussy through Stravinsky*. New York: W. W. Norton, 1966.

Bamberger, Carl, ed. *The Conductor's Art*. New York: McGraw-Hill, 1965.

Bergmann, Leola Nelson. *Music Master of the Middle West: The Story of F. Melius Christiansen and the St. Olaf Choir*. New York: Da Capo Press, 1968.

Blume, Friedrich. *Geschichte der evangelischen Kirchenmusik*. Second revised edition, edited in collaboration with Ludwig Finscher et al. Kassel: Bärenreiter, 1965.

Blume, Friedrich. *Renaissance and Baroque Music: A Comprehensive Survey*. Translated by M. D. Herter Norton. New York: W. W. Norton, 1967.

Blume, Friedrich. *Two Centuries of Bach: An Account of Changing Taste*. Translated by Stanley Godman. London: Oxford University Press, 1950.

Boult, Adrian Cedric. *A Handbook on the Technique of Conducting*. New edition. Oxford: Hall, 1943.

Boult, Adrian Cedric, and Emery, Walter. *The St. Matthew Passion: Its Preparation and Performance*. London: Novello, 1949.

Bukofzer, Manfred F. *Music in the Baroque Era*. New York: W. W. Norton, 1947.

Chase, Gilbert. *America's Music from the Pilgrims to the Present*. Revised second edition. New York: McGraw-Hill, 1966.

Coward, Henry. *Choral Technique and Interpretation*. London: Novello, [1914].

Cowell, Henry, and Cowell, Sidney. *Charles Ives and His Music*. New York: Oxford University Press, 1955.

Daniel, Ralph T. *The Anthem in New England before 1800*. Evanston, Ill.: Northwestern University Press, 1966.

Dart, Thurston. *The Interpretation of Music*. Harper Colophon Books. New York: Harper & Row, 1963.

Davison, Archibald T. *Choral Conducting*. Cambridge, Mass.: Harvard University Press, 1940.

Davison, Archibald T. *Church Music: Illusion and Reality*. Cambridge, Mass.: Harvard University Press, 1952.

Davison, Archibald T. *The Technique of Choral Composition*. Cambridge, Mass.: Harvard University Press, 1945.

Dean, Winton. *Handel's Dramatic Oratorios and Masques*. London: Oxford University Press, 1959.

Deutsch, Otto Erich. *Handel: A Documentary Biography*. London: Adam and Charles Black, 1955.

Dikenmann-Balmer, Lucie. *Beethoven's Missa Solemnis und ihre geistigen Grundlagen*. Zurich: Atlantis, 1952.

Dix, Gregory. *The Shape of the Liturgy*. Second edition. London: Dacre Press, 1945.

Dolmetsch, Arnold. *The Interpretation of the Music of the XVII and XVIII Centuries Revealed by Contemporary Evidence*. [New edition.] London: Novello, 1946.

Donington, Robert. *The Interpretation of Early Music*. [Second edition.] London: Faber and Faber, 1963.

Dorian, Frederick. *The History of Music in Performance: The Art of Musical Interpretation from the Renaissance to Our Day*. New York: W. W. Norton, 1966.

Drinker, Sophie. *Brahms and His Women's Choruses*. Merion, Pa., 1952. Privately published.

Ehmann, Wilhelm. *Choral Directing*. Translated by George D. Wiebe. Minneapolis, Minn.: Augsburg, 1968.

Einstein, Alfred. *The Italian Madrigal*. Translated by Alexander H. Krappe, Roger H. Sessions, and Oliver Strunk. 3 volumes. Princeton, N. J.: Princeton University Press, 1949.

Ellinwood, Leonard. *The History of American Church Music*. New York: Morehouse-Gorham, 1953.

Emery, Walter. *Editions and Musicians: A Survey of the Duties of Practical Musicians and Editors Towards the Classics*. London: Novello, 1957.

Essays on Music in Honor of Archibald Thompson Davison by His Associates. Cambridge, Mass.: Harvard University, Department of Music, 1957.

Fellerer, Karl Gustav. *The History of Catholic Church Music*. Translated by Francis A. Brunner. Baltimore: Helicon Press, 1961.

Fellerer, Karl Gustav. *Der Palestrinastil und seine Bedeutung in der vokalen*

Kirchenmusik des achzehnten Jahrhunderts. Augsburg: B. Filser, 1929.

Fellowes, Edmund Horace. *English Cathedral Music from Edward VI to Edward VII*. Fourth edition. London: Methuen, 1948.

Fellowes, Edmund Horace. *The English Madrigal Composers*. Second edition. London: Oxford University Press, 1948.

Fields, Victor Alexander. *Training the Singing Voice: An Analysis of the Working Concepts Contained in Recent Contributions to Vocal Pedagogy*. Morningside Heights, N. Y.: King's Crown Press, 1947.

Finn, William J. *The Art of the Choral Conductor*. Boston: C. C. Birchard, 1940.

Finn, William J. *The Conductor Raises His Baton*. New York: Harper and Brothers, 1944.

Friedrich, Annette. *Beiträge zur Geschichte des weltlichen Frauenchores im 19. Jahrhundert in Deutschland*. Regensburg: Gustav Bosse, 1961.

Fuhr, Hayes M. *Fundamentals of Choral Expression*. Lincoln, Nebr.: University of Nebraska Press, 1944.

Gajard, Joseph. *The Rhythm of Plainsong According to the Solesmes School*. Translated by Aldhelm Dean. New York: J. Fischer, 1945.

Geiringer, Karl. *The Bach Family: Seven Generations of Creative Genius*. London: George Allen & Unwin, 1954.

Geiringer, Karl. *Haydn: A Creative Life in Music*. Second edition, revised and enlarged. Berkeley, Calif.: University of California Press, 1968.

Geiringer, Karl. *Johann Sebastian Bach: The Culmination of an Era*. New York: Oxford University Press, 1966.

Green, Elizabeth. *The Modern Conductor*. Englewood Cliffs, N. J.: Prentice-Hall, 1961.

Haas, Robert. *Aufführungspraxis der Musik*. Potsdam: Akademische Verlagsgesellschaft Athenaion, 1931.

Hines, Robert Stephan, ed. *The Composer's Point of View: Essays on Twentieth-Century Choral Music by Those Who Wrote It*. Norman, Okla.: University of Oklahoma Press, 1964.

Howerton, George. *Technique and Style in Choral Singing*. New York: Carl Fischer, 1957.

Hughes, Anselm, ed. *The New Oxford History of Music*, Vol. II: *Early Medieval Music up to 1300*. London: Oxford University Press, 1954.

Hughes, Anselm, and Abraham, Gerald, eds. *The New Oxford History of Music*, Vol. III: *Ars Nova and the Renaissance, 1300-1540*. London: Oxford University Press, 1960.

Hume, Paul. *Catholic Church Music*. New York: Dodd, Mead & Company, 1957.

Hutchings, Arthur. *Church Music in the Nineteenth Century*. London: Herbert Jenkins, 1967.

Jacobs, Arthur, ed. *Choral Music: A Symposium*. Baltimore: Penguin Books, 1963.

Keller, Herman. *Phrasing and Articulation: A Contribution to a Rhetoric of Music*. Translated by Leigh Gerdine. New York: W. W. Norton, 1965.

Kennedy, Michael. *The Works of Ralph Vaughan Williams*. London: Oxford University Press, 1964.

Kerman, Joseph. *The Elizabethan Madrigal: A Comparative Study*. New York: American Musicological Society, 1962.

Klein, Joseph J. *Singing Technique: How to Avoid Vocal Trouble*. Princeton, N. J.: D. Van Nostrand, 1967.

Kross, Siegfried. *Die Chorwerke von Johannes Brahms*. Berlin: Max Hesse, 1958.

Lang, Paul Henry. *George Frideric Handel*. New York: W. W. Norton, 1966.

Larsen, Jens Peter. *Handel's Messiah: Origins, Composition, Sources*. London: Adam and Charles Black, 1957.

LaRue, Jan, ed. *Aspects of Medieval and Renaissance Music: A Birthday Offering to Gustave Reese*. New York: W. W. Norton, 1966.

Lawson, James Terry. *Full-Throated Ease: A Concise Guide to Easy Singing*. Vancouver: Western Music Co., 1955.

La Huray, Peter. *Music and the Reformation in England, 1549-1660*. London: Herbert Jenkins, 1967.

McElheran, Brock. *Conducting Technique for Beginners and Professionals*. New York: Oxford University Press, 1966.

Marshall, Madeleine. *The Singer's Manual of English Diction*. New York: G. Schirmer, 1953.

Mellers, Wilfrid. *Music and Society*. 2nd ed. New York: Roy Publishers, 1950.

Moe, Daniel. *Basic Choral Concepts*. Minneapolis, Minn.: Augsburg, 1972.

Moe, Daniel. *Problems in Conducting*. Minneapolis, Minn.: Augsburg, 1968.

Moser, Hans Joachim. *Heinrich Schütz: His Life and Work*. Translated by Carl F. Pfatteicher. St. Louis: Concordia, 1959.

Newlin, Dika. *Bruckner, Mahler, Schoenberg*. Morningside Heights, N. Y.: King's Crown Press, 1947.

Palmer, Larry. *Hugo Distler and His Church Music*. St. Louis: Concordia, 1967.

Parrish, Carl. *The Notation of Medieval Music*. New York: W. W. Norton, 1959.

Pfautsch, Lloyd. *English Diction for the Singer*. New York: Lawson-Gould/G. Schirmer, 1971.

Pfautsch, Lloyd. *Mental Warmups for the Choral Conductor*. New York: Lawson-Gould/G. Schirmer, 1969.

Reese, Gustave. *Music in the Middle Ages*. New York: W. W. Norton, 1940.

Reese, Gustave. *Music in the Renaissance*. Revised edition. New York: W. W. Norton, 1959.

Robertson, Alec. *Requiem: Music of Mourning and Consolation*. New York: Praeger, 1967.

Routley, Erik. *The Church and Music*. London: Gerald Duckworth, 1967.

Routley, Erik. *Twentieth Century Church Music*. London: Herbert Jenkins, 1964.

Sachs, Curt. *Rhythm and Tempo: A Study in Music History*. New York: W. W. Norton, 1953.

Salzman, Eric. *Twentieth-Century Music: An Introduction*. Englewood Cliffs, N. J.: Prentice-Hall, 1967.

Scherchen, Hermann. *Handbook of Conducting*. Translated by M. D. Calvo-coressi. London: Oxford University Press, 1933.

Scott, Charles Kennedy. *Madrigal Singing*. London: Oxford University Press, 1931.

Shaw, Watkins. *A Textual and Historical Companion to Handel's "Messiah."* London: Novello, 1965.

Smallman, Basil. *The Background of Passion Music: J. S. Bach and His Predecessors*. London: S. C. M. Press, 1957.

Stevens, Denis. *Tudor Church Music*. Second edition. London: Faber and Faber, 1966.

Stevenson, Robert. *Protestant Church Music in America*. New York: W. W. Norton, 1966.

Strunk, Oliver. *Source Readings in Music History from Classical Antiquity through the Romantic Era*. New York: W. W. Norton, 1950.

Suñol, Gregory. *Text Book of Gregorian Chant According to the Solesmes Method*. Translated from the sixth French edition with an introduction by G. M. Durnford. Tournai: Desclée, 1930.

Terry, Charles Sanford. *Bach: The Mass in B Minor*. Second edition. London: Oxford University Press, 1958.

Tovey, Donald Francis. *Essays in Musical Analysis*, Vol. V: *Vocal Music*. London: Oxford University Press, 1956.

Vennard, William. *Singing: The Mechanism and the Technic*. Revised edition, greatly enlarged. New York: Carl Fischer, 1967.

Waite, William G. *The Rhythm of Twelfth-Century Polyphony: Its Theory and Practice*. New Haven, Conn.: Yale University Press, 1954.

Werner, Eric. *In the Choir Loft: A Manual For Organists and Choir Directors in American Synagogues*. New York: Union of American Hebrew Congregations, 1957.

Werner, Eric. *Mendelssohn: A New Image of the Composer and His Age*. Translated by Dika Newlin. New York: Free Press of Glencoe, 1963.

Werner, Eric. *The Sacred Bridge: The Interdependence of Liturgy and Music in Synagogue and Church during the First Millenium*. New York: Columbia University Press, 1959.

Werner, Jack. *Mendelssohn's "Elijah": A Historical and Analytical Guide to the Oratorio*. London: Chappell, 1965.

Whittaker, W. Gillies. *The Cantatas of Johann Sebastian Bach*. 2 volumes. London: Oxford University Press, 1959.

Wienandt, Elwyn A. *Choral Music of the Church*. New York: Free Press, 1965.

Wilcox, John C. *The Living Voice: A Study Guide for Song and Speech*. Revised edition. New York: Carl Fischer, 1945.

Young, Percy M. *The Choral Tradition*. New York: W. W. Norton, 1971.

Zimmerman, Franklin B. *Henry Purcell, 1659-1695: His Life and Times*. London: Macmillan, 1967.

PERIODICALS

American Choral Review [Volumes I-III titled: *Bulletin of the American Choral Foundation*]. New York: American Choral Foundation, 1958- .

The Amor Artis Bulletin. New York: Amor Artis, 1962- .

The Choral Journal. Tampa: American Choral Directors Association, 1959- .

Church Music. St. Louis: Concordia, 1968- .

Journal of the American Musicological Society. Richmond, Va.: American Musicological Society, 1948- .

Memo, Nos. 1- . New York: American Choral Foundation, 1959- .

Music and Letters. London: Oxford University Press, 1920- .

Music Library Association Notes: A Magazine Devoted to Music and Its Literature. Washington: Music Library Association, 1943- .

The Musical Quarterly. New York: G. Schirmer, 1915- .

The Musical Times. London: Novello, 1844- .

Musik und Kirche. Kassel: Bärenreiter, 1929- .

Sacred Music [prior to 1965, titled: *Caecilia*]. Latrobe, Pa.: Church Music Association of America, 1874- .

ARTICLES

Adler, Samuel H. "Music in the American Synagogue." *American Choral Review*, VI (April, 1964), 7-9 and (July, 1964), 3-6.

Baker, Helen A. "Arthur Honegger and 'King David'." *Amor Artis Bulletin*, VII (January, 1968), 1-2 + 10-12.

Ballard, William. "Toward a More Artistic Performance of the Madrigal." *Bulletin of the American Choral Foundation*, III (March, 1961), 7-10.

Barbour, J. Murray. "Billings and the Barline." *American Choral Review*, V (January, 1963), 1-5.

Berger, Jean. "Interpretation of Twentieth Century Choral Music." *Choral Journal*, VII (March-April, 1967), 15-17.

Berger, Jean. "Our Choral Heritage." *Choral Journal*, II (May, 1962), 18-20.

Brewer, Richard H. "The Polychoral Style of Michael Praetorius." *Choral Journal*, VIII (March-April, 1968), 15-21.

Bright, Houston. "The Composer Looks at the Choral Director." *Choral Journal*, VII (January-February, 1967), 24-25.

Brindle, Reginald Smith. "La tecnica corale di Luigi Dallapiccola." *Quaderni della Rassegna musicale*, II (1965), 47-58.

Cambon, Elise. "Sacred Music by Francis Poulenc." *American Guild of Organists Quarterly*, VIII (October, 1963), 123-28 + 142-45 + 152.

Camillucci, G. "Appunti per un corso di direzione di coro." *Musica Sacra*, XCI (July-September, 1967), 82-91, and (October-December, 1967), 140-58.

Christman, Bernard E. "The Placement of the Choir in Modern Catholic Church Architecture." *Sacred Music*, XCV (Spring, 1968), 5-19.

Clark, J. Bunker. "The A Cappella Myth!" *Choral Journal*, IX (January-February, 1969), 29-31.

Commanday, Robert Paul. "Repertory for Men's Choruses: Renaissance Music." *American Choral Review*, V (October, 1962), 1-3.

Copley, I. A. "Peter Warlock's Choral Music." *Music and Letters*, XLV (October, 1964), 318-36.

Cudworth, Charles. "George Frideric Handel's *Theodora*." *Amor Artis Bulletin*, III (November, 1963), 1-2 + 7-9.

Diercks, Louis H., and Boone, E. Milton. "The Individual in the Choral Situation—with Mathematical Justifications." *Choral Journal*, VII (March-April, 1967), 25-29.

Ehmann, Wilhelm. "'Concertisten' und 'Ripienisten' in der H-moll-Messe Joh. Seb. Bachs." *Musik und Kirche*, XXX (March-April, 1960), 95-104, and (May-June, 1960), 138-47, and (July-August, 1960), 227-36, and (September-October, 1960), 255-73, and (November-December, 1960), 298-309.

Ehmann, Wilhelm. "Heinrich Schütz: Der Psalmen Davids, 1619, in der Aufführungspraxis." *Musik und Kirche*, XXVI (July-August, 1956), 145-71.

Ehmann, Wilhelm. "Performance Practice of Bach's Motets." *American Choral Review*, VII (September, 1964), 4-5, and (December, 1964), 6-7, and (March, 1965), 6, and (June, 1965), 8-12.

Freedman, Frederick. "Ernst Toch and the *Cantata of the Bitter Herbs*." *Amor Artis Bulletin*, II (December, 1962), 1 + 8-10.

Gelles, George. "Mozart's Version of *Messiah*." *American Choral Review*, X (Winter, 1968), 55-65.

Gelles, George. "Schoenberg's Choruses Opus 50." *American Choral Review*, XI (Fall, 1968), 17-22.

Gerow, Maurice. "Criteria of Choral Concert Program Building As Related to an Analysis of the Elements of Musical Structure." *Journal of Research in Music Education*, XII (Summer, 1964), 165-71.

Gottlieb, Jack. "The Choral Music of Leonard Bernstein." *American Choral Review*, X (Summer, 1968), 156-77.

Greenberg, Noah. "The Choirmaster and the Renaissance Choral Repertory." *Bulletin of the American Choral Foundation*, II (October, 1959), 1-3.

Haberlen, John. "Microrhythms: The Key to Vitalizing Renaissance Music." *Choral Journal*, XIII (November, 1972), 11-14.

Halsey, Louis. "Britten's Church Music." *Musical Times*, CIII (October, 1962), 686-89.

Johnson, Marlowe W. "The Choral Writing of Daniel Pinkham." *American Choral Review*, VIII (June, 1966), 1 + 12-16.

Keenze, Marvin H. "Singing City Choirs." *Journal of Church Music*, X (September, 1968), 8-10.

Kirby, F. E. "Hermann Finck on Methods of Performance." *Music and Letters*, XLII (July, 1961), 212-20.

Lawler, Fred D. "The Electronic Personal Pitch for Singers: An Aid in Learning Choral Music." *Choral Journal*, VIII (March-April, 1968), 6.

McEwen, Douglas R. "Interview with Roger Wagner." *Caecilia*, LXXXIX (Fall, 1962), 83-128.

Merkel, Byron M. "Applied Physiology." *Choral Journal*, VI (May-June, 1966), 20-22 + 26.

Mohr, Ernest. "Willy Burkhard: Swiss Composer." *Amor Artis Bulletin*, III (February, 1964), 1-2 + 7.

Nathan, Hans. "William Billings: *The Continental Harmony* (1794)." *American Choral Review*, V (July, 1963), 1 + 5-9.

Newlin, Dika. "Arnold Schoenberg as Choral Composer." *American Choral Review*, VI (July, 1964), 1 + 7-11.

Newlin, Dika. "The Role of the Chorus in Schoenberg's 'Moses and Aaron'." *American Choral Review*, IX (Fall, 1966), 1-4.

Norden, N. Lindsay. "Untempered Intonation." *Organ Institute Quarterly*, III (Autumn, 1953), 16-23.

Orga, Ates. "Penderecki: Composer of Martyrdom." *Music and Musicians*, XVIII (September, 1969), 34-42 + 76.

Ottman, Robert W. "Vocal Chamber Music." *Choral Journal*, VII (March-April, 1967), 30-32.

Pinkham, Daniel. "Intonation, Dissonance and Sonority." *Bulletin of the American Choral Foundation*, III (March, 1961), 6-7.

Pritchard, W. Douglas. "The Choral Style of Jean Berger." *American Choral Review*, VIII (September, 1965), 4-5 + 15.

Riemer, Otto. "Der Chorkomponist." *Musica*, XIV (October, 1960), 638-45.

Seigle, Cecilia Segawa. "The Choral Music of Vincent Persichetti." *American Choral Review*, VII (March, 1965), 4-5.

Shearer, C. M. "A Look at Choral Music in the Nineteenth Century." *Choral Journal*, VIII (January-February, 1968), 27-29, and (March-April, 1968), 24-26.

Skinner, Howard. "Some Comments on Rhythm." *Choral Journal*, VIII (May-June, 1968), 22-25.

Skinner, Howard. "Words and Music." *Choral Journal*, VII (May-June, 1967), 6-9, and (July-August, 1967), 13-15.

Somary, Johannes. "Presenting Music from Switzerland." *Amor Artis Bulletin*, III (February, 1964), 1 + 7-10.

Steinberg, Michael. "Erich Leinsdorf on Choral Music and Performance." *American Choral Review*, VII (September, 1964), 7-8.

Steinitz, Paul. "On Rehearsing a Choir for the 'Canticum Sacrum' [of Stravinsky]." *The Score* (March, 1957), pp. 56-59.

Stevens, Halsey. "The Choral Music of Zoltán Kodály." *Musical Quarterly*, LIV (April, 1968), 147-68.

Stevenson, Robert. "The English Service." *American Choral Review*, VI (October, 1963), 1 + 5-8, and (January, 1964), 5-7.

Stevenson, Robert. "Tomás Luis de Victoria: Unique Spanish Genius." *American Choral Review*, VIII (March, 1966), 1-3 + 7, and (June, 1966), 1-3 + 6 + 18.

Szell, George, and Lang, Paul Henry. "A Mixture of Instinct and Intellect." Interview published in *High Fidelity*, XV (January, 1965), 42-45 + 110-12.

Thomas, Arnold R. "A History of the Male Glee Club." *Music Journal*, XXV (September, 1967), 84-87 + 100.

Thomas, Kurt. "Über die Arbeit des Chorleiters mit dem Orchester." *Musik und Kirche*, XXX (July-August, 1960), 206-9.

Tircuit, Heuwell. "Alan Hovhaness: An American Choral Composer." *American Choral Review*, IX (Fall, 1966), 8.

Toch, Ernst. "The *Cantata of the Bitter Herbs* and the Haggadah." *Armor Artis Bulletin*, II (December, 1962), 1 + 9-10.

Trowell, Brian. "*Semele*: Opera and Oratorio." *Amor Artis Bulletin*, II (March, 1963), 1-2 + 8 + 11.

Walsh, Stephen. "Stravinsky's Choral Music." *American Choral Review*, X (Spring, 1968), 99-112.

Wilkey, Jay W. "Igor Stravinsky's Cantata: *A Sermon, a Narrative, and a Prayer*." *Choral Journal*, X (September-October, 1969), 14-19.

Williamson, John Finley. "Choral Singing: [articles individually titled]." Twelve articles in *Etude*, LXVIII and LXIX (April, 1950-October, 1951).

Young, Percy M. "The English Madrigal Tradition." *American Choral Review*, VII (September, 1964), 1-3 + 5-6 + 8-12.

Zimmerman, Franklin B. "An Experiment in Integrated Musical Learning." *College Music Symposium: Journal of the College Music Society*, VII (Fall, 1967), 19-23.

MISCELLANEA

Bukofzer, Manfred. "The Beginnings of Choral Polyphony." *Studies in Medieval and Renaissance Music*. New York: W. W. Norton, 1950.

Bukofzer, Manfred. "On the Performance of Renaissance Music." *Proceedings of the Music Teachers National Association*, XXXVI (1941), 225-35.

Choral Editing Standards Committee of the American Choral Directors Association. Walter Collins, Chairman. "Resolution." *Choral Journal*, VIII (May-June, 1968), 14.

Christiansen, F. Melius. "Ensemble Singing." *Yearbook of the Music Supervisors National Conference, 1932*. Chicago: Music Supervisors National Council, 1932.

Dailey, William Albert. "Techniques of Composition Used in Contemporary Works for Chorus and Orchestra on Religious Texts.... Works... Considered: 'Canticum Sacrum'—Stravinsky, 'Prayers of Kierkegaard'—

Barber, 'Magnificat'—Hovhaness." Unpublished Ph.D. dissertation, Catholic University of America, 1965.

Darrow, Gerald Fanning. "The Nature of Choral Training as Revealed Through an Analysis of Thirty-Three Years of Published Writings." Unpublished Ed.D. thesis, Indiana University, 1965.

De Angelis, Michael. *The Correct Pronunciation of Latin According to Roman Usage*. Second edition revised and corrected by Nicola A. Montani. Philadelphia: St. Gregory Guild, 1937.

Editing Early Music: Notes on the Preparation of Printer's Copy. "Introduction" signed by Thurston Dart (Stainer and Bell), Walter Emery (Novello), and Christopher Morris (Oxford University Press), 1963.

Ehmann, Wilhelm. "Voice Training and Sound Ideal as a Means of Musical Interpretation in Choral Music." *Festschrift Theodore Hoelty-Nickel: A Collection of Essays on Church Music*. Edited by Newman W. Powell. Valparaiso, Ind.: Valparaiso University Press, 1967.

Faugerstrom, Eugene M. "The Dramatic Function of the Chorus in English Oratorio from 1880 to the Present." Unpublished Ph.D. dissertation, Northwestern University, 1964.

Gatti, Guido M., ed. *Quaderni della Rassegna musicale*, Vol. I: *L'opera di Goffredo Petrassi*. Torino: Giulio Einaudi, 1964.

Gatti, Guido M., ed. *Quaderni della Rassegna musicale*, Vol. II: *L'opera di Luigi Dallapiccola*. Torino: Giulio Einaudi, 1965.

Geiringer, Karl. "The Church Music." *The Mozart Companion*. Edited by H. C. Robbins Landon and Donald Mitchell. London: Rockliff, 1956.

Godwin, Robert Chandler. "Schumann's Choral Works and the Romantic Movement." Unpublished D.M.A. thesis, University of Illinois, 1967.

Grout, Donald Jay. "On Historical Authenticity in the Performance of Old Music." *Essays on Music in Honor of Archibald Thompson Davison by His Associates*. Cambridge, Mass.: Harvard University, Department of Music, 1957.

Haydon, Glen. "Musicology and Performance." *Proceedings of the Music Teachers National Association*, XXXV (1940), 80-87.

Herz, Gerhard. "Historical Background." *Cantata No. 4 — Christ lag in Todesbanden*: J. S. Bach. Edited by Gerhard Herz. New York: W. W. Norton, 1967.

Herz, Gerhard. "Historical Background." *Cantata No. 140—Wachet auf, ruft uns die Stimme*: J. S. Bach. Edited by Gerhard Herz. New York: W. W. Norton, 1972.

Hillis, Margaret. "At Rehearsals: [Pamphlet of Instructions for Members of the Chicago Symphony Chorus]." Barrington, Ill.: American Choral Foundation, 1969.

Horton, John. "The Choral Works." *Schumann: A Symposium*. Edited by Gerald Abraham. London: Oxford University Press, 1952.

Kumlien, Wendell Clarke. "The Sacred Choral Music of Charles Ives: A Study in

Style Development." Unpublished D.M.A. thesis, University of Illinois, 1969.

Mendel, Arthur. "Introduction." *The Passion According to St. John: J. S. Bach.* Edited by Arthur Mendel. New York: G. Schirmer, 1951.

Mendel, Arthur. "Note on Performance." *Missa Brevis in F Major (1774—K. 192)*: W. A. Mozart. Edited by Arthur Mendel. New York: G. Schirmer, 1955.

Mendel, Arthur. "[Preface]." *A German Requiem*: Heinrich Schütz. Edited by Arthur Mendel. New-York: G. Schirmer, 1957.

Mendel, Arthur. "Remarks on the Performance of The Christmas Story." *The Christmas Story*: Heinrich Schütz. Edited by Arthur Mendel. New York: G. Schirmer, 1949.

Pankratz, Herbert Raymond. "The Male Voice in German Choral Music of the Renaissance." Unpublished Ph.D. dissertation, Northwestern University, 1961.

Pisciotta, Louis Vincent. "Texture in the Choral Works of Selected Contemporary American Composers." Unpublished Ph.D. dissertation, Indiana University, 1967.

Pooler, Frank, and Pierce, Brent. *New Choral Notation (A Handbook).* New York: Walton Music Corporation, 1971.

Redlich, Hans. "The Choral Music." *Benjamin Britten: A Commentary on His Works from a Group of Specialists.* Edited by Donald Mitchell and Hans Keller. New York: Philosophical Library, 1953.

Regier, Berhard Wayne. "The Development of Choral Music in Higher Education." Unpublished D.M.A. dissertation, University of Southern California, 1963.

Rosenthal, C. A., and Loft, Abram. "Church and Choral Music." *The Music of Schubert.* Edited by Gerald Abraham. New York: W. W. Norton, 1947.

A Simple Introduction to Plainsong, Being a Reprint of the "Rules for Interpretation" given in the "Liber Usualis." Tournai: Desclée, [1935].

Thomas, Kurt. *The Choral Conductor.* English adaptation by Alfred Mann and William H. Reese. [Published as a special issue of the *American Choral Review*, XIII, Nos. 1 and 2.] New York: Associated Music Publishers, 1971.

Veld, Henry. "Choral Conducting." *Proceedings of the Music Teachers National Association*, XXIX (1934), 46-56.

Williamson, John Finley. "Training the Individual Voice through Choral Singing." *Proceedings of the Music Teachers National Association*, XXXIII (1938), 52-59.

Zimmerman, Franklin B. *The Anthems of Henry Purcell.* [Published as a special issue of the *American Choral Review*, XIII, Nos. 3 and 4.] New York: Associated Music Publishers, 1971.

REFERENCE MATERIALS

Adler, Samuel H. *A List of Music for the American Synagogue*. American Choral Foundation *Memo*, No. 49. April, 1964.

Apel, Willi, ed. *Harvard Dictionary of Music*. Second edition, revised and enlarged. Cambridge, Mass.: Harvard University Press, 1969.

Axworthy, Suzanne. *Bibliography of the Choral Music of Vincent Persichetti*. American Choral Foundation *Memo*, No. 58. June, 1965.

BBC Music Library: Choral and Opera Catalogue. 2 volumes. London: British Broadcasting Corporation, 1967.

Bittinger, Werner, ed. *Heinrich Schütz Werke Verzeichnis*. Kassel: Bärenreiter, 1960.

Blom, Eric, ed. *Grove's Dictionary of Music and Musicians*. Fifth edition. 9 volumes. London: Macmillan, 1954. Supplement, 1961.

Blume, Friedrich, ed. *Die Musik in Geschichte und Gegenwart*. 14 volumes. Kassel: Bärenreiter, 1949-68.

Burnsworth, Charles C. *Choral Music for Women's Voices: An Annotated Bibliography of Recommended Works*. Metuchen, N. J.: Scarecrow Press, 1968.

Buszin, W. E., et al. *A Bibliography on Music and the Church*. New York: National Council of Churches of Christ, 1958.

Campbell, Frank C. *A Critical Annotated Bibliography of Periodicals*. American Choral Foundation *Memo*, No. 33. July, 1962.

Carroll, J. Robert. *Compendium of Liturgical Music Terms*. Toledo, Ohio: Gregorian Institute of America, 1964.

Case, James H. *A List of Contemporary American Choral Music for Men's Voices*. American Choral Foundation *Memo*, No. 39. March, 1963.

Case, James H. *A List of Contemporary American Choral Music for Mixed Voices*. American Choral Foundation *Memo*, No. 46. January, 1964.

Case, James H. *A List of Contemporary American Choral Music for Women's Voices*. American Choral Foundation *Memo*, No. 43. September, 1963.

Deutsch, Otto Erich. *Schubert: Thematic Catalogue of All His Works in Chronological Order*. London: J. M. Dent & Sons, 1951.

Diamond, Wilfrid. *Dictionary of Liturgical Latin*. Milwaukee: Bruce Publishing Co., 1961.

Doe, Paul. "Register of Theses on Music." *R[oyal] M[usical] A[ssociation] Research Chronicle*, No. 3 (1963), pp. 1–25. ["Amendments and Additions" have appeared in the same journal: No. 4 (1964), pp. 93–97, and No. 6 (1966), pp. 51–58.]

Duckles, Vincent. *Music Reference and Research Materials: An Annotated Bibliography*. Second edition. New York: Free Press, 1967.

Engel, Lehman. *A Select List of Choral Music from Operas, Operettas, and Musical Shows*. American Choral Foundation *Memo* No. 41. June, 1963.

Ford, Wyn K. *Music in England before 1800: A Select Bibliography*. London: Library Association, 1967.

Gates, Crawford, comp. *Catalogue of Published American Choral Music.* Second edition. New York: National Federation of Music Clubs, 1969.

Gerboth, Walter. "Index of Festschriften and Some Similar Publications." *Aspects of Medieval and Renaissance Music: A Birthday Offering to Gustave Reese.* Edited by Jan LaRue. New York: W. W. Norton, 1966.

Godman, Stanley, comp. "A Classified Index of Bach Articles." *Music Book,* Vol. VII. Edited by Max Hinrichsen. London: Hinrichsen Edition Limited, 1952.

Greenberg, Noah. *A Selective List of XV and XVI Century Netherlandish Choral Music Available in Practical Editions.* American Choral Foundation *Memo,* No. 13. March, 1960.

Griswold, Robert. "A Guide to Current Practices in English Cathedral Choral Music." *Diapason,* LV (September, 1964), 43-47, and (October, 1964), 39-45.

"A Guide for the Choral Conductor to Articles and Books That Describe Performance Practices During the Baroque and Classical Periods." *Bulletin of the American Choral Foundation,* III (March, 1961), 13-14.

"A Guide for the Choral Conductor to Books Describing Analytic and Composition Techniques." *Bulletin of the American Choral Foundation,* II (October, 1959), 7-8.

Hartley, Kenneth R. *Bibliography of Theses and Dissertations in Sacred Music.* Detroit: Information Coordinators, 1966.

Hatchett, Marion J. *Music for the Church Year: A Handbook for Clergymen, Organists, and Choir Directors.* New York: Seabury Press, 1964.

Hayes, Morris D. *A Selected List of Music for Men's Voices.* American Choral Foundation *Memo,* Nos. 42 and 52. August, 1963, and September, 1964.

Heaton, Charles Huddleston, comp. "A Church Music Bibliography." *Music: The A.G.O. and R.C.C.O. Magazine,* III (January, 1969), 38-39, and (March, 1969), 24-25, and (April, 1969), 52-53.

Hewitt, Helen, comp. *Doctoral Dissertations in Musicology.* Fifth edition, edited by Cecil Adkins. Philadelphia: American Musicological Society, 1971. [Supplement in the *Journal of the American Musicological Society,* XXV (Fall, 1972), 428-67.]

Heyer, Anna Harriet, comp. *Historical Sets, Collected Editions, and Monuments of Music.* Second edition. Chicago: American Library Association, 1969.

Hopkinson, Cecil. *A Bibliography of the Musical and Literary Works of Hector Berlioz.* Edinburgh: Edinburgh Bibliographical Society, 1951.

Howerton, George, et al, compilers. *Contemporary Music: A Recommended List for High Schools and Colleges.* Washington, D.C.: Music Educators National Conference, 1964.

Hughes, Anselm. *Liturgical Terms for Music Students: A Dictionary.* Boston: McLaughlin and Reilly, 1940.

Jessup, B. L. *Bibliography of the Choral Music of Daniel Pinkham.* American Choral Foundation *Memo,* No. 65. June, 1966.

Kinsky, Georg. *Das Werk Beethovens thematische-bibliographisches Verzeichnis seiner sämtlichen vollendeten Kompositionen*. Munich: G. Henle, 1955.

Kirk, Colleen J. "Choral Materials." *Journal of Research in Music Education*, VII (Spring, 1959), 41-68.

Klyce, Stephen. *A List of Twentieth-Century Madrigals*. American Choral Foundation *Memo*, No. 76. February, 1968.

Knapp, J. Merrill. *Selected List of Music for Men's Voices*. Princeton, N. J.: Princeton University Press, 1952.

Köchel, Ludwig Ritter von. *Chronologisch-thematisches Verzeichnis sämtlicher Tonwerke Wolfgang Amadé Mozarts*. Sixth edition, revised by Franz Giegling, Alexander Weinmann, and Gerd Sievers. Wiesbaden: Breitkopf & Härtel, 1964.

Krohn, Ernst C. *The History of Music: An Index to the Literature Available in a Selected Group of Musicological Publications*. St. Louis: Washington University, 1952.

LaRue, Jan, and Vinton, John. *A Selective List of Choral Compositions from the Classical Period in Practical Editions*. American Choral Foundation *Memo*, No. 24. June, 1961.

Locke, Arthur W., and Fassett, Charles K. *Selected List of Choruses for Women's Voices*. Third edition, revised and enlarged. Northhampton, Mass.: Smith College, 1964.

Major Choral Works by Contemporary Composers. New York: American Music Center, [1954].

Messerli, Carlos R. "The Church Musician's Five-Foot Shelf: Basic Books in Worship, the Liturgy, and Church Music." *Church Music*, 1968, pp. 43-47.

Modisett, Katherine Carpenter. "Bibliography of Sources, 1930-1952, Relating to the Teaching of Choral Music in Secondary Schools." *Journal of Research in Music Education*, III (Spring, 1955), 51-60.

Morris, Renée. *Bibliography of the Published Choral Music of Alan Hovhaness*. American Choral Foundation *Memo*, No. 66. November, 1966.

The Music Index: The Key to Current Music Periodical Literature. Detroit: Information Service, 1949- .

National Jewish Welfare Board, Bibliography Committee. *Bibliography of Jewish Vocal Music*. New York: National Jewish Music Council, 1948.

Protestant Episcopal Church in the U.S.A., Joint Commission on Church Music. *Service Music and Anthems for the Nonprofessional Choir*. Greenwich, Conn.: Seabury Press, 1955.

Rasmussen, Mary, comp. "A Bibliography of Choral Music with Horn Ensemble Accompaniment, as Compiled from Eleven Selected Sources." *Brass Quarterly*, V (Spring, 1962), 109-13.

Rasmussen, Mary, comp. "A Bibliography of Choral Music with Trombone Ensemble Accompaniment, as Compiled from Eleven Selected Sources." *Brass Quarterly*, V (Summer, 1962), 153-59.

Rasmussen, Mary, comp. "A Bibliography of 19th- and 20th-Century Music for Male Voices with Wind- or Brass-Ensemble Accompaniment." *Brass Quarterly*, VII (Winter, 1963), 67-77, and (Spring, 1964), 124-32.

Rasmussen, Mary, comp. "A Bibliography of 19th- and 20th-Century Music for Mixed Voices with Wind- or Brass-Ensemble Accompaniment." *Brass Quarterly*, VI (Spring, 1963), 120-30, and (Summer, 1963), 179-86; and VII (Fall, 1963), 34-44.

RILM [i.e., Répertoire international de la littérature musicale] : *Abstracts of Music Literature*. New York: International Musicological Society; International Association of Music Libraries; and American Council of Learned Societies, 1967-.

Sasse, Konrad, comp. *Händel Bibliographie*. Second, improved edition. Leipzig: Deutscher Verlag für Musik, 1967.

Schmieder, Wolfgang, ed. *Thematisch systematisches Verzeichnis der musikalischen Werke von Johann Sebastian Bach*. Leipzig: Breitkopf & Härtel, 1950.

Steere, Dwight. *Music for the Protestant Church Choir: A Descriptive and Classified List of Worship Material*. Richmond, Va.: John Knox Press, 1955.

Vagner, Robert. "A Selective List of Choral and Vocal Music with Wind and Percussion Accompaniments." *Journal of Research in Music Education*, XIV (Winter, 1966), 276-88.

Valentin, Erich. *Handbuch der Chormusik*. 2 volumes. Regensburg: Gustav Bosse, 1953-58.

Vinquist, Mary, and Zaslaw, Neal, eds. *Performance Practice: A Bibliography*. New York: W. W. Norton, 1971.

Whitwell, David. "On the Repertory for Chorus and Band: Introductory Notes." *American Choral Review*, VII (March, 1965), 12. [Lists introduced in this article are published separately and under various titles in American Choral Foundation *Memo*: Nos. 53 (December, 1964); 56 (April, 1965); 61 (December, 1965); and 64 (May, 1966).]

Zaslaw, Neal, ed. *Current Musicology*, No. 8: *Bibliography of Performance Practices*. New York: Columbia University, Department of Music, 1969.

Zimmerman, Franklin B. *Henry Purcell, 1659-95: An Analytical Catalogue of His Music*. London: Macmillan, 1963.

INDEX